NORTH CAROLINA SLAVES
AND
FREE PERSONS OF COLOR

BURKE, LINCOLN AND ROWAN COUNTIES

William L. Byrd, III
and John H. Smith

HERITAGE BOOKS
2008

HERITAGE BOOKS
AN IMPRINT OF HERITAGE BOOKS, INC.

Books, CDs, and more—Worldwide

For our listing of thousands of titles see our website
at
www.HeritageBooks.com

Published 2008 by
HERITAGE BOOKS, INC.
Publishing Division
100 Railroad Ave. #104
Westminster, Maryland 21157

Copyright © 2000 William L. Byrd, III
and John H. Smith

All rights reserved. No part of this book may be reproduced or transmitted in any form or by any means, electronic or mechanical, including photocopying, recording or by any information storage and retrieval system without written permission from the author, except for the inclusion of brief quotations in a review.

International Standard Book Numbers
Paperbound: 978-0-7884-1530-2
Clothbound: 978-0-7884-7685-3

ANNE LICEAT INVITOS IN SERVITUTEM DARE?

IS IT RIGHT TO MAKE SLAVES OF OTHERS AGAINST THEIR WILL?[1]

---

[1] George W. Alexander, *Letters on the Emancipation* (1842; reprint, New York: Negro Universities Press, 1969): 4

contents

INTRODUCTION	IX
ACKNOWLEDGEMENTS	XI
CHAPTER ONE	**1**
LINCOLN COUNTY	1
PETITIONS TO SELL SLAVES	*1*
CHAPTER TWO	**3**
LINCOLN COUNTY	3
CRIMINAL ACTIONS	*3*
CHAPTER THREE	**57**
LINCOLN COUNTY	57
RUNAWAYS	*57*
CHAPTER FOUR	**59**
LINCOLN COUNTY	59
HIRING OF SLAVES	*59*
CHAPTER FIVE	**61**
LINCOLN COUNTY	61
PATROL RECORDS	*61*
CHAPTER SIX	**65**
LINCOLN COUNTY	65
CORONER'S INQUESTS	*65*
CHAPTER SEVEN	**75**
LINCOLN COUNTY	75
MISCELLANEOUS RECORDS	*75*
CHAPTER EIGHT	**77**
BURKE COUNTY	77

BILLS OF SALE	77
CHAPTER NINE	**87**
BURKE COUNTY	87
CIVIL AND CRIMINAL ACTIONS	*87*
CHAPTER TEN	**115**
BURKE COUNTY	115
WEAPON PERMIT	*115*
CHAPTER ELEVEN	**117**
BURKE COUNTY	117
BASTARDY BONDS	*117*
CHAPTER TWELVE	**119**
BURKE COUNTY	119
TRADING WITH SLAVES	*119*
CHAPTER THIRTEEN	**121**
ROWAN COUNTY	121
CRIMINAL AND CIVIL ACTIONS	*121*
CHAPTER FOURTEEN	**199**
ROWAN COUNTY	199
SLAVE PATROL RECORDS	*199*
CHAPTER FIFTEEN	**201**
ROWAN COUNTY	201
DEPOSITIONS	*201*
CHAPTER SIXTEEN	**203**
ROWAN COUNTY	203
STEALING OF SLAVES	*203*
CHAPTER SEVENTEEN	**205**
ROWAN COUNTY	205
HIRE OF SLAVES	*205*
CHAPTER EIGHTEEN	**209**

ROWAN COUNTY 209
    DEED OF GIFT OF SLAVE *209*

CHAPTER NINETEEN **211**
ROWAN COUNTY 211
    MORTGAGE OF SLAVES *211*

CHAPTER TWENTY **213**
ROWAN COUNTY 213
    LETTER OF INTENT REGARDING SLAVES *213*

CHAPTER TWENTY-ONE **215**
ROWAN COUNTY 215
    COHABITATION RECORDS *215*

CHAPTER TWENTY-TWO **217**
ROWAN COUNTY 217
    BILLS OF SALE *217*

CHAPTER TWENTY-THREE **223**
ROWAN COUNTY 223
    PETITION EX PARTE *223*

CHAPTER TWENTY-FOUR **229**
ROWAN COUNTY 229
    RUNAWAYS *229*

CHAPTER TWENTY-FIVE **243**
ROWAN COUNTY 243
    TRANSPORTING SLAVES *243*

INDEX **253**

introduction

The records in this volume were transcribed from originals located in the North Carolina State Archives. The records are listed under general headings as "Slaves and Free Negroes," or "Slaves and Free Persons of Color." In some cases they are listed under the heading of "Miscellaneous Records."[2]

These particular records were gleaned from the North Carolina Counties of Lincoln, Burke and Rowan. Many of these records are faded, torn and missing part of the original text. Every attempt has been made to transcribe them accurately. The text in some of the records may be irretrievable in a few years.

Included are an extensive array of civil and criminal actions pertaining to slaves and free persons of color. Interaction between all races is represented, and sometimes it is displayed on an intimate level. The interwoven history of Black and White is far more complex than is generally known. These records bring to light the interactions through legal and other papers.

---

[2] Thornton W. Mitchell, "Preliminary Guide to Records Relating to Blacks in the North Carolina State Archives," *Archives Information Circular* 17(June 1980): 3-4.

Acts of the General Assembly governed the handling of slaves. Many of these acts are referred to in this volume. The Acts of the General Assembly are available for research at the North Carolina State Archives, and the University of North Carolina at Chapel Hill.

The records in this book are arranged in categories listed below:

Petitions to Sell Slaves	Criminal Actions	Runaways
Hiring of Slaves	Patrol Records	Coroner's Inquest
Miscellaneous Records	Bills of Sale	Civil Actions
Weapons Permits	Bastardy Bonds	Trading with Slaves
Depositions	Stealing of Slaves	Mortgage of Slaves
Cohabitation Records	Transporting of Slaves	Petition Ex Parte
Deeds of Gifts of Slaves	Letters of Intent Regarding Slaves	

A table of cases for criminal and civil actions has been compiled at the back of this book for reference. (See Table of Cases.)

Many of these slaves and free persons of color left North Carolina and spread out across the entire United States both before and after Emancipation. It is hoped that this book will bring to light these rather obscure records.

acknowledgements

The publishing of this book would not have been possible without the valuable help and assistance of the the staff of the North Carolina State Archives. Their courteous service is more appreciated than they can imagine.

Lincoln County

Chapter One

Lincoln County

PETITIONS TO SELL SLAVES

Petition to Sell Slave

No. Carolina   }   Co. of Pleas & Quarter Sessions
Rowan County }   Nov. 1851

To the worshipful Justices of said Court. The Petition of David and Isaac Earnheart: Guardian of Philip Earnheart show unto your worships that he is the owner of a negro girl named Esther and that owing to his indulgence towards her she is now, and will continue to be of very little value to his Estate. They therefore pray your worships to grant unto them an order to sell said negro girl, upon such terms as to your worships may seem right.
And as in duty bound they will ever pray

Craige & Caldwell for Petitioners

Lincoln County

Chapter Two

Lincoln County

CRIMINAL ACTIONS

State
Vs.
Abner (a Slave)

Lincoln 25 January 1840
Mr. Henderson Forsyth
      Exr. of John A. Forsyth
Sir
      Take notice that at the next Superior Court of Law to be held for the County of Lincolnton on the Second Monday after the Third Monday in February 1840 Abner a negro slave late the property of John A. Forsyth will be put upon his Trial for his life before said Court upon a Charge of Murdering his Master John A. Forsyth
Jas R Dodge   Solicitor

Negro Abner was committed to Jail on the 12 day of November for killing of his Master John A Forsythe and was taken out on the 3 of April 1840 which makes 144 days at 35 cents day $ 50.40
    April 4 1840   fees   .60
                                                          $ 51.00
Henry Linard for Apprehending him   5.00
                                                          $ 56.00
                    Paul Kistler   Jailor

The State   }   Superior Court of Law March
   vs.   }   Term 1840 Isaac Holland charges
Abner a slave }   the State as Extra Services

Lincoln County

for going out after four witnesses wanted for the State two Dollars as per the Judges order

                    Isaac Holland

The Examination of the Negroes of John A. Forsyth respecting his death taken on the ground Novr. 11th 1839

Gracey States
    That the Negro Abner was restless through the night and passing about the fire & tent & she saw him unbutton the tent in which Forsyth lay & look in same tent, & then come around the fire & set down at the door of the Negroes tent for some time with his head down - he then got up & went round the negroes tent & she saw nothing more of him until she heard a pop She then saw Abner running by the tent near his feet half bent & passed on to the Carry all, & soon returned & lay down in the Negros tent, she some time after heard her Master making a given noise & called up Phillis stating that something was the Matter with her Master - they went & looked & saw their masters Brains on the tent Pillow & further saith that Abner lay in his tent & never went to look at his Master

Phillis States
    that she saw nothing nor heard nothing until they were waked up with the noise of their Masters breathing then went to the tent & said his brains knocked out

Dave States
    That Aunt Gracey called him up & said, Dave what is the Matter with your Master & Phillis said, Dave jump up & see what is the Matter with your Master & he jump & got alight & run to the tent & saw some one had killed his Master & states that Abner was then lying in the tent & didn't get up to see his master

Samson States
    the Same in Substance that Stephen does, that Abner had been chained to Stephen the nights previous & plead with his Master to be at liberty that night his master said it was play they take it time about & set him loose he also states that Abner went to bed & was up in the night making fires

Stephen States
    That he saw Abner sitting by the fire in a _____ position after the fire had been made in the night & after that noticed him sitting down in

Lincoln County

the tent he also states that with some difficulty he go & Abner to go to a house near & he came & back & said the man wouldn't come Till day Light And went to another & come back said they would come till day light but said that the man said the most valuable things must be taken to the house & that he (Abner) must take a horse & go to another house & he took a horse & went off & did not return

The above taken down by   Larkin Stowe
be fore me I. Holland JP

State of North Carolina }
Lincoln County   }

To any Lawful officer to Execute and Return Whereas information hath been made to me James T. Alexander an Acting Justice of the Peace of said County that John A. Forsyth hath been feloniously killed and Murdered within the bounds of this County and it is further believed that his own Slaves Abner & Dave and others whose names are unknown killed and Murdered him This is therefore to command You to take the bodies of said Abner & Dave and the others concerned names unknown and them have before me or some other Justice of the Peace for said County to be dealt with according to Law. Witness my hand & Seal this 13 November 1839
Summons for the State } J. T. Alexander J.P. (Seal)
Larkin Stowe
Leroy Stowe
Henry Fulenwider
and the Negroes of J. A. Forsyth
that were present on the Ground
get their names from Miss Stowe
Stephen Absalom
Gracey Philis Nancy
Dave

---

know all men by these presents that we Henderson Forsyth & James B. Gracey & Leroy Stowe acknowledged ourselves Indebted to the State of North Carolina in the Sum of one Thousand Dollars each to be void on conditions that David, Sampson, Gracey, Fillis, four slaves do appear at our next Superior court of Law to be held in Lincolnton (March Term) to

Lincoln County

Give evidence in behalf of the state against Abner in the within case & not depart the Court without leave given under our hand & Seals this 14th of Novr 1839   H. Forsyth   (LS)
                Jas. B. Gracey   (LS)
                    State
                      vs.
               Abner & Dave
                   Slaves
              Executed on Dave
              Abner in Jail. H.
         Fulenwider not summon'd
             W. R. Clark   Clk

Novr 14th 1839 after Examining the negroes of the Deceast (John A. Forsyth) and no evidence Leaking out against any but Abner, the others so far as is necessary is made Safe by bonds the cost of this warrent is $1.80.
                      I. Holland   JPLeroy Stowe was bound in the Sum of one thousand Dollars for the appearance of five negroes to give evidence for the State against Abner a Slave charged with the murder of John A. Forsyth $1000
Larkin Stowe bound as a witness in $100
Leroy Stowe also bound as a witness - $100

State of North Carolina   }   Superior Court of Law
Lincoln County   }   March Term A.D. Eighteen hundred and forty.
The Jurors for the State upon their Oath present that Abner a Slave late of said county not having the fear of God before his eyes, but being moved and seduced by the instigation of the Devil on the thirteenth day of November in the year of our Lord One Thousand Eight hundred and Thirty Nine with force and Arms in the County of Lincoln aforesaid, in and upon one John A. Forsyth in the peace of God and the State then and there being, feloniously, wilfully and of his Malice aforethought did Make an assault And That the said Abner with a Certain Axe of the Value of six pence which he the said Abner in both his hands then and there had and held the said John A. Forsyth in and upon the top of the head of him the said John A. Forsyth then and there feloniously, wilfully, and of his

Lincoln County

Malice aforethought did strike, giving to the said John A. Forsyth one Mortal wound of the length of three inches and of the depth of one inch, of which said Mortal wound the said John A. Forsyth then and there instantly died And so the Jurors aforesaid, upon their Oath aforesaid do day That the said slave Abner, the said John A. Forsyth then & there in Manner and form aforesaid feloniously wilfully and of his Malice aforethought did kill and Murder Against the Peace and dignity of the State

       James R Dodge Sol

        State
        Vs.
       Abner a Slave
       Ind. Murder

Pal Cr[??er??]
James Queen
Larkin Stowe
Henry Fulenwider
David   }
Sampson } Slaves
Tracy   }
Phillis   }

James Tracey
All Sworn & Sent
Henry Fulenwider & James Tracey Bound in $100 to Appear from day to day
John Michal
A True Bill
John Killian Foreman

State of North Carolina	}	Superior Court of Law
Lincoln County	}	Spring Term 1840
State	}	
Vs	}	Murder
Abner a Slave	}	

Lincoln County

The prisoner Abner being brought To the bar & asked What he hath to say Why Judgment of death should not be pronounced against him sayeth Nothing Whereupon it is Ordered and adjudged by the Court that the prisoner at the bar Abner be taken to the public Jail of the County & there kept without bail or/as _____ untill friday the third day of April next upon Which day between the hours of Ten in the forenoon & three oclock of the Afternoon the Sheriff take him to the place of Public Execution & then & there that the said Abner be hung by the neck untill he be dead.

I John Michal Clerk of the Superior Court of law Lincoln County do hereby Certify that the foregoing is a true & correct copy of the record & sentence a pronounced upon the Said Abner a Slave at the aforesaid Time In testimony Whereof I have hereunto set my hand and affixed the seal of office this 3rd day of April 1840.
John Michal   Clk

****

State
Vs.
Ben & Edmund

Subpeona

State of North Carolina
To the Sheriff of Lincoln County Greeting: you Are Hereby Commanded to Summon Alexander a Slave (Instanter) personally to be and appear before the Judge of our Superior Court of Law, at the next Court to be held for our said County, at the Courthouse in Lincolnton, on the 6th Monday after the 4th Sept. next then and there to testify, and the truth to say, in behalf of Edmond a Slave in a certain matter of controversy before said Court depending, and then and there to be tried, wherein The State is plaintiff, and Edmond is defendant
And this you shall in no wise omit, under the penalty prescribed by law.

Witness, L. Henderson Clerk of our said Court, at office, the 6th Monday after 4th Sept, 1835, and in the 60 year of our Independence.
L. Henderson
by B S Shuford   D Clk

Subpeona

State of North Carolina
To the Sheriff of Lincoln County Greeting:

Lincoln County

You are hereby Commanded to summon Michael Sherrill Thomas Long & Jacob Gabriel personally to be and appear before the Judge of our Superior Court of Law, at the next Court to be held for our said County, at the Court house in Lincolnton, on the 6th Monday after the 4th Monday in Sept next then and there to testify, and the truth to say, in behalf of the State in a matter of controversy before said Court depending, and then and there to be tried wherein The State is plaintiff, and Edmon a Slave and others is defendant
And this you shall in no wise omit, under the penalty prescribed by law.
  Witness, Lawson Henderson Clerk of our said Court, at office, the 6th Monday after the Monday in March, 1835, and in the 59th year of our Independence
      Lawson Henderson Clk
      by B S Johnson D Clk

State of North Carolina } Superior Court of Law &
Lincoln County   } Equity Fall Term 1835

      The State
       Vs
     Ben & Edmond

Wilson Gabriel
  Charges the State as a witness on this case 3 days at 60cs
per day   1.80
Mileage to Court & home 39 miles at 2cs   .78
Ticket   .10
                $ 2.68

Sworn to before me at
office Novr 14th 1835
     B S Johnson Clk

State of North Carolina } Superior Court of Law &
Lincoln County   } Equity fall Term 1835
         { The State
         { Vs
         { Ben & Edmond

Eli Sherrill

Lincoln County

Charges the State as witness on this case 3 days at 60 cs.
per day   1.80
Mileage 44 Miles Traveling 02 cs   .88
Ticket   .10
Sworn before me at $ 2.78
office Nov 14th 1835

            B S Johnson   Clk

State of North Carolina   }   Superior Court of Law &
Lincoln County   }   Equity Fall Term 1835
                               {   The State
                               {   Vs
                               {   Ben & Edmond
Turner Abernathy for
Emberson a slave
      charges the State on this Case for attending as a witness 3
days at 60 cs per day   1.80
Mileage to Court & home 36 miles at 2 cs   .72
Ticket   .10
                                                $ 2.62
Sworn to before me at office
Novr 14th 1835
                  B. S. Johnson   Clk

                       Subpeona
State of North Carolina

      To the Sheriff of Lincoln County Greeting: You are hereby commanded to summon Jim a Slave the property of Robt Abernathy Senr & Philip & Zilpha slaves the property of Michael Sherrill personally to be and appear before the Judge of our Superior Court of Law, at the next Court to be held for our said County, at the Courthouse in Lincolnton, on the 6th Monday after the 4th Monday in Sept next then and there to testify, and the truth to say, in behalf of The State in a certain matter of controversy before said Court depending and then and there to be tried, wherein The State in plaintiff and Edmon a slave and others is

Lincoln County

defendants. And this you shall in no wise omit, under the penalty prescribed ny law.

Witness, Lawson Henderson Clerk of our said Court, at office, the 6th Monday after the 4th Monday in March, 1835, and in the 59th year of our Independence. Lawson Henderson Clk
by B H Shuford D Clk

State of North Carolina

To the Sheriff of [Blank] County Greeting: you are Hereby Commanded to Summon Wilson Gabriel & Abraham Gabriel personally to be and appear before the Judge of our Superior Court of Law, at the next Court to be held for our said County, at the Courthouse in Lincolnton on the 6th Monday after the 4th Monday in Sept next then and there to testify, and the truth to say, in behalf of Edmon a Slave the property of Tho L Mays in a certain matter of controversy before said Court depending, and then and there to be tried, wherein the State is plaintiff and Edmon is defendant
And this you shall in no wise omit, under the penalty prescribed by law.

Witness, Lawson Henderson Clerk of our said Court, at office, the 6th Monday after the 4th Next 1835, and in the 59th year of our Independence.
Lawson Henderson Clk
by B H Shuford D Clk

State of North Carolina } Superior Court of Law
Lincoln County   } Fall Term 1835

The Jurors for the state upon their oath aforesaid that Edmund a slave the property of one Thomas L Mays and Ben a slave the property of one Abraham Gabriel both late of the County of Lincoln and state aforesaid on the 9th day of Novemner AD 1835 with force and arms in the County aforesaid _____ Iron of the value of Ten dollars of the goods and Chattels of one Moses D Abernathy then and there seeing found then and there feloniously did steal and Take and Carry away against the peace and dignity of the State
Wm. J Alexander
Solr

Lincoln County

State of North Carolina   Lincoln Cty
to any Lawful officer to Execute
this day Came M N Abernathy before me Alexander Ward one of Justices of the peace for said County and made oath in Due form of Law that Moses D Abernathy had his Iron house Broke open on the Night the 4th Friday in May and on the friday Night following Broke open again and Did steal and felloniously carry away the first Night I suppose three hundred weight and on the second Night He would suppose between four and five hundred lbs Iron I have Just Reasons Sespect Ben a Negro Slave belonging to Abraham Gabriel and Edmund a Negro slave belonging to Thomas L. Mays and Abram a Negro slave belonging to the above named Moses Abernathy to be gilty of the above Charge these are therefore to Command to apprehend the said Ben Edmund and Abram and Cause them to appeare before some Justice of the peace to answer the said Charge and further Delt with as the law Directs given under my hand and seal this 20th June 1835
       Alexander Ward   JP

Summon for the State
Albert
Moses
David
Zilpha
Jim
philip
Emberson
Joe

I Authorize and depute Isaac Douglass to execute this warent for me and in My Name - Isaac   Thomas Ward   Shff 20th   1835

Moses Abernathy   } acknowledged them selves
Frederick Abernathy   } indebted to the state of
North Carolina in the sum of one hundred dollars Each to be levied of the Goods and Chattles Land and Tenements to be void on condition that Tom   Moses & Alfred appear at the next Superior Court to be held for the county of Lincoln at the court house in Lincolnton on the 6th Monday after 4th Monday in September next to give Evidence in behalf of the state

Lincoln County

against Ben a Slave the property of Abraham Gabriel and Edmond Slave the property of Thomas L. Mays
Turner Abernathy also bound in the Sum of one hundred dollars that David & Emerson slaves appear at the next Superior Court to be held for the county at the court house in Lincolnton on the 6th Monday after the 4th Monday of Sept next to Give Evidence in behalf of the state against Edmund slave the property of Tho. L. Mays & Ben a slave the peoperty of Abraham Gabriel
Eli Sherrill also bound in sum of $100 to appear at the next Superior Court to Give Evidence in the above Case in behalf of the State
Nath Edwards JP this 24 of June 1835
Alexander Ward JPExecuted By Thomas Ward Sheriff By Me
Isaac Douglas

State of North Carolina
Lincoln County
  Abraham Gabriel & Thomas L. Mays Acknowledges them selves indebted to the State of North Carolina in the Joint sum of five hundred lbs Each to levy of there goods and Chattles lands and tenaments Void on Conditions that Abraham Gabriel Negro Ben and Thomas L. Mays Negro Edmond make there personal appearance before the Judge of our Next Superior Court of Law to be held for the County of Lincoln at the Court house in Lincolnton to answer a Charge of state and Not Depart the with out lease
      June the 24th 1835

Alexander Ward   JP
Nath Edwards   JP
Jno J Shuford   JP

Abraham Gabriel &
Thomas L Mays
Bond   B.D. 1835

****

      State
      Vs.
    Abraham (a Slave)

Lincoln County

State of North Carolina
    To the Sheriff of Lincoln County, Greeting you are hereby commanded to summon Philip Baker to produce James his slave & Cause him personally to be and appear before the Judge of our Superior Court at the next Court to be held for the county of Lincoln at the Court-house in Lincolnton on the 2nd Monday after 3rd in August instanta, then and there to testify, and the truth to say, in behalf of the state in a certain matter of controversy before said Court, depending and there to be tried, wherein the state is plaintiff and Abraham a slave is defendant. And this in no wise omit under the penalty prescribed by law.
    Witness John Michal Clerk of our said court, at office, the 2nd Monday after 3rd Monday in August and in the 62 year of our Independence, A.D. 1837
                    John Michal Clk

****

                    State
                     Vs.
              Abel (a Slave)

                  Subpeona

State of North Carolina
    To the Sheriff of Lincoln County Greeting: You Are Hereby Commanded to Summon Martin Knipe J. D. Harmon Polly Hunsicker, Michal Hefner (Dave & Jane slaves the property of Jas. Hunsicker) personally to be and appear before the Judge of our Superior Court of Law, at the next Court to be held for our said County, at the Court house in Lincolnton, on the 2d Monday after the 3d in Augt. next then and there to testify, and the truth to to say, in behalf of The State in a certain matter of controversy before said Court depending, and then and there to be tried, wherein The State is plaintiff, and Abel a Slave the property of George Sigman is defendant. And this you shall in no wise omit, under the penalty prescribed by law.

    Witness B. S. Johnson Clerk of our said Court, at Office, the 2nd Monday after 3rd in Feby, 1837, and in the 61 year of our Independence.
                  B S Johnson Clk

Lincoln County

State of North Carolina } Superior Court of Law
Lincoln County } Fall Term, 1837

{ In the suit of
Michael Heffner   { State
{ Versus
{ Abel a Slave

Charges the State in this cause for attendance as a Witness 5 days at 60 per day	$ 3.00
Mileage to court and home 46 miles at 2 per mile	.92
Ferriage Ticket	.10
	$ 4.02

Sworn to before me at office, the 9th day of Septr 1837

John Michael   Clk

George Sipe - had rented the place from the owner of Negro Abel - George Sigman - was to pay 40 bushels Corn standing rent. him & his wife & children all left the House fastened the Door with something - was his dwelling house 3 beds in it & furniture - 10 or 11 oclock in Morning got word the House was on fire - When he came back all burnt up Sunday burning. Monday from some information next [??] to Joseph Honeysicker found his rasor and a Veil in black Daves possession - Abel wanted to sell a Handkerchief
Martin Canup
Daniel Harman
Michel Heffner as to confessions
Frederick Hoke Esqr & Squire Sigman turned him loose

Mr Canup started to go from home to young John Laws & had to go by the house - 1/2 mile from Sipes House met Abel - 9 or 10 o'clock - Abel told him he had been in his Masters Old field feeding his hogs - Abel had nothing in his hands - heard somebody hollow asked Negro where it was

Lincoln County

he said he did not - Negro then sat down together & talked. The Negro said he believed Sipes house was afire. Wit said he reckoned not negro said yes it was. Wit go and look - went together up & it was afire -

Daniel Harmon
James - belong to Philip on Sunday got up to Mr. Sigmans. The boy was gone from home - came to the house in the afternoon - boy asked him to go to the barn. Children were there - asked him to come round & in his hat - was a green Veil & a hankerchief - the same - said he got them at the Battalion Muster - he showed him the razor & looking glass which he also said he got at the muster.

State of North Carolina } Superior Court of Law Fall
Lincoln County   } Term Eighteen Hundred Thirty Seven

The Jurors for the State upon their Oath present, that Abel a slave the property of George Sigman late of said County & not having the fear of God before his eyes but being moved and seduced by the instigation of the Devil on the Twenty eighth day of May in the year of Our Lord One Thousand eight Hundred and Thirty-seven, with force and Arms in the County of Lincoln aforesaid, feloniously wilfully and Maliciously did set fire to and burn a certain Dwelling house of one Joseph Sipe there situate, against the Peace and dignity of the State
                        Jas R Dodge Sol

State of North Carolina } to any Lawful officer to
Lincoln County   } Execute & Return according
to Law whereas Joseph Sipe hath this Day appeared Before me Fr. Hoke one of the Justices of the peace for said County and made oath that Able a Negro of George Sigman By all accounts Did on the 24th inst maliciously And feloniously set fire to the Dwelling house of him the said Joseph Sipe with intent to Burn and Destroy the same and Did Consume the same thereby these are therefore to Command you to apprehend him the said Able negro & Bring him Before me or some other Justice for the said County to Bee Delt with according to Law given under my hand And seal this 30th of May 1837
summons   Fr. Hoke (Seal)

Lincoln County

Martin Knup
Polly hunsicker
Michael Hefner
&
Dave   negro of Joseph Hunsicker
& Jani   all for the state

May 31st 1837
witnesses   }   Martin Knup and J. Daniel Herman
                           each Bound in $100

now if the above Bounden persons do make their personal appearance at our next superior Court held for the County of Lincoln and state of North Carolina at the Court House in Lincolnton there the above Recognizance to be void other wise to Remain in full force and virtue
         Acknowledged before me
            Henry Cline   JP

                         The State against
                         Abel a Negro of
                         George Sigman
                         Executed by
                         J. D. Herman
                         officers fees $1.80

                         Subpeona
State of North Carolina,
       To the Sheriff of Lincoln County Greeting: you Are Hereby Commanded To Summon Martin Zimmerman personally to be and appear before the Judge of our Superior Court of Law, at the next Court to be held for our said County, at the Courthouse in____ , on the 2nd Monday After the 3rd in August then and there to testify, and the truth to say, in behalf of The State in a certain matter of controversy before said Court depending, and then and there to be tried where in The State is plaintiff, and Negro Abel is defendant. And this you shall in no wise omit, under the penalty prescribed by law

Lincoln County

Witness, B S Johnson Clerk of our said Court, at office, the 2d Monday after 3rd in February, 1837, and in the 61st year of our Independence.

                B S Johnson   Clk

Mr George Sigman
     Take notice that at the next Superior Court of Law of Lincoln County to be held at Lincolnton on the Second Monday after the Third Monday of August (instant) a negro Slave named Abel Your property will be put up his trial in a State prosecution affecting his life This is to notify you to attend the same
1 August 1837   Jas R Dodge   Sol

State of North Carolina,
     To the Sheriff of Lincoln County, Greeting: you are hereby commanded to summon Burrell Allen personally to be and appear before the Judge of our Superior Court at the court to be held for the county of Lincoln at the Court-House in Lincolnton on the 2nd Monday after the 3rd in Augt. Instanter, then and there to testify and the truth to say, in behalf of The State in a certain matter of controversy before said court depending, and there to be tried, wherein The State is plaintiff and Abel a Negro Slave is defendant. And this you shall in no wise omit under the penalty prescribed by law
     Witness John Michal Clerk of our said Court, at office Monday after 3rd in August and in the 62 year of our Independence, A.D. 1837
                John Michal   Clk

State of North Carolina
     To the Sheriff of Lincoln County, Greeting: you are hereby commanded to summon Burwell Allen personally to be and appear before the judge of our Superior Court at the next Court to be held for the county of   at the Court-House in Lincolnton on the Instanter, then and there to testify, and the truth to say, in behalf Abel a Slave in a certain matter of controversy before said Court, depending and there to be tried, wherein State is plaintiff and Abel Slave is defendant. And this you shall in no wise omit under the penalty prescribed by law.

Lincoln County

Witness John Michal Clerk of our said court, at office, the 2d Monday after 3rd next in Aug 1837 and in the 62 year of our Independence, A.D. 1837   John Michal   Clk

****

State
Vs.
William Hager & Others

State of North Carolina, Lincoln County   Know All Men By These Presents, That William C Hager Sherod Little all of the County of Lincoln are held and firmly bound unto Tho Ward Sherriff of our said county, in the sum of one Hundred dollars, current money of this State; to the which payment well and truly to be made and done, we bind ourselves, our heirs, executors and administrators, jointly and severally, firmly by these presents. Sealed with our seals, and dated this 7th day of Sept Anno Domini 1835

The Condition of the above obligation is such, That if the above Bounded William C Hager do make his personal appearance before the Judge of our next Superior Court to held for the county of Lincoln at the Court-House in Lincolnton on the 6th after Monday the 4th in Sept nxt, then and there to answer The State to bill of Indictment for A.B. committed on Body of Will a slave the Property of R H Burton and there to abide by the judgment of said Court, and not depart the same without leave first had; and if the securities shall well and truly discharge themselves. as special bail, of **[Blank]** then this obligation to be void - else to remain if full force and virtue.

Signed, Sealed And Delivered   }
In The Presence of   }
D McGee   Wm C Hager   (Seal)
                               Sherod S Little (Seal)

I   Sheriff of   Lincoln County, do hereby assign the above obligation and condition to the plaintiff therein named, his executors and administrators, to be sued for according to the statute in such case made and provided. In witness whereof, I have hereunto set my hand and seal, the **[Blank]** day of **[Blank]** Anno Domini 1835

                    Tho Ward   (Shff Seal)

Lincoln County

State of North Carolina
Lincoln County

Know All Men By These Presents, That William M Hager & George Kincade all of the County of Lincoln are held and firmly bound unto Thomas Ward Sheriff of our said County, in the sum of one Hundred dollars, current money of the State; to the which payment well and truly to be made and done, we bind ourselves, our heirs, executors and administrators, jointly and severally, firmly by these presents. Sealed with our seals, and dated this 7th day of Sept Anno Domini 1835. The Condition of the above obligation is such, That if the above bounden William Hager do make his personal appearance before the judge of our next Superior Court to be held for the County of Lincoln at the Court-House in Lincolnton on the 6th Monday after the 4th in Sept nxt, then and there to answer The State to a bill of indictment for an A.B. Committed on the Body of Will a slave The property of R. H. Burton and there to abide by judgment of said Court, and not depart the same without leave first had; and if the securities shall well and truly discharge themselves, a special bail, of **[Blank]** then this obligation to be void - else to remain in full force and virtue.

Signed, Sealed And Delivered,　　}Wm M. Hager　　　(Seal)
In The Presence of　　　　　　　 }George W. Kincade　(Seal)
　　D. McGee

I **[Blank]** Sheriff of **[Blank]** County, do hereby assign the above obligation and condition to the plaintiff therein named, his executors and administrators, to be sued for according to the statute in such case made and provided. in witness whereof, I have hereunto set my hand and seal, the **[Blank]** day of **[Blank]** Anno Domini 1835
　　　　　　Tho Ward　(Seal)

State of North Carolina　}　　Superior Court of
Lincoln County　　　　　 }　　Law Spring Term 1835

Lincoln County

The jurors for the state upon their oath present that William M Hager   William C. Hager and Simon Hager all late of said county on the first day of April in the year of our Lord one thousand eight hundred and Thirty five with force and Arms in said County in and upon one Will a slave the property of Robert H. Burton an assault did make and this said Will them and these did beat wound and ill treat to his great damage and against the peace and dignity of the State.

       William J. Alexander
       Sol

State   Witness Bound $100
 Vs
Wm H Hager   A True Bill
 & Others   Jno Reinhardt   Forman
 Ab
Robert H Burton
Abraham P. Joy
  Wit
Sworn
B Johnson   SC

****

State
Vs.
Catherine Barringer

State of North Carolina } At a Superior
Lincoln County   } Court of Law opened
and held for the County of Lincoln on the fourth Monday after the fourth Monday of March eighteen hundred and fifteen -

The Jurors for the State upon their Oath present that Catherine Barringer of the County of Lincoln maried Woman not having the fear of God before her eyes but being moved and Seduced by the instigations of the Devil on the twenty fifth day of January in the year one thousand eight hundred and fifteen with force and arms in the County of Lincoln aforesaid in and upon a female Negro slave **[Note: the word "child" marked through]** by the name of Clary in the peace of God and the State then and there being

Lincoln County

feloniously wilfully and of her malice aforethought did make an assault and that Said Catherine Barringer a certain stick which she the Said Catherine Barringer in her right hand then and there had and held and then and there feloniously wilfully and of her malice aforethought did the said female Negro [Note: the word "child" marked through] Slave Clary [Note: the words "did strike and beat" marked through] in and upon the head stomach Back and Sides of her the Said female Negro [Note: word "Child" marked through] Slave named Clary then and there feloniously wilfully and of her malice aforethought did strike and beat giving to the said female Negro [Note: "child" marked through] slave Clary by stroking and beating with the stick aforesaid in manner and form aforesaid several mortal bruises of which several mortal bruises the said female Negro [Note: "child" marked through] slave Clary from the twenty fifth day of January in the year aforesaid untill the twenty sixth day of January in the same year in the County of Lincoln aforesaid did languish and languishing did live on which said twenty sixth day of January in the said year one thousand eight hundred and fifteen the said female Negro [Note: "child" marked through] slave Clary in the County of Lincoln aforesaid of the several Mortal Bruises aforesaid died: and so the Jurors aforesaid upon upon their Oath aforesaid do say that the Said Catherine Barringer the said female Negro [Note: "child" marked through] Clary in manner and form aforesaid feloniously wilfully and of her malice aforethought did kill and Murder contrary to the statute in that case made and provided and against the peace and dignity of the State.

J. Wilson Sol

And the Jurors for the state aforesaid upon their oath aforesaid do further present that the aforesaid Catherine Barringer Maried Woman As aforesaid in the County aforesaid not having the fear of God before her eyes but being moved and seduced by the instigation of the Devil on the said twenty fifth day of January in the year one thousand eight hundred and fifteen aforesaid with force and arms in the County of Lincoln aforesaid in and upon a female Negro Slave named Clary in the peace of God and the State then and there being feloniously wilfully and of her malice aforethought did make an assault and that the said Catherine Barringer a certain stick which she the said Catherine Barringer in her right hand then and there had and held in and upon the right side of the head near the right temple of the said female Negro Slave Clary then and there feloniously wilfully and of her malice aforethought did strike and

Lincoln County

penetrate giving to the said female Negro Slave Clary then and there with the stick aforesaid in and upon the aforesaid right side of the head Near the right temple of the said female Negro Slave Clary one mortal wound of the length of one inch of which said mortal wound the said female Negro Slave Clary from the said twenty fifth day of January eighteen hundred and fifteen untill the twenty sixth day of the same month in the County aforesaid did languish and languishing did live on which said twenty sixth day of January in the year aforesaid the said female Negro Slave Clary in the County aforesaid of the said mortal wound Died: And So the Jurors aforeaid upon their Oath aforesaid do Say that the Said Catherine Barringer the said female Negro Slave Clary in manner and form aforesaid feloniously wilfully and of malice aforethought did kill and Murder contrary to the act of Assembly in that case made and provided and against the peace and dignity of the State

                                J. Wilson   Sol

State
Vs
Catherine Barringer   A True Bill
20 April 1815   Peter Link   forman
Governor Pro[???]
                          David Warlick
                          Absalom Warlick
                          John Norman   wit.
                          William Shenter
                          Philip Hyne
                          Mary Hyne
            Polly Labron[???]name marked through]
                          Elizabeth Shenk
                          James Bivins
                          Sworn & Sent
                          Lwn. Henderson   Clk

****

State
Vs.
Bob (a Slave)

Lincoln County

Mr. Nathaniel McClurg
    I hereby notify you that a true Bill of indictment for Arson have been found by the Grand Jury at the last Superior Court of law held for Lincoln County at the Courthouse in Lincolnton on the fourth Monday AD 1827 against your Negro Man Slave Bob, and that the said Negro Man Slave Bob will be tried for said offences at the next Superior Court of law to be held for Lincoln County at the Courthouse in Lincolnton on the 4th Monday after the 4th Monday of September next when & where you may attempt to defend him if you think proper
                          June the 28th AD 1827
H. Cansler

                          The State
                              Vs
                          Bob a Slave
                      The Property of
                      Nathl McClurg
                          Notice
                 To Octbr Term 1827
                 Copy delivered the
                    28 of June 1827
                H. Cansler Pltff

State of North Carolina
Lincoln County
                Superior Court of Law
                April Term 1827
    The Jurors for the State upon their oath present that Bob a Negro man Slave the property of Nathaniel McClurd not having the fear of God before his eyes but being moved and seduced by the instigation of the Devil on the first day of April in the year of our Lord one thousand eight hundred and twenty seven with force and arms in the County of Lincoln aforesaid a certain house commonly called a Barn of one Adam Kiser there situate feloniously wilfully and maliciously did set fire to and the same house commonly called a barn having five Bushels of Rye corn therein then and there by such firing as aforesaid he Commonly wilfully and maliciously did burn and Consume against the peace and dignity of the State
                    N. Wilson Sol

Lincoln County

State of North Carolina
Lincoln County
     Superior Court of Law
      April Term 1827

The Jurors for the State upon their Oath present that Bob a Negro man Slave the property of Nathaniel McClurd on the first day of April in the year of our Lord one thousand eight hundred and twenty seven with force and arms in the County of Lincoln aforesaid a certain house of one Abram Mooney there situate the same having Rye Corn therein it being a house commonly called a Barn feloniously wilfully and maliciously did set fire to, and the same house then and there by such firing as aforesaid feloniously wilfully and maliciously did burn and consume against the peace and dignity of the State
       N Wilson Sol

dismissed Apr   State
Term 1828   Vs
      Bob a Slave
       Arson
    Abram Mooney Plaint

     Dick a Slave
     Jim a Slave wit
     Peter a Slave
     Liran[???]
     D. A. Ramsaur Foreman
     Lwn Henderson Clk

****

       State
        Vs.
      John Collins

State   } James Martin Swears that in the
Vs   } year 1817 John Collins went to the

Lincoln County

John Collins   }   house of this deponent and asked
Charge   }   him to walk with him to Esqr
Corn Stealing   }   Abner Mcafee's he consented and
                         while on the way on a near rout
                         that he generally walked there said
                         John Collins told him that he was
                         going after corn but that he was
not going to get the corn of McAfee but of Mat (who is one of his negro men) that he saw said Collins go to a hollow chestnut Tree and take he thinks a petticoat out of the Tree and proceeded on toward Mcafee's that after they had went on together to certain log he refused to go any further with him (Collins) upon any such business - that he (Martin) sac[Torn] at some body walking and thought it to be said Collins and Esqr. Mcaffee expecting that Mcafee had caught him (Collins) getting the corn from Mat the negro fellow but on their coming nearer he heard one of them whistle upon which he said come on. and when they came to him he found it to be Collins and Mat. but that they then had no corn That they went on near to the path that led to Bradley's old place and before getting quite to the path Mat told Collins and him Martin to stop there till he came back. And after being gone long enough to go to the crib and get corn he Mat came back with the same petticoat (as so took it to be) that sd. Collins got out of the hollow chestnut tree with he thinks about a bushel of corn in it in the say as I so took it to be and delivered it to the said John Collins then they started on together till they came to my path then I refused to go any further with him while on any such business. and he (Collins) said he would take the corn home. and I left him - that said John Collins told him (Martin) that he (Collins) has got fifteen bushels of Mcaffees wheat from Mat in one year but what year he does not know. And further says that he believes all this was done without the knowledge and consent of the said Abner Mcafee as he (Collins) told him that he would not do so any more if he wouldn't tell on him   Bill Dru/awn[??]

****

State
Vs.
Peter Best

Lincoln County

State of North Carolina }   Superior Court of Law
Lincoln County   }   October term 1812

    The Jurors for the state upon their oath present That at a Court of Pleas and quarter Sessions held for the County of Lincoln at the Court house in Lincolnton on the third Monday of January in the year one thousand eight hundred and nine, there was pending and at issue a certain charge and cause the state against one Campble a negro slave the property of William Row (Rose) Sadler, for grand larceny for stealing certain goods the property of one Michael Schenck from the waggon of one Andrew Hovis: And the Juror aforesaid said upon their oath aforesaid do further present That on the heal of said charge against the said negro slave Campble to wit, on Saturday of the said January Court that is to say on the twenty first day of January in the year aforesaid Peter Best late of the County of Lincoln planter was introduced as a witness in behalf of the state gainst the said negro Campble and that the said Peter Best being so introduced and coming before the said Court of please and Quarter Sessions then and there holden as aforesaid, he the said Peter Best, then and there in open Court did take his corporal oath upon the Holy Gospel of God the Justices of the said Court of Pleas and quarter Sessions then and having sufficient and competent Power and authority to administer said oath to the said Peter Best in that behalf and that the said Peter Best not having the fear of God before his eyes, but being moved and seduced by the instigation of the Devil and no wise regarding the laws and statutes of the state but wickedly intending and to aggrive[sic]? and impin[sic]?the said negro slave Campble with forse and arms then and there, to wit, on the said twenty first day of January in the year aforesaid before the said Court of Pleas and quarter Sessions then and there holden as aforesaid upon his oath, aforesaid, falsely, maliciously, wilfully, corruptibly, and feloniously did say swear and declare (among other things) in substance and to the effect following, That is to say That he the said Peter Best gave three certain bonds to the amount of five hundred dollars, on the fifth day July in the year one thousand eight hundred and eight to the aforesaid Andrew Hovis in order to save himself (the said Peter Best) from being sent to Jail and not in consideration of the articles and goods which the said Andrew Hovis had lost and for the stealing of which the said negro slave Campble, then and there as aforesaid stood charged [Note: the word "indebted" marked through & replaced with

Lincoln County

"charged"] and that one Thomas McGee threatened on the said fifth day of July in the year one Thousand eight hundred and eight, that if he the said Peter Best did not sign and deliver, the said then Bonds amounting as aforesaid to five hundred dollars to the said Andrew Hovis he the said Peter Best should be committed to Jail; and that he the said Peter Best did not promise and agree, offer and propose some time after the aforesaid goods were stolen, to give the aforesaid Michael Shenck the owner of said goods one hundred dollars in consideration of the advance and profit, which he the said Michael Shenck might have made upon the articles and goods, whereas in fact and in truth the said Peter Best did not give three bonds amounting to five hundred dollars, on the fifth day of July in the year one thousand eight hundred and eight to the said Andrew Hovis, in order to save him the said Peter Best from being sent to Jail; and whereas in fact and in truth the said Peter Best did give the said three bonds amounting to five hundred dollars to the said Andrew Hovis in consideration of the articles and goods which the said Andrew Hovis had lost and for the stealing of which the said negro slave Campble then and there stood charged and whereas in truth and in fact the said Thomas McGee did not threaten on the said fifth day of July in the year one thousand eight hundred and eight, if he, the said Peter Best did not sign and deliver said bonds amounting to five hundred dollars to the said Andrew Hovis, he the said Peter Best should be committed to Jail; and whereas in truth and in fact he, the said Peter Best, did offer amd propose, promise and agree sometime after the said articles and goods were stolen from the aforesaid Andrew Hovis, to give the said Michael Shenck the owner of said goods, one hundred dollars in consideration of the advances profit which he the said Michael Shenck might have made on said articles and goods, all which facts was aforesaid from to by the said Peter Best [?] material and important to and in the trial of the said charge against the said negro slave Campble And to the Jurors aforesaid on their oath aforesaid do say that the said Peter Best then and there to wit on the twenty first day of January in the year aforesaid one thousand eight hundred and nine, in the County of Lincoln aforesaid in and before the said Court of Pleas and quarter Sessions (They the said Court then and there having sufficient and competent power and authority to administer said oath to the said Peter Best in that behalf) by his own act and consent and of his own most wicked and corrupt mind and disposition in manner and form aforesaid, did falsely, wickedly, willfully, maliciously,

Lincoln County

feloniously and corruply commit wilful and corrupt Perjury, to the great displeasure of Almighty God, to the [evil?/ill?] example of all others in the like case offending against the form of the act of Assembly in such case made and provided and against the peace and dignity of the State

                      Edwin Jay Osborn Sol. P.S.

State   }   A true Bill
Vs   } Indict   Alexander Moore
Peter Best   }   forman
Perjury
To October Term 1812
Govrnor Prosr

Thos McGee   }
Michl Schenk   }
                    } Witnesses
Js. McKee   }
Jn Sadler   }
Andw Hovis   }
Sworn & Sent
Lwn. Henderson Clk

****

State
Vs.
Ramsour & Others

State of North Carolina
Lincoln County
                    Superior Court of Law
                      April Term 1827

The jurors for the state upon their oath present that Jacob Ramsour John Michel Martin Zimmerman and George Shuford all of the County of Lincoln on the 26th day of April 1827 with force and arms in the County of Lincoln upon the body of Charles a Negro Slave the property of Christian Arney did make an assault and him the said Charles then and

Lincoln County

there did wound beat and ill treat against the peace and dignity of the State

State
Vs
Ramsour and others
A.B.
Christian Arney }
[?] Shank }
Jacob Reinhardt }
Daniel Shuford }
Henery[?] Shank }
Jacob Rush[?] }
Sworn & sent
Lwn Henderson Clk

Wilson Sol

Henderson
A True Bill as restricts[?]
Ramsour & Michael
Wit
D A RAMSOUR Foreman

****

State
Vs.
Dick (a Slave)

State }
Vs }
Dick a Slave the }
property of H. Fulenwider }
& R. H. Burton }

J. P. Hood a witness being Sworn, states that as he was going from the Forge towards this House passed by the Blacksmith Shop Where Deft was at work where he saw the deceased who was a Hammer man in the forge with a piece of Iron drawn against Dick who had retreated from his Anville Block when Adam the decd persued him & struck him Dick with the Iron Dick then picked up a pair of Tongs when witness told him to lay then down he then towards Adam but did not go near him deceased then pursued him with the Bar of Iron Dick took the Iron from decd the decd then clinched Deft and deft threw him down on a Tub of Water in which the Tongs were setting the Deft Made no attempt to hurt decd after having threw him down Witness told Deft to get up and took hold of him and he got off of deceased the deceased sprung up immediately after him and run him Round the Shop When witness found

Lincoln County

that which he decd had a wound on his forehead which he supposed was [?? ??] by Deft Dropping the Bar of Iron which he had to defend himself

---

State Of North Carolina
Lincoln County. Whereas by information of Robert H. Burton, it is made known that Adam a negro man slave the property of Henry Fulenwider & Robert H Burton is dead, & from information died of wounds received in a fight with Dick a negro man slave also the property of said Hy. Fulenwider & Robert H Burton - These are therefore to command you to arrest the body of said negro man slave Dick & have him before me or some other Justice of the peace for said county to be dealt with according to law
Given under my hand & seal March 15th 1839
D. Reinhardt   J.P. (Seal)
J. P. Hood
Doct J. P. Simpson
& negro Bob witnesses
service of this warrant acknowledged March 15th 1839
       Robt H Burton

Doctr J. P. Simpson being sworn states that he attended decd that he believes if his death was occasioned by either of his wounds it must have been by the one produced by falling on the Tongs that the wound on the forehead was slight he further states that deceased told him shortly before he died that he punched Dick with a piece of Iron first that he would tell no lie about it But that his own impression is that his death was not occasioned by either of the wounds
We the subscribers having heard the foregoing evidences do believe that the defendant was Justifiable in acting in his own defense as we understand he did by the evidence and therefore discharge him of the within charge
15th March 1839   B S Johnson (J.P.)
           Jno Hoke   J.P.
           D. Reinhardt J.P.
           Carlos Leonard J.P.
           J. S. Alexander J.P.

Lincoln County

Bob a witness being cautioned as to the consequences of an Oath was sworn & deposeth as follows States that Adam Decd came to the shop with a chisel to be sharpened Dick told him that he wished to bend his waggon tyne that he was in the fire first decd told Dick that if he did not sharpen his chisel he would go & tell Mr. Ramsour and Dick said he would do it as soon as he bent his Tyne Adam then commenced cursing Dick & Dick cursed Adam Adam then said if he did not mind he would knock him down with a Barr of Iron Dick said he was not afraid & Dick Retreated Adam then Drew his Iron at which time Mr. Hood came in

****

State
Vs.
Edward Mobly
Owner of Bob (a Slave)
State of North Carolina

To the Sheriff of Lincoln County, Greeting: You are hereby commanded that of the goods and chattels, lands and tenements of Edward Mobly (owner of the negro slave Bob) if to be found in your bailwick, you cause to be made the sum of seven Pounds and seven pence which in the Superior Court of Law, held for the County of Lincoln at the Court-house in Lincolnton The State recovered against him for costs and charges in the said suit expended, whereof the said Edward Mobly is liable, as appear to us of record: besides your fees for this service. And have you the said monies before the Judge of our said Court at Lincolnton on the fourth Monday after the 4th Monday of March next; then and there to render the said State for costs and charges as aforesaid. Herein fail not, and have you then and there this writ.

Witness, Lawson Henderson Clerk of the said Court at Office the fourth Monday after the 4th Monday of Septr in the XLVII year of American Independence, Anno Domini 1822

Lwn Henderson

Lincoln County

Come to hand Novr 11th 1822 J. Coulter Shff

The State	Indictment	£ 0 : 10 : 0
Vs	3 Recognizances	[?] : 6 : 0
Edward Mobly the	Seal and Copy }	
owner of the Slave	of Sentence }	0 : 18 : 0
Bob convicted of	Judgment and }	
Felony &	execution for court}	0 : 11 : 3
Housebreaking		£ 2 : 5 : 3
	Solr. J W Wilson $5	
		2 : 10 : 0
Fe Fa	Peter Hoyle	
		0 : 14 : 7
To April Term 1823	Rudolph Rodes	
		0 : 14 : 7
		£ 6 : 4 : 7
	J. Zimmerman	}
	[??] arrest & [??]	}
		0 : 16 : 0
		£ 7 : 0 : 7
	Equal to	$ 14.06
	Commiss	35
	Levy fee	75
		$ 15.16

State	}	Bill of costs	
Vs	}	Clerks fees	£ 2 : 5 : 3
Edward Mobley	}	Solr JW $5	2 : 10 : 0
the owner of	}	Peter Hoyle Witness	0 : 14 : 9
the Slave Bob	}	Rudolph Rodes	0 : 14 : 7
		John Zimmerman	0 : 16 : 0
			£ 7 : 0 : 7
		equal to	$ 14 : 6-
107.21		add $5 Sol fee	5
2			19 -6

Lincoln County

214.42   1.60
 53.60   17.46
268.02
Bill of costs
The State
  Vs
Edward Mobly the
owner of the slave
Bob

****

State
Vs.
Joseph Wear

State of North Carolina } To John Zimmerman
Lincoln County   } Jailer
you are hereby Commanded to receive into your Jail the body of Joseph Wear in consequence of a charge of the State of Burglary, for being accessary in breaking the Store of Jacob Ramsour of Lincolnton the sd Joseph Wear safely to keep untill discharged by a due course of Law Given under our hands this 8th day of Novr. 1825
                    C. E. Reinhardt JP
                    Jas. Bivings   JP

[Editor's Note: Part of the below document is missing.]

Present that the said Joseph Wier after words   on the same first day of April in the said year of our Lord one thousand and eight hundred and twenty six in the County of Lincoln aforesaid with force and arms in the said County of Lincoln the said Negro man Slave June feloniously did receive harbour conceal and Maintain he the said Joseph Wier then and there well knowing the said Negro man Slave June the said felony and Burglary aforesaid to have done and committed in manner and form aforesaid contrary to the statute in that case made and provided and against the peace and dignity of the State
                    W. Wilson

Lincoln County

State   }   Evidence of Henry A.
Vs   }   Langford -
Joseph Wier   }

Says that it is a month or more since Wier asked him if he would not assist on getting to a place of money & sd the place was at one Summeys & sd one Summey had some Thousands of Dollars in his store & sd he could contrive a way to get it & put in (Langfords) on a way he (Wier) appointed a time when they (Wear & Langford) should come and see the place They met at Mr Ramsours but Wier sd it was Mr. Summeys Wier took me Langford in to show me the situation of the store we staid in Mr Ramsours store until we were satisfied I went back to our horses Wier sd I might go on home & he Wier would go on his journey to Statesville & sd he would be back home on Saturday & also that he would be back in time on Saturday night to fix & legalate business to get in to Summeys Store. Wier did not get back until Saturday evening too late to get it done as things were not in fix he (Wier) sd that it had to be done the next night - or not at all for the man would go away on Monday & I under stood the man Ramsour or Summey as Wier called him was to take his money away on Monday. On Sunday he Wier came over to an out-house where I staid & sd the tools must be fixed he Wier picked out & sorted tools he thought would be necessary & sent Negro June to fix a piece of Iron to lift the chop piece of the door it was fixed & we Langford & June returned back to the house again we had not been there long untill Wier came over He Wier there directed as on to Ramsours store to get that money & sd that it was in a drawer under the counter where Wier generally stood when Wier & me were in the store the Thursday before & sd that the main body lay there but the small change was on the opposite side in a small drawer & told us to go on & get it if we could & bring it to him & he would have it exchanged for other kind of money & pay us our part. We came & Wier furnished us with horses.

1   Question How much money did Wear tell you was there
       A five six or Eight Thousand Dollars & that he had seen it put away there
2   Q who made the instruments to open the door
       A June

Lincoln County

3   Q who assisted on making the instruments
     A Mr. Wier crooked one piece & direct
     June how to make the rest like it
4   Q Was Wier to come an himself to assist in breaking open the store
     A He still allowed he would be untill the last th sent his Negro June
5   Q What saddle did you ride
     A It was Mr. Wiers sadle & Wier direct me to take his saddle
6   Q is or is not this saddle Wiers & the one you rode
     A It is Wiers Saddle & the one he told me to take
7   Q When he Wier come an with you to Town to show you Summeys store house he took you to
     Ramsours store did or did he not direct you to measure certain parts of sd store & what parts did he direct you to measure
     A he told me as he stept in at the door on the left hand side he would set his saddle bags & I
     Langford should set a hickery on the same side at the half steeple on the left hand side as we
     went in to see where the steeple would strike the hickery
8   Q did you Lock the door of the house you lived in when you left home
     A I did & put the key in a crack of the house in Mr Wiers presence
9   Q did you take the measure of the Steeple of the door & retain it & by that measure open the
     door as Wier had directed you
     A I took the measure on home & kept it until we June & I brought it back & by that measure got into the house
     Q did or did not Wier direct his Negro Boy June to open the door
     A he did
     Q did June open the door
     A he did
11   Q Where did you hitch your horses
     A about 100 yards on the Right hand of the road as we come & about 200 yards on the other side
     of Col Daniel Hokes fence

Lincoln County

12   Q What directions did Wier give to you to act when you came on
A he directed us to pull our hatts & shoes off before we went into the store house & we done so

13   did the negro take away any thing out of the store
A June said he had found some money on the opposite side where Wier told us the small change was

Questions by deft
Q What horses did you ride
A two Horses a stud horse, & a mare
Q What was the name of the mare
A you & your family called her the cane filly she was a dark coulored beast
Q What time was it in the night that you & June came on here
A It was some thing after 12 Oclock on last Sunday night the 6th of Novr June rode the cane filly
Q Where did you lay the keys of the house & was it a common place to put them
A I put the keys in a crack & it was not a common place but according to appointment as Wier was to be there when we got back & sd may be he might come & want to get in before we got

---

Evidence of Henry Cansler

Says that Mr Wier told them that his saddle was in Langford and Junes house & that this saddle found there is that same saddle that is sworn to by Langford to be Wiers, & that a stirrup Iron was found on the way mateing the one that was found on the saddle the house was locked when we got there & by Mr Wiers consent the Steeple was drawn & the saddle found

Daniel Hoke states that he went with Langford to the place that Langford described that the horses were ties & found the cutting of the limb as described by Langford the rest of his evidence as to the saddle corresponds with that of Mr Canseller

                    C.E. Reinhardt   JP

Jas Bivings   JP
                        State

Lincoln County

Vs
June a Slave&
Joseph Wier
Burglary

Jacob Ramsour
P. S. Wit
Mo Haffner
Henry Cansler
Henry Landford
Sworn & sent
Lwn Henderson

State of North Carolina }   Superior Court
Lincoln County   }   April Term 1826

The jurors for the State on their oath present June (a negro man Slave the property of Joseph Wier) of the County of Lincoln on the first day of April in the year of our Lord one thousand eight hundred and twenty six about the hour of ten in the night of the same day with force and arms in the County of Lincoln aforesaid the dwelling house of Jacob Ramsour there situate feloniously and burglariously did break and enter with intent the goods and chattels of the said Jacob Ramsour in the said dwelling house then and there being found then and there feloniously and burglariously to steal take and carry away against the peace and dignity of the State

     And the jurors aforesaid upon their oath aforesaid do further present that Joseph Wier late of the same County of Lincoln before the said felony and Burglary was committed in form aforesaid to wit on the first day of April in the year aforesaid with force and arms in the County of Lincoln aforesaid did unlawfully and feloniously counsel aid abet and procure the said June to do and commit the said felony and burglary against the peace and dignity of the State. And the Jurors Aforesaid upon Their Oath Aforesaid do further

---

North Carolina }   Superior Court of Law
Lincoln County   }   April Term 1826

Lincoln County

The State vs Joseph Wier - Defendant swears that on yesterday for the first time, he was advised that a certain John   would be a material witness for his defense, since which time he has not had it in his power to have summoned, as he lives about 21 or 22 miles distant from this place - He expects to have him at next Court

        Sworn to in open Court   Joseph Weir
        April 28th 1826
        Lwn Henderson   Clk

Deponent further swears that he expects to prove by said witness that negro June was at his house at work during the day that this deponant was arrested, until after the arrest of this deponant & he was taken away by the officer

                      Joseph Wier

Sworn to and subscribed
in open Court 29th April
AD 1826 Lwn Henderson   Clk

                      State
                      Vs
               Joseph Wier
           Examination of
               Witnesses

****

                      State
                      Vs.
               Morgan Jones

State of North Carolina }   Superior Court of Law
Lincoln County   }   October Term 1826

The jurors for the state upon their oath present that Morgan Jones of the county of Lincoln on the twenty sixth day of October in the year of our Lord one thousand eight hundred and twenty six with force and arms in the county of Lincoln aforesaid one negro male slave by the name of Altimore of the value of one hundred dollars the goods and chattels and property of William Graham then and there being found did then and there feloniously seduce steal take and convey away with an intention to

Lincoln County

appropriate and dispose of to the own proper use of the said Morgan Jones against the form of the Statute in that case made and provided and against the peace and dignity of the state - And the jurors aforesaid upon their oath aforesaid do further present that Morgan Jones aforesaid of the County aforesaid on the aforesaid twenty sixth day of October in the year of our Lord one thousand and eight hundred and twenty six with force and arms in the county aforesaid one negro male slave by the name of Altimore of the value of one hundred dollars the goods and chattels and property of William Graham then and there being found did then and there feloniously steal take seduce and convey away with an intention to sell and dispose of to one John Wintz against against the form of the Statute in that case made and provided and against the peace and dignity of the State

J. Wilson Sol

State
Vs
Morgan Jones
Felony
William Graham
John Wintz
Witnesses
Sworn & sent.

Lwn Henderson Clk

A True Bill
Daniel Hoke

State of North Carolina

State	}	
Vs	}	on a charge of negro stealing
Morgan Jones	}	The county of Lincoln to Benjamen Sherwood

jailor of Davidson County DE to maintaining this defendant as a prisoner from the 22nd of May last, to the 3rd of August, seventy three days at thirty seven and a half cents per day is $ 27.37 1/2
receiving and discharging said prisoner   <u>60</u>
                                          27.97 1/2

Lincoln County

B Sherwood, jailor

State of North Carolina }   December Session 1826
Davidson County   }   I David Mock clerk of the court of pleas and quarter sessions for Davidson County do certify that Benjamen Sherwood jailor of said county exhibited, and Swore to the above amount in open court
      In testimony whereof I have hereunto set my hand affixed the Seal of my office the 22nd day of December 1826
               D. Mock   CCC

Lexington   }   paid 10
Dec 25   }Clerk of the Superior Court of Lincoln County
The State
    Vs
Morgan Jones

Jailors Acct

State of North Carolina }   October Term, 1826
Lincoln County   }

State versus Morgan Jones
William Kesiah charges the Pltff for attending as a witness in this suit 5 days
at 1 dollar per day $ 5.00
104 miles travelling at 1.00 per 30 miles   3.46 2/3
Ferriage, Ticket, 10 cts   .10
                                                  $ 8.56 2/3
Sworn to before me at officethis 27 day of October 1826
               Lwn. Henderson   Clk

State of North Carolina }   October Term, 1826
Lincoln County   }
       State versus Morgan Jones
John Wintz charges the Pltff forattending as a witness in thus suit 5 days
at 1.00 per day $ 5.00
98 miles travelling, at 1.00 per 30 miles   3.26 2/3

Lincoln County

Ferriage, Ticket, 10 cts   .10
                                                                $ 8.36 2/3
Sworn to before me at officethis 27th day of October 1826
                          Lwn Henderson   Clk

I assign the within to the use of Paul Keistler for value recd- of him
October 27th 1826
           his
   William   X   Kesiah
           mark

State of North Carolina   }   October Term, 1826
Lincoln County   }
       State versus Morgan Jones
Dunning Kesiah charges the Pltff for attending as a witness in this suit 5 days
at 1.00 per day $ 5.00
98 miles travelling, at 1.00 per 30 miles   3.26 2/3
Ferriage, Ticket, 10 cts   .10
                                                  $ 8.36 2/3
Sworn to before me - at office this 27th day of October 1826
                       Lwn Henderson   Clk
I assign the within to the use of Paul Keistler for value recd
October 27th 1826
Dunning Kesiah

****

State
Vs.
Negro Man

State   }   Bill Of Costs
Vs   }
Negro Man   }   Indictment   £ 0 6 0
12 Recognizance   1 4 0
Order of Commitment Released   4 0

Lincoln County

dismission & Bill of Costs	11	3
	2 5	3
Cons Eli Perkins	8	0
Shff Coulter treat 1/6 taking in		
Custody 7/6	9	0
Sentence of Court	10	0
Atto Geo McCullock	2 0	0
	£ 5 12	3
Witness L. Lorance	2 1	2
" E. Lorance	2 2	0
	£ 9 15	5
	$ 19.54	

The State
Vs
Negro Man
Bill of costs
Satisfyed
Jno Coulter Shff These to be filed with the Executions to April Sessions 1832

****

State
Vs.
Daniel (a Slave)

State of North Carolina
      To the Sheriff of Bumcomb County Greeting:
you are hereby commanded to summon Maxamillian Harris personally to appear before the Judge of our Superior Court of Law, at the next court to be held for the County of Lincoln at the court house in Lincolnton on the 4th Monday after the 4th Monday of March next; then and there to testify and the truth to say in behalf of The State of No. Carolina in a certain cause then and there depending, and to be tried; between said State plantiff, and Negro Daniel defendant. And this you shall in no wise omit under the penalty prescribed by law. Herein fail not, and have you then and there this writ.

Lincoln County

Witness Lawson Henderson Clerk of our said court at office the 4th Monday after the 4th Monday of September 1820 and in the XXXXV year of our Independence.

Lwn Henderson

State of No. Carolina } To the Gaoler of Lincoln
Bumcombe County   } County you are hereby

commanded to Take the body of Daniel a negro slave and him safely keep in your custody untill discharged by Law. Whereas said Daniel is charged by the State for feloniously stealing and carrying Away from the said County of Lincoln one Roan horse
Pros. by William Abernathy given under my hand and Seal 2nd of march 1821

J. H. Poteet   (Seal)

State
Vs
Daniel

State of North Carolina } Superior Court of Law
Lincoln County } April term 1821

The Jurors for the State upon their oath of the County of Lincoln present that Daniel (a Negro slave the property of Blake Piercy) on the first day of April in the year of our Lord eighteen hundred and twenty one woth force and arms in the County aforesaid one roan horse of the value of ten dolars the goods and chattles of William Abernaty then and there being found did feloniously steal take and had away against the peace and dignity of the State

Wilson Sol.

State   A True Bill
Vs   Alexander Moore
Daniel a Slave   fore Man
  Larceny
William Abernathy

Lincoln County

James Abernathy
Jno Wheeler
Maxamillian Harris
Francis a Slave   wit
Sworn & sent
Lwn Henderson

State of North Carolina   }   Superior Court of Law
Lincoln County   }   April Term, A. D. 1821

   State
  Vs.
Negro Daniel

Jas. Abernathy charges the State in this cause, Dr.
To attendance as a Witness,
2 days at 6 per day   12.   0
Traveling to Court and home again 36 miles at 6
per 30   7.   2
Ferriage   Ticket 10 cents   1.   0
                                               £ 1.   0.   2

Sworn to before me, the 27th day of April A. D. 1821
                        Wallace A. Henderson   D. Clk.

State of North Carolina   }   To some Lawful Officer to
Buncombe County   }   Execute and return as the Law directs
         Whereas William Abernathy Appears before me James H. Poteet acting Justice for said county and made Oath in due form of Law that he has Just Reason to believe that a certain Negro Slave named Daniel Belonging to Blake Piercy of Buncombe County did feloniously steal and carry away from the county of Lincoln County One Roan horse the property of said Abernathy contrary to the Law and dignity of the State these are therefore to comand you to Apprehend Said Negro Daniel and Safely keep so he may Be delt with as the Law directs given Under my hand And Seal this 2d day of March 1821
Jurors for the State   J. H. Poteet   (Seal)

Lincoln County

Ephraim Piercy
[Two names marked through]
Joseph Shepherd [Marked through]

State of North Carolina } Superior Court of Law
Lincoln County   } April Term, A.D. 1821
State
 Vs
Negro Daniel
Wm. N. Abernathy charges the state in this cause,
Dr. To
attendance as a Witness, 2 days at 6 per day   12.   0
Traveling to Court and home again 30 miles
at 6 pr 30   7.   2
Ferriage   Ticket 10 cents   1.   0
                                          £ 1.   0.   2

Sworn to before me, the 27th day of April A.D. 1821
                Wallace A Henderson   D Clk

State of North   } To any Lawful Officer
Lincoln County   } or Martin Shuford
    Whereas William Abernathy has complained to me on oath one of the Justices of the peace for the County of Lincoln that Negro Daniel claimed by Blair McGee on the night of the 20th of February 1821 did feloniously steal tak and carry away one Roan Horse of the proper good & Chattels of the said William & against the peace and dignity of the State
    This is therefore to command you to take the body of said Negro Daniel & have him before me or some other Justice of the peace for said County that he may be dealt with as the law directs
Given under my hand & seal
This 12th March 1821   Daniel Hoke   JP

State of North Carolina } We & each of us acknowledge
Lincoln County   } ourselves indebted to the

Lincoln County

State of North Carolina in the sum of fifty Pounds each to levied of our goods and chattels Lands & tenements to be void on condition that William Abernathy & Blair McGee [This name marked through] make their personal appearance at the next Superior Court of Law to be held for the County of Lincoln on the 4th Monday of April next then & there to give evidence against Negro Daniel & not departeth Court without cause
 Witness   Wm Abernathy   (Seal)
   12th day of March 1821
        Daniel Hoke   JP
Executed & released by me
Martin Shuford
State
 Vs
Negro Daniel
Bill Drawn

State of North Carolina }   Superior Court of Law
Lincoln County   }   April Term, A.D. 1821

 State   Negro Francis
  Vs
 Negro Daniel

charges the State in this cause, Dr.
To attendance as a Witness, 3 days
 at 10/ - per day   1: 10: 0
Traveling to Court and home again
  130 miles at 10/ - per 30   2: 3: 4
   Ferriage Ticket 10 cents   1: 0
                     3: 14: 4

Sworn to before me, the 27th day of April A.D. 1821
        Wallace A Henderson   D Clk
 State
  Vs
 Negro Daniel
 To be filed & when
 collected to be paid

Lincoln County

to R. H. Burton for use
of Mrs. Young on Frank

State of No Carolina   }   We Each of us do hereby
Buncombe County   }   acknowledge Our Selves
Indebted to the State of No Carolina in the Just Sum of Fifty pounds Each To be levied Of our goods and chattles Lands and Tenements of Void On condition that we make our personal appearance before the Judge Of the Superior Court yo be holden for the county of Lincoln at the court house in Linclonton the Third monday After the fourth monday in March next then and There to give Evidence in behalf of the State against Daniel a negro Slave the property of Blake Piercy[?] and not depart the court without leave then this obligation Void Otherwise remain in Full force and Virtue of Law Given Under Our hands and Seals this 2nd day of march 1821

                Wm. Abernathy   (Seal)
Attest
J. H. Poteat   Ephraim Piercy[?]   (Seal)

    State
    Vs
Daniel Recognizance

State of North Carolina
    To the Sheriff of Burke County Greeting: you are hereby commanded to Summon Negroe Frank (a Slave the property of Neomy Young) personally to appear before the Judge of our Superior court of Law, at the next Court to be held for the County of Lincolnton on the 4th Monday after the 4th Monday of March; then and there to testify and the truth to say in behalf of The State of No Carolina in a certain cause then and there depending, and to be tried; between The said state - plaintiff, and Negroe Daniel defendant, And this you shall in no wise omit under the penalty prescribed by law. Herein fail not, and have you then and there this writ.

Lincoln County

    Witness Lawson Henderson Clerk of our Said court at Office the 4th Monday after the 4th Monday of September 1820 and in the XXXXV year of our Independence

                      Lwn. Henderson

Executed Mark
Brittain H Shff
  By   The State
John Harden   Vs
                    Negro Daniel
                    Subpeona
                    To April Term 1820
                    Burke
                    Come to hand 27th March
                    Thos G[???]   Shff

State of North Carolina
Lincoln County
    Superior Court of Law
    April Term 1821
The Jurors for the State upon their oath present that Daniel a Negro man Slave the property of Blake Piercy[?] on the 22d day of April 1821 with force and arms in the County of Lincoln aforesaid one Kirb Bridle of the value of fifty cents the goods and chattles of David Phillips then and there being found then and there did feloniously steal take and carry away against the peace And dignity of the State
                          J. Wilson   Sol

State
Vs
Daniel a slave   A true Bill
  P.L.   Alexander Moore
                      fore Man

David Phillips
  P.Q. wit.
Wm Abernathy
Francis a Slave
Sworn & sent

Lincoln County

Lwn. Henderson Clk

****

State
Vs.
Isaac & Cyrus (Slaves)

Commitment of
Isaac Slave

State of North Carolina }   Mettimus for Felony
Lincoln County   }

Peter Summey one of the Coroners for said County To the keeper of the Jail for said County Whereas Isaac (a slave formerly the property of Joshua M. Irby Decd.) being before me on a charge of the Murder of the said Joshua on the finding of a Jury of inquest on the day of the date hereof These are here for commanding you to keep the body of said Slave Isaac safely in your jail so that you have him before the Judge of our next Superior Court of laws for said County that he may be further dealt with according to law Given under My hand & Seal this 22nd day of May 1828

       P. Summey Coroner

State of North Carolina }   Oct Term 1828
 Lincoln County   }
  versus   }   Wm. McCullock
 Isaac slave   }
 charges the State   }   for
attending as a witness in this suit 4 days at
.60 per day, $ 2.40
44 miles traveling, at .60 per 30 miles   .88
Ferriage 12 1/2 Tickets 10 cents,   .22 1/2
                                            $ 3.50 1/2

Sworn before me C. C. Henderson at office this 22 day of Oct 1828
     Lwn Henderson Clk

State of North Carolina }   To any Lawful Officer
Lincoln County   }

Lincoln County

To Execute and make return These are to require you immediately upon sight hereof to summon twenty four good and lawful men of the said county to be and appear before Peter Summey one of the Coroners of the said county at the late residence of Joshua M Irby in the said County by Nine o-clock on this day Then and There to enquire of do and execute all such things as on behalf of the said State shall be lawfully given then in charge touching the death of Joshua M. Irby and be you then & there to testify certify what you shall have done in the premises and further to do and execute what in behalf of the said State shall be then & there enjoined you
Given under my hand & Seal the 22nd day of May A.D. 1828
     P Summey   Coroner

Witnesses Sumoned	Jury of Inquest -
Will. McCulloch	Executed
Rachael McCulloch	by Summoning as
Robert McCulloch	directed 24 Jurors
Will. Irby	& Summoned
Joseph Irby	6 Witnesses for State
Cyrus a Slave	H. Cansler Shff
B.J.J. D.S.	B. J. Johnson D.S.

State of North Carolina } Mr. James L. Adams
Lincoln County   }
Whereas two negro men viz Isaac & Cyrus late in the possession of Joshua M. Irby deceased have been Committed to the Jail of said County on a Charge of Murder. You are therefore hereby Notified to appear at our next Superior Court of Law to be held for the County of Lincoln at the Court House in Lincolnton 4th Monday after the 4th Monday in Sept. last past And show cause if you can why said negroes should not be Tried for said charge.
       H. Cansler   Shff
October 8th 1828

 State
  Vs
 Isaac & Cyrus

Lincoln County

notices to
James L. Adams
Copy delivered
by W. J. Wilson on
Monday 12th Oct 1828
H. Cansler   Shff

State of North Carolina }   An Inquisition indented
Lincoln County }   taken at Dwelling house
of Joshua M. Irby late in the Said County of Lincoln the 22nd day of May in the Year of Our Lord 1828 before Peter Summey - one of the coroners of & in said County upon the view of the body of Joshua M. Irby then & there lying dead upon the Oaths of William J. Wilson, Isaac Holland, Thomas Ferguson, James D. Hill, John Massey, Clizby Cobb, Philip Cansler, James Quin, John Hill, William Moore, John Noland, John Bell, Andrew Ferguson, David McCulloh, John McCulloh, Andrew Falls, James A. Robinson, James Wright, Jr., John Patterson, John Gibson, Thomas Graves, Robert Craig, Paul Setzer, & James McClure good & lawful men of the County aforesaid, who being Sworn and charged to enquire on the part of the State aforesaid, when, where, how, And after what Manner the said Joshua M. Irby came to his death, do say upon their Oath that the said Joshua Came to his death by acts of Violence, and believes from Circumstances that Isaac a Slave the property of said Joshua, was the Perpetrator of the Deed & it is the Opinion of the Jurors that he the sd Joshua came to his death by a Mortal wound on his left breast together with Several others viz. a wound on his chin & neck resembling that of being choaked & other bruises. In Witness whereof as well the aforesaid Coroner as the Juror aforesaid have to the Inquisition put thus on the day and year aforesaid and at the place aforesaid
    P Summey   Coroner   William J. Wilson Foreman

1	William J. Wilson	Foreman
2	Isaac Holland	(Seal)
3	Thomas Ferguson	(Seal)
4	James D. Hill	(Seal)
5	John Massey	(Seal)
6	Clizby Cobb	(Seal)
7	Philip Cansler	(Seal)

Lincoln County

	8 James Quin	(Seal)
	9 John Hill	(Seal)
	10 William Moore	(Seal)
	11 John Noland	(Seal)
	12 John Bell	(Seal)
	13 Andrew Ferguson	(Seal)
The State vs Isaac a slave	14 David McCulloh	(Seal)
Cyrus a Witness for the State	15 John McCulloh	(Seal)
gives as security for his	16 Andrew Falls	(Seal)
appearance at next Superior	17 James A. Robinson	(Seal)
Court for Lincoln County	18 James Wright, Jr.	(Seal)
Mary H Irby and Joseph	19 John Patterson	(Seal)
Irby who jointly & severally	20 John Gibson	(Seal)
acknowledge themselves	21 Thomas Graves	(Seal)
indebted to the State of	22 Robert Craig	(Seal)
North Carolina in the sum	23 Paul Setzer	(Seal)
of Six Hundred dollars	24 James McClure	(Seal)
for the appearance of		
said Cyrus May 22nd 1828		
Test		
William J. Wilson JP	M. H. Irby	
	Joseph Irby	

State of North Carolina
Lincoln County

Mr. Wm. J. Wilson, administrator of the Estate of Joshua M Irby deceased
Take notice That whereas two negro men, viz Isaac & Cyrus The property of Said Joshua M Irby have been committed to the Jail of Said County for murder, you are therefore hereby notified as administrator of Said Joshua M Irby deceased to appear at our next Superior Court of Law to be held for Said County at the Court House in Lincolnton on the 4th Monday after the 4th Monday in September last, past, then & there to show cause if any you can, why said negroes should not be tried for committing Said Murder
Given under my hand & Seal
October 8th 1828

H Cansler   Shff

Lincoln County

State
Vs
Isaac & Cyrus
(negro men)
Notice to Wm. J. Wilson

AdministratorExecutedby delivering a copy of the within Notice to Wm J Wilson on the 8th Oct 1828
H Cansler Shff

State of North Carolina } Superior Court of Law
Lincoln County   } October Term 1828

The Jurors for the State upon their oath present that Isaac a negro man slave of the County of Lincoln not having the fear of God before his eyes but being moved and seduced by the instigation of the devil on the first day of October in the year of out Lord one thousand eight hundred and twenty eight with force and arms in the County of Lincoln aforesaid in and upon the body of Joshua M Irby in the peace of God and the state then and there being feloniously wilfully and of his malice aforethought did make an assault - and that the said negro man slave Isaac a certain Iron Hammer which he the said negro man slave Isaac in his right hand then and there had and held to, against and upon the said Joshua M Irby then and there feloniously wilfully and of his malice aforethought did cast and throw and that the said negro man slave Isaac with the Iron Hammer aforesaid so cast and thrown him as aforesaid the said Joshua M Irby in and upon the breast of him the said Joshua M Irby then and there feloniously wilfully and of his malice aforethought did strike and wound giving to the said Joshua M Irby then and there with the Iron Hammer aforesaid so as aforesaid by the said negro man slave Isaac cast and thrown in and upon the breast of him the said Joshua M Irby **[Faded]** wound of the length of three inches and of the depth of one inch of which said mortal wound the said Joshua M Irby then and there instantly died and so the Jurors aforesaid upon their oath aforesaid do say that the negro man Slave the said Joshua M Irby in manner and form aforesaid feloniously wilfully and of his malice aforethought did kill and murder against the peace and dignity of the State

J Wilson Solr

Lincoln County

[#] 25
  State
   Vs   A True Bill
 Isaac a (Slave)   Danl Conrad forem
  Murder
    Gov. O_er[?]
    Wm. J. Wilson
    Cyrus a witness
    Jacob a witness
    Phillis a wit
    Sworn & sent
    Lwn Henderson Clk
    William McCulloh
    Tried Octr 1828

Chapter Three

Lincoln County

RUNAWAYS

State of North Carolina }   To the Jailor of
Lincoln County   }   said County
      Whereas John Whitesides brought before me a Mullato boy who says his name is Peter & that he is a free Man; before his examination it appears he is a runaway you are hereby commanded to confine him in said Jail. Until he is released According to Law. Given under My hand & Seal 1st of August 1825
                  H. Cansler   (J Peace)
                  To John Zimmerman
                        Jailor of
                    Lincoln County
                 Confined on Monday
                  1st August 1825

****

State of North Carolina }   to the keeper of the
Lincoln County   }   Common Gaol for

said County you are hereby Commanded to receive into the Gaol of Said County the body of Thomas Oliver, who was found in possession of a negro man who he offered to sell, which negro is believed to be a Runaway, and he the said Oliver Safely keep until discharged by due Course of Law given under Our hands & Seals this 27th day of February 1836
D Reinhardt   JP (Seal)
Jno Hoke   JP (Seal)

Lincoln County

A white man who says his name is Thomas Oliver that he lives in Mecklenburg, No. Carolina, on the road leading from Charlotte to Salisbury 7 or 8 miles from Charlotte on the head waters of Sugar Creek, that he left home on last Monday was a week in company with his brother Wm. Oliver, with stall fed cattle to sell 21 in number, the negro in company, negros name is Sam, that he passed through Charlotte with his cattle, & crossed the Catawba River, at Moore's ferry where the River is called Catawba, that he sold all his cattle in Columbia S. Carolina to at six a pound, cannot tell the amount of sale, that he sent all his money, except five dollars by his brother home **[Fold in paper]** had no clothes with him, except what he wore. That the negro in his possession belongs to him & his brother William Oliver, that he was raised by his father & willed to them, That he has now but twenty five cents with him, that his father died in Mecklenburg County, that after he sold his cattle in Columbia, he set out with the negro Sam, to sell, that he passed through Winnsboro & Yorkville, & along to Fulenwider forge - That he never offered to sell the negro till yesterday at Fulenwider furnace, That he asked then $700 -

signed & acknowledged before me	his
Robt. H. Burton J.P. Feby 27th 1836	Thomas W Oliver
	mark

****

A negro man who says his name is Anthony that he belongs to Saml. Gibson in Waxaw settlement near 12 mile Creek said he was raised by Nathaniel Barret[?], who sold him to Gibson, fall a year ago, & proved that he runaway from Gibson before last harvest -

Lincoln County

Chapter Four

Lincoln County

HIRING OF SLAVES

North Carolina }   Articles of agreement entered
Lincoln County }   into & concluded between
Jacob Reinhardt of the one part Martin C. Phifer of the other part both of said County & state Witnesseth that the said Jacob Reinhardt hath hired & by these presents doth hire to the said Martin C. Phifer, a negro fellow belonging to the said Reinhardt named York, to work as blacksmith as far as he is able and capable in his shop for the said Phifer for one year commencing on the 2d day of February next, and to work the usual hours & times that are customary for servants, apprentices & the said Reinhardt further agrees to furnish the said York with clothing, boarding & lodging at his own table & house for which the said Phifer is to pay tha said Reinhardt One hundred & forty four dollars one half at the end of six months & the other half at the end of the year In witness whereof they have hereunto set their hands & seals the 31st day of January 1829

Test   M. C. Phifer   (Seal)
J. P. Reinhardt   Jacob Reinhardt   (Seal)

****

Know all Men by these presents that I Edward Boyd Am held and firmly bound unto Robert MCall in the Sum of Three hundred & Seventy six dollars & Thirty one cent which I the Said Edwd. Boyd doth Let the said Robt MCall have a Negroe Girl Named Betsey for the Interest of the above Sum of $376.31 and as long as the said Boyd Lets the Said MCall have the Said Negro Girl Betsey the Said McCall is not to push the Said Boyd for the said Money and the Said Robt. MCall is to clothe the said Negro Girl with all Necessary Clothing Bothe for the Winter & Summer and pay the taxes of Said Negro Girl Betsey and when Ever the Said Boyd Tenders

Lincoln County

the Money Either in Silver Currency or Bank Notes in the Different Banks the said MCall shall Deliver to the Said Boyd the Said Girl Betsey and her Clothing witness my hand and Seal this 19th day of March 1816
Witness   Edward Boyd (Seal) John Herman John Henry

Lincoln County

Chapter Five

Lincoln County

PATROL RECORDS

State N Carolina   }   To James McCombs Constible
Lincoln County   }   you are hereby commanded to

take the Body of Nancy Grice and her safely deliver to the jailer of your county that she may be kept safely until the next Court in October - To answer a complaint of the state against her - The circumstances are these, said Nancy Grice was brought this morning before me John Abernathy a Justice of the Peace for this County. by the Patrol - who upon being qualified made oath that they found in her House at a late hour in the night a Negro fellow belonging to William Johnston Called Fred - which Negro made his escape but she the said Nancy Grice give up a part of his clothes which were in her possessions - Further it is generally believed that she is married to this fellow and that he has been regularly in the habit of visiting her at all times contrary to his master intention or permission & that the owner of the said fellow does consider that he is seriously injured in consequence of this elicit intercourse   Agust 29th 1825

John Abernathy   (JP)

William Garner William Fike Robert Riley Henry Hansel bound in twenty pounds Each To appear and giver Evidence against Nancy Grice

John Abernathy   (JP)

Commitment

Lincoln County

Nancy Grice
Executed By
James McConely
Court
1 Arrest
4 Summons
Bill Drawn
Nancy Grice
Confined on
the 29th August
1825 on the
within Charge

****

State of North Carolina }
Lincoln County } We do hereby Certify
that Wilson Gabriel, Jacob Gabriel, Franklin Abernathy, & John B. Abernathy & Logan Sherrill, did Serve as patrollers in Capt Longs Company. One year in 1832
      John D Abernathy
      Patroll Committee for
Capt Longs Company

****

Patrollers in Capt Collins Company   1837 notified and [??] not living in the Company will not act
James Quin   Shff
by J. M. Roberts   Shff

****

This will Certify that Mr Abram Scott personally came before me the subscriber duly qualified as one of our patroll for one year this 10th June 1833 In Capt Hannahs Company
      R Gasten   SP

Lincoln County

****

John H. Robison Wm A Acott Alexander Rankin Junior attended on a summons by the pattrol committee for Capt Hannas district was duly sworn as a patrole company for one year by the Subscriber

Robt. Gasten SP

****

July 23rd 1834 I further Certify that the above named Patrollers served as such for 1 year in Said Company   Robert Gasten SP
for the Committee
Patroll Committee

****

State of North Carolina }   January Sessions 1837
Lincoln County   }   Ordered by Court that
William Long, John Roberson, A. P. Roberson, Isaac Sherrill, Joseph Gabriel, Thomas Mcorkle, Freeman Howard, Frederick Lineberger, be appointed patroller in Capt. Abernathys Company for one year
Witness   M W Abernathy

****

John Michaels Petition

To their Worships the Judges of the County Courts held for the County of Lincolnton, the subscribers begs the liberty of stating, that he finds it impossible to discharge the duties of Patroller, which duties were assigned him at their Sessions in April. He fondly hopes that his punctuality in the discharge of the duties desolving upon him as a citizen, of which at least one of your Worshipful Body has been an observer will afford satisfactory evidence that it is imperious necessity which is the cause of his pleading exception. He begs leave to state that he is attending as time and opportunity will admit to the study of geography under the direction of the Principal of the Academy of this place. In this study, in the above manner the subscriber was employed previous to his appointment as Patroller. Of this circumstance he presumes your worships were ignorant and from this he hereby presumes that your Honors will be induced to excuse him from

Lincoln County

the duties of Patroller and by so doing the subscriber will consider himself under increased obligations and as in duty bound shall ever pray
Signed this 19th of July A.D. 1822
Jhn Michael July session 1822 after taking into consideration the facts above stated ordered that Jno Michael be excused

Lincoln County

Chapter Six

Lincoln County

CORONER'S INQUESTS

State of North Carolina }
Lincoln County }
We the undersigners Justices of the Peace in and for said County for want of a Coroner do Appoint Elkanah Shuford to Set as Coroner in a Case Now before us viz as Negro Man found Dead in the said County on the Premises of Enos Sherrill, he the said Elkanah Shuford is Hereby Authorized to summons twelve freeholders to Examine & Act Agreeable to Act of Assembly Made & provided in Such Cases
Sworn to & Subscribed before us
      Elkanah L. Shuford
Jno J Shuford   (JP)
J L Lowrance   (JP)
Miles W Abernathy (JP)

Jurors summoned on the Above Coroners Inquest And A_____d
Elisha Bridges Isaac Anderson
James Bridges John Shinn

Wm Rankin
Alpherd Bridges
Jonas Ramsour
Eli Sherrill
Lawson Lowrans
Mason Sherill
Nicholas Carpenter
Enos Sherill[marked through]
Isaac Robinson
Reuben Hamelton

Lincoln County

David Smith

****

Novr the 3rd 1831
We the under sined Jurors were Legally Summoned to Examine the Body of a dead negro man found on the premises of Enos Sherrells in Liles Creek near the mouth of sd Creek to examine Some witnesses Entroduced

1st Examined Hoseah Sherell & he stated that he Saw a Smoke from the house in the Botum field & he Suspected it was Edmond an out Lying Negro formerally belonging to Wm Rankin & him And Austin Sherill went to see & when drew near to the place the fire [?] saw & is negro a runing about 60 or so yds from me he put the dogs on the track he then got out of [?] site when he got down the Creek Bank he ran to the Creek & he saw him with his hed out in an upright position he Said to the dogs Bigon & Junk he [?] no more of him the dogs did not Tuch him the above was the 1st novr 1831 next morning myself & Wm Rankin Austin Sherill & Lewis L Sherell went to the place I saw him Last & hunted for him & we found him about 3 rod Below where I seen him Last we Rased him out of the water & Lade him on the Bank   Elkanah Shuford
                    Hosea W Sherrill
2nd We Examined Austen Sherill & hestated he saw a Smoke on the Bottum field he also suspected it was Edmond & the above & him Self Hoseah Sherill went Down to See & we parted one one Each side of a Certain Dich & Came near where the smoke was the first he herd was Hosah Calling the dog he ran Down the Dich till he Could Cross & then stoped & herd Hosah say here is in the Creek he Ran to the Creek But Seed nothing of the Negro & next morning an hunted for him & found him about 3 rod from where Hosah said he seen him we Rased him out of the Creek & Lade him on the Bank
Elk L Shuford   H W Sherrell
3rd Wm Rankin stated that on the 1st of novr 1831 Austin Sherill Came down to his house for the Canoe & said they saw a negro suspected to be Edmond & that he thout he was Drownded [?] the negro & the next morning we went up the River in the Canoe to the place Hosah saw him in the Creek & we serched & found him & Rose him out of the Creek & Lade him on the Bank this was Lilses

Lincoln County

Creek near the mouth where it Emties in the Catawba
Wm Ranken

4th Lewis S Sherell states that he was Enformed at Hosah Sherells that he Saw a negro in the Creek & he Suspected he was Drounde & them Austin Sherrill Hosah Sherill & Wm Ranken went to hunt & found him in about 2 or 3 rods from where Hosah Sheril said he saw him Last in Lilses Creek we Rose him out of the water & Lade him on the Bank
Elk L Shuford   David L. Sherrill

We Examined the Body of Said negro found in the Creek viz Lilses Creek and he was Cleare of marks of violens & of course we must Belive he was Drownded in trying to make his Escape this negro We Belive to be a Sertain negro man named Edmond formerally owned by Wm Ranken of Said County & now Said to Be the property of James Allon of Buncom County N C   Signed by Us We the Jurors this Day & year above Riten in presants of

Wm Ranken	James Bridges	Lwn Lowrance
Reuben Hamilton	Nicolas Zimmerman	Isaac Anderson
Mason Sherrill	David Smith	
Jonas Ramsour	John Shinn	
Alfed Bridges	Eli Sherrill	
tested	Isaac Robinson	
Elk L Shuford Coroner	Elish Bridges	

****

State of North Carolina   }
Lincoln County   }   We Jacob Helderman
Franklin M Reinhardt & Jonas W Derr acting justices of the peace for said County do appoint & constitute Rufus M Helderman as Coroners to hold an inquest over the body of a Negro Boy named Sauco the property of Elisha Purkins found in the old field on the land of Aaron Goodson on Tuesday the 19th of Febr 1861 Given under our hands & seals the day & year above written

                          J Helderman   (JP)
                          F M Reinhardt   (JP)
                          Jonas W Derr   (JP)

Lincoln County

The boy Sauco the subject of this inquest has been known to be crasy for sometime frequently leaving home & be gone wandering about for several days at a time, he was found dead in an old field on the plantation of Aaron Goodson by Aaron Goodson he was lying on his back streached at full length with some clothing on, a shirt a pair of pants and a sock on his left foot is the position that Aaron Goodson testifies he found him inThe undersigned Jurors have made a careful examination of the person of the Boy Sanco and gives as their Verdict that he died a Natural death This 19th of February 1861

Charles Kelley	J. S. Bynum	S. Finger
Langdon A Loftin	M. L. Loftin	Alfred Garrison
J. M. Michal	F. L. Lehmons	
Jacob Goodson	James Mullen	
John F. Helderman	Henry M Goodson	

[Eds. note: the first two references to the deceased look to be "Sauco," while the third is clearly "Sanco."]

****

We the undersigned having been summoned and duly sworn to hold an inquest over the body of a Negro (by the name Hope) the property of Jas. L. Russ which sd body was found in the kitchen [Note: "the kitchen" marked out] an out house belonging to the same The cause of his death we believe to be in consequence of the many bruises on his body. Frost bitten Feet & a partial dislocation of the neck, who has done it we know not. so say us all
Jan. 12th 1845

William Nance   foreman
Robert Johnston
Alex Davis
John Davis
Jackson Kelley
Saml W Venable
Isaac Nixon

Lincoln County

Henry Hager
John H Hager
Robert Mendinghall
James Hager
John Robinson
Green D Abernathy
Sharad Little
Soloman Lifford
Edward McGinnis
Green W Cox
John B Freeman
****

State of N. C. Lincoln Co
Decr 1. 1864
Near Michael Fingers Mill

Having received intelligence of a dead body being found Near this place & summoned the following

To wit
Maj Jo R Blackburn
A. L. Hobbs
Robt Haynes [**J. J. Blackburn marked through**]
Levi Shrum
Daniel Shrum
Daniel Halman
L. Keever [**Leander Steward marked through**]
Michael Finger
M. Campble
Sol. Carpenter
James Sumrow [**Wm. Blackburn marked through**]
D. Finger

Who after examination having been Duly
Sworn maketh the fol report
W. H. Alexr. Connor

Lincoln County

$10 ordered to be paid

****

dec 1. 1864

We the Jury of Inquest having been Sworn by Robert Blackburn Esqr being hear to report that a body recognized as a Coloured Man thought to be a Slave man found this morning by Daniel Shrum in a hollow near Michael Fingers Mill on the waters of Lockharts[?] Creek in Lincoln County Eaten up intirely except one foot which was enclosed in a shoe - the hair & hat was [Faded] some forty - yards up the hill & a trail down the hill leaving some remnants of clothing was traced down to the hollow where his clothes foot & a harer sack was found. We are fully convinced said boy has been with the Army. he had a yankey pr pants on with a Confederate Coat. The Jury are of opinion he came to his death by some unknown cause or the usual visitation of God

Summons to the Jury -
Joseph R Blackburn
James Summerrow
A L Hobbs
Milos Campbell
Daniel Finger
Levi Shrum
Michael Hagar
Daniel Holman
Solomon Carpenter
Lawson Keever
Robert G. Haynes

****

State of North Carolina }   To any lawfull
Lincoln County   }   officer to execute
you are hereby Commanded to Summon eighteen good & lawful Jurers to attend instantly at the dwelling house of Jas. L. Ross in order to hold a

Lincoln County

Jury of inquest over the body of a Negro boy Who is there lying dead, here in fail not given under our hands & seals Janr 1st 1845

Also summons Dr T H Johnston or Dr Wm [???] or Dr Jas Abernaty or any two physicians to be had We do depute H. W. Burton to execute the above summons   J D King   (JP)   J W [???]   (JP)   Janr 12th 1845

J. D. King   (JP)
J. W. [???]   (JP)

1. Robert Johnston Senr
2. William Nance Senr. Foreman
3. Solomon Sifford
4. Green S. Abernathy
5. Robert Mendenhall
6. John Freeman
7. Sherod Lyttle Junr
8. Isaac Nixon
9. John Robison
10. James Hagar
11. John Hagar
12. James Bryant [Marked out; replaced with Edward McGinnis]
13. Henry Hagar
14. John Davis
15. Alex. Davis
16. Green Cox
17. Jackson Kelly
18. Saml Venable

Jan 12th 1845
The within Summons
executed by me
H W Burton   Dpt
Constable

18 Jurors
Officers fees for summoning 18
Jurors at 20 cts Each $3.60
I depute Ezekiel Abernathy
to summons the physician or
physicians named in the written
warrant   J. D. King   (JP)

The above witness was   }
summoned by me E. Abernathy   }

Lincoln County

on Dr. Abernathy.   } officers fees 20 cts

****

State of NC   }
Lincoln County   }
The following persons were summoned as a Jury of inquest Examin in to the cause of the death of Peter a Slave belonging to the heirs of John Henderson Decst Examination at Noah Maury[??] on the night of 3d April 1848
R. E. Johnston
T R Shuford   }   Witnesses Sworn
Wm R Edwards   }   and Examined
Danl Butts   }   Noah Maury[???]
Thos Stuard   }   Levy Havner
John Alexander   }   Isabella A Slave
A L Hoke   }   wife of the Corpse
James Taylor
Franklin Taylor
Henry Buff
And Hauss
Alexr Moore

The Jury Sworn and preceded to the Examination of the body
After Due Examination the Jury find that the body under Examination came to its death by the visitation of God

R. E. Johnston   Foreman   Daniel Butts
Thos R Shuford   John Y. Alexander
A L Hoke   A. J. Hause
W R Edwards   James Taylor
N. T. Stuard   Franklin Taylor
Alexander Moore   Henry Buff

I John M. Jacobs Coroner for the County of Lincoln have proceeded to Summon the sd. foregoing Jury of August on this 3rd day of April 1848 and after having qualified and Empanneled them to examine said Corpse reported as thereunto set forth
                    J. M. Jacobs   Cor

Lincoln County

12 Jurers summoned at 20 ea	$ 2.40
3 Witnesses a 20	.60
Inquisition	2.40
	$ 5.40

Lincoln County

Chapter Seven

Lincoln County

MISCELLANEOUS RECORDS

List of Jurors
[Jurors -- case unknown]

Danl. Rowe	chal'd for cause	
Fred Dellinger	chal'ged " "	
Wash. Lowe	chal'ged " "	
And. H. Shuford	chal'ged without cause	1
Neman Alexander	chal'ged for cause	
Lewis Dellinger	chal'ged without cause	2
Boston Best	1	
David Carpenter	chal'ged without cause	3
Spencer Shelton	chal'd for cause	
John Rudesil	chal without cause	4
Elisha Berdges	chal for cause	
Thos. Wilson	chal " "	
David Settlemyer	2	
James Holesclaw	3	
John Yount	4	
George Moony	chal'gd without cause	
J. W. Moore	chal'ed without cause	
Major Hull	5	
John Falls	for cause	
David Reinhardt	chal'ged for cause	
John Linebarger	chal'd for cause	
Absalom Hoover	chal'd without cause	
John Coulter	6	
R. H. Burton	7	
Absalom Sherrall	chal'd for cause	
Ephraim Fryday	chal'd without cause	

Lincoln County

David Abernathy	chal'd for cause
David Ramsour(Sen)	8
Rob. Johnson	chal'gd for cause
Wesly Monday	chal'gd for cause
Lyman Woodford	" " "
John Motz Jr.	cha'd for "
Jesse Penny	cha'd without cause
Alex. McCorcle	9
James Cowan	chal'd for cause
Eph. Goodson	chal'd without cause
John D. Rankin	chal'd for cause
Lawson Carpenter	chal'gd without cause
David Smith	chal'gd _____
John Smyer	10
Fred Linbarger	chal'd for cause
Richard Birch	11
George Little	chal'd without cause
Levi Killian	chal'd " "
Peter Hoke	12

Burke County

Chapter Eight

Burke County

BILLS OF SALE

State of North Carolina }
} July Sessions 1804
Burke County }
The within bill of Sale was duly proved in open court by the oath of Robert Williamson & recorded.
       Attest   J. Erwin Clk
       Thos: Patton
       Bill of Sale
       2 Negroes

Know all men by these presents That I Thos. Patton of the County of Wilkes in the State of North Carolina have bargained Sold & delivered unto Ben Smith of Burke County in the state aforesaid one negroe boy slave by the name of Rye for and in consideration of the Sum of four hundred Dollars to me in hand paid by the said B. Smith which said Boy is about the age of sixteen years also one other Negroe Boy slave about fifteen years of age by the name of Ned for & in consideration of the sum of four hundred Dollars money of the United States to me in hand paid by the said Smith and I do hereby bind my self my Excrs. & admrs. to the said B. Smith his heirs exrs. & admrs. to warrant the said two Negroe Boys Rye & Ned from all & every lawful claim of any person whatsoever and also Warrant them to be sound serviceable and clair of all impediments Whatsoever in witness whereof I have hereunto Set my hand & Seal July the 16th day 1804
       Thos. Patton (Seal)
       Robert Williamson Jurat

Burke County

****

Articles of agreement made and entered into the fourth day of March one thousand eight hundred and three between James Murphy of Burke County in the State of North Carolina of the one part, and Christian Horn of the same County of the other part Witnesseth, That the said Murphy on his part doth hereby promise and agree to put under the care and management of the said Christian Horn the following hands, Viz., Negroes Derry, Charles, Toney, Lucy
and Mary or in case Lucy and Mary or either of them should at any time be kept from the employment of said Horn, the said Murphy is to supply their place with some other hand or hands in lieu thereof, and the said Murphy doth also agree on his part to find and put under the care of said Horn four work horses with harness and sufficient number of ploughs hoes axes Viz. for said Horn and the hands aforesaid to work with, and for the purpose of raising a crop on said Murphy's plantation this present year, and the said Murphy doth further agree to find the said Horn one hundred weight of pork and to lend him one cow and calf during the time he shall stay with said Murphy, And the said Murphy for and in consideration of the labour care and management of the said Christian Horn herein after to be expressed and hereafter to be performed by the said Horn, doth further promise and agree to let the said Horn have the one sixth part of all the corn and corn blades, and one half of the corn tops which said Horn with the hands aforesaid shall raise and secure on said Murphy's plantation and also one sixth part of the wheat now growing on said place except a small lott called a turnip patch and the said Horn is to have one sixth part of the oats that shall grow on twenty acres of Land and the sixth part of all the cotton and potatoes which he shall raise on said plantation with the hands aforesaid, and the said Murphy doth further agree to let said Horn have one half acre of Land in the Meadow field for flax and Horn is to find his own seed &C

The said Christian Horn doth hereby promise and agree on his part to take charge of the Negroes horses ploughs hoes and axes above mentioned for the express purpose of working with them and raising a crop on said Murphy's plantation this present year, and does promise covenant and agree with the said Murphy to plant with corn in good time and in good order all the cleared land on said plantation lying on the South West side of Canoe Creek and also the cleared land lying on the North East side of said Creek between said Creek and a branch runing through said plantation nearly North and South except about thirteen

Burke County

acres lying the highest up said branch which the said Murphy reserves for pasture and the said Horn is also to plant in corn about six acres of land south East of said Murphy's house part of which is yet to clear, and he is also to sow and put in in good time and in good order one acre and an half of flax for said Murphy in any part of the plantation the said Murphy shall choose and all the remaining part of said land shall be sowed in oats except what may be thought necessary for a garden and for potatoes Cabage cotton and the meadow, And the said Christian Horn doth hereby promise covenant and agree with the said Murphy for and in consideration of the shares heretofore mentioned to take proper care of the things which shall be committed to his charge and also the hands which are to worke with him in attending and taking care of said crop And said Horn doth further promise and agree that he himself with the hands horses and utensils aforesaid will give the said crop of what kind soever due and good attendance, and that he will make and repair whatever fencing may be necessary to save said crop of corn wheat oats &c from being destroyed by stock of any kind and that he will gather and divide the same agreeably to the shares above mentioned, and that he with the hands above named will take of all said Murphy's Meadow, Mow the same make and house or stack the hay in good time and order, and that he with the hands aforesaid shall take care of said Murphy's stock of Horses Cattle Hogs and Sheep and feed the same agreeably to said Murphy's directions and to get firewood make fires &c And that he will also in the month of August or the first ten days of September sow and plow in, in good order nine or ten acres of wheat on any part of the plantation said Murphy may choose and the wheat now growing is to be threshed by said Horn before it is divided.

The said Horn is to engage in the said business on the tenth instant and to be discharged as soon as the whole of the crop is gathered and housed, at which time he is to divide up the aforesaid hands, horses and utensils together with the aforesaid Cow and Calf.

For the true performances of the several promises and engagement herein made we bind ourselves to each other in the sum of one hundred pounds to be paid by the party failing to the party injured.

Signed sealed and delivered this 4th day of March 1803 in presence of

Danl. Morgan	James Murphy	(seal)
Hugh Tate	his	

Burke County

Christian Horn (seal)
mark

****

State of North Carolina }
          } July Session 1807
Burke County   }
The within Bill of Sale was duly proved in Open Court by John McDowell and recorded
   Attest J. Erwin Clk

Know all men by these presents that I David Witherspoon of Wilks County & State of North Carolina Bargined and Sold unto Kenneth McKenzie a Negroe Girl Named Clase which Negroe I do warrant and for Ever Deffend from me my heirs &c from the lawful clames of all persons whatever witness my hand and seal this 2 Day of May 1807.
Test   D. Witherspoon (seal)
J. McDowell Jurat

****

Ann Bowman
to
Elisabeth Bowman
Bill of Sale

State of North Carolina }
          } January Session 1811
Burke County   }
This bill of Sale was duly proved in Open Court by the oath of Sherwood Bowman Subscribing witness thereto recorded andOrdered to be Registered
Attest J. Erwin Clk

Know all men by these Presents that I Ann Bowman of the County of Burke State of No. Carolina for Various Considerations & good Causes Me thereto Moving has this Day Bargained & Sold unto my Daughter Elizabeth Bowman one Negro Girl Named Dise aged four years for the

Burke County

Sum of fifty Pounds to me in hand Paid by Said Elizabeth Bowman at the Sealing and Delivery of these Presents the receit Whereof is hereby acknowledged that I Myself am fully Satisfied & Paid and that I the said Ann Bowman for myself my heirs Executors Administrators & assigns Do warrant & Defend the said Negro free of all gifts grants Bills of Sale Deeds of Gifts Rigts of Legacy or Rigt of Legatee Wills or Incumbrances of any Kind made Done or had by any Person or Persons Whatsoever & at the sealing & Delivery of these Presents that the said Elizabeth Bowman is hereby Put in Possession of said Girl In witness Whereof I the said Ann Bowman has hereunto Set my hand & affixed my Seal this 25th Day of July in the year 1808

Witness Present
Wm Crye   Jurat
Sherwood Bowman   Jurat

her
Ann   Bowman   (seal)
Mark

****

Ann Bowman
to
Groves Bowman
Bill of Sale

State of North Carolina } January Session 1811
                         }
Burke County   }

The within bill of sale was duly proved in Open Court by the Oath William Cry a Subscribing Witness thereto recorded and Ordered to be Registered
Attest   J. Erwin   Clk

Know all Men by these Presents That I Ann Bowman of Burke County State of North Carolina Hath Bargained & Sold unto My Son Groves Bowman of Said County & State affsd. one Negro man Named Sam aged twenty five Years in Consideration of the Sum of five Hundred Dollars to be paid according as an obligation Bearing Date with these Present represents & Sets forth given by Sd. Groves Bowman to Said Ann Bowman, the Receit whereof is in this wise given that at the Sealing & Delivery of these Presents I Anne Bowman Doth Deliver the above Negro

Burke County

Sam unto Said Groves Bowman free & Clear of all Rights Titles Claims Wills Deeds of gifts Rights of Legacy or Claim of Legatee or any other Claim of Person or Persons Whatsoever before the Sealing & Delivery of these Presents & That I the said Ann Bowman hath full Right & Absolute Authority in myself & for my heirs to Warrant & Defend the said Negro by these Presents to him the said Groves Bowman his heirs Executors Administrators or Assigns free & Clear of all Incumbrances Suits Costs Charges, Done hereafter or suffered to be Done Either by me or any of the above Mentioned in my Name or any other Person or Persons Whatsoever In Testimony Whereof I the said Anne Bowman have hereunto Set my hand & affixt my Seal this Thirteenth Day of July in the year 1808.

Signed Sealed & Delivered   her
in Presence of   Anne   Bowman (seal)
Wm Crye Jurat   Mark
Sherwood Bowman   Jurat

****

Charles Wakefield
to
Charles Collet
Bill of Sale

State of North Carolina }
                                   } October Sessions 1811
Burke County   }
This Bill of Sale was duly proved in Open Court by the oath Charles Wakefield recorded and Ordered to be Registered
Attest J. Erwin Clk

North Carolina Burke County   This Indenture Made and Entered this the third Day of April in the Year of Our Lord 1811 Between Charles Wakefield Senior of the one Part and Charles Collet of the other Part Boath of County and State afore said Witness that I Charles Wakefield Do Sell Unto Charles Collet a negro Boy that is Known By the name of Bill for the sum of one hundred and fifty Dollars in witness hereof I set my hand and seal.
Charles Wakefield (Seal)

Burke County

Test
Charles Wakefield Jurat
Ambrose Parks

****

Nicholas Day
to
Nicholas Day Jr.
Bill of Sale

State of North Carolina }
} January Session 1816
Burke County }
This Bill of Sale was duly proved in open Court by the oath of James Day a witness thereto recorded and Ordered to be Registered
attest J. Erwin Clk

Burke County North Carolina
Know all Men by these Presents that I Nicholas Day hath bargained and sold and by these Presents I do bargin and sel unto Nicholas Day Jr. One Negro girl names Cloe for and in consideration of forty five Dollars to me in hand paid the Rec't Heare of I do heareby acknowledge and do Warrant And Defend the same unto Nicholas Day Junr. His heirs and assigns for Ever against the Claim or Claims of any other persons What Ever in witness My hand and Seal this 21 Day of January 1815

Test   Nicholas Day (seal)
James Blair
James Day Jurat

****

Bill of Sale

State of North Carolina }
} January Session 1816
Burke County }

Burke County

This Bill of Sale was duly proved in open Court by the oath of James Day a witness thereto recorded and Ordered to be Registered
attest J. Erwin Clk

Burke County North Carolina
Know all Men by these presents that I Nicholas Day hath Barganed and Sold and by these presents I do bargin and sel unto John Day my son one Negro Girl named diner for and in Consideration of forty five Dollars to me in hand paid the Rec't Heare of I do heareby acknowledge and do Warrant And Defend the same unto John Day my son His heirs and assigns for Ever against the Claime or Claims of any other person What Ever as witness My hand and Seal this 21 Day of January 1815
test   Nicholas Day (Seal)
James Day Jurat
James Blair
****

[Editors Note: This Bill of Sale is badly damaged]

John Townsends
Bill of Sale
Registerd.

[Large section torn]
       This deed was duly proved in Open Court by the oath of Leu Estes a witness thereto recorded and Ordered to be Registered
Attest J. Erwin ClkRegistered in the registry of Burke County in Book No. 14 page 203 the 17th Feby. 1823
Wm. McEntire Clk
To all Persons whence it may concern know ye that I John Brown of the County of Washinton for & in Consideration of the sum of three hundred & fifty Dollars Good and Lawful Money to me in hand paid By John Townsen of the County of Burk No. Carolina recept. whereof I do hereby acknowledge have bargand and sold Made over and Delivered & by these presence according To due form of law do bargan sell and Make Over And confirm to the said John Townsen one [Faded] Girl by the name of Sara to have and to hold [Editors Note: Large section torn]unto the said John Townsen forever defend Witness whereof I have [Faded] hand and

Burke County

seal this 25th Day of August [Torn] Signed sealed and Delivered In Presence of
Test   John Brown Junr. (seal)
Leu Estes Jurat
Le Ze Cea[?] Estes

****

to
**Ephraim M. Greenlee
Wm Roane
bill of sale for
Jenny aged 17 or 18
4th Decr. 1833
Registered**

Registered in the registers office of Burke County in Book No. 23 Page 466 this 16th January 1839.
Wm. McEntire Clk
For and in consideration of the Sum of four hundred dollars to Ephraim M. Greenlee in hand paid by William Roane the receipt of which is hereby acknowledged the Said E.M. Greenlee hath bargained and sold unto said William Roane a negro girl named Jenny now in the possession of Jacob Dole Senr. to have and to hold said girl to said Roane his heirs and assigns forever and the said Greenlee doth Covenant and warrant that said girl is a slave for life in testimony whereof he doth hereunto set his hand and seal this the 4th day of December 1833.
E.M. Greenlee (seal)
William Walker
ack'd

State of North Carolina   }Court of Pleas & quarter
Burke County   }Sessions October Term 1838
      The execution of the within bill of sale was duly acknowledged in open Court by the conveyor. It also appearing to the satisfaction of the Court that the parties to said bill of sale were at the time of the execution and delivery of the same Citizens residing in the County of Burke and

Burke County

State of North Carolina it thereupon ordered that the same be recorded and ordered to be registered.
Test   S.S. Erwin   Clerk

Burke County

Chapter Nine

Burke County

CIVIL AND CRIMINAL ACTIONS

Patsey Williams
Vs.
Wm. & Nancy Presswood

Original Bill

Wm. J. & N.W. Alexander for Complt.

The Clerk & Master of Equity for the County of Burke will issue an injunction & writ & sequestration according to the prayer of the forgoing bill with directions to the Sheriff to release the Slaves when taken upon defendants entering into bond with Sufficient Security in the sum of two thousand five hundred dollars, conditioned that they Comply with such decree as the Court may make upon the final hearing of the cause - this upon Complainants entering into bond the equity at least in the Sum of the thousand dollars Conditioned by the payment of Such damages as may be recovered by the Defendants hereafter for the filing of this bill or Suing out the process hereby awarded & the performance of whatever decree the Court of Equity may make in this Cause.

Henry Sca[?] JSCE
April 22d 1833

State of North Carolina }
                              } In Equity
Burke County   }
      To the Honorable the Judge of the Superior Court of Equity in and for the County of Burke aforesaid the Bill of Complaint of Patty

Burke County

Williams of the District of Darlington and State of South Carolina Against Nancy Presswood and William Presswood both of the County of Burke and State of North Carolina humbly complaining sheweth unto your Honor that some years ago she acquired Title to a certain negro girl slave called Biner from her grandfather William Presswood - that now at this time she has a good and valid
Title to the said negro girl with her increase which amount to six in number known by the following names Willis - Sylvia - Eliza - Harriet - Ira - and John that these negroes are in the possession of the said William Presswood and Nancy Presswood and are of the value of between eighteen hundred and two thousand dollars that your Orator brought her action at law to deliver against the said defendants by writ returnable to the next Superior Court of Burke County on said negroes - that the writ aforesaid has been executed by the Sheriff of the County aforesaid - that since the service of the writ aforesaid the said William Presswood and Nancy Presswood have there [al?] to remove the negroes aforesaid beyond the limits of this State and beyond the jurisdiction of the Court of this State - that they have actually attempted so to remove them and now have the negroes aforesaid concealed in the woods ready to be removed beyond the control of the courts aforesaid - Your Orator further charges that the said William Presswood and Nancy Presswood have no other property of any value in their possession except the negroes aforesaid - that the said William fraudulently to deprive your Orator out of the same secretly removed the Mother of said negroes and her children that she had at the time from the State of South Carolina - your Orator has constituted and appointed James Money of the State of South Carolina her agent and true and lawful attorney bearing date 22nd day of February 1833 - for that therefore that your Orator fears that the said William Presswood and Nancy Presswood will remove the said negroes beyond the jurisdiction of the State and beyond the reach of the process of its Courts and because your Orator may be entirely deprived of the benefit of her suit at Law in the County aforesaid against said defendant for recovery of said negroes object of which is to recover specifically in as much as the said defendants are not worth anything and intend as your Oratrix believes to remove said slaves as aforesaid - May it please your Honor to grant unto your Oratrix the States Writ of Subpoena directed to the said Nancy and William Presswood commanding them to be and appear at the next Superior Court of Equity to be holden for Burke County aforesaid on the 4th Monday of

Burke County

September next then and there upon their Corporal Oaths full true direct and perfect answer make to all and singular the allegations in this your Oratrix Bill contained and that as fully as tho the same were again repeated and they thereunto particularly interrogated and may it please your Honor to decree that the said Nancy Presswood and William Presswood be forthwith restrained from removing the said negroes aforementioned beyond the jurisdiction of the Courts of this State and that your honor order and decree that the said Nancy Presswood and William Presswood give bond with sufficient security for the delivery and forthcoming of the negroes aforesaid upon the determination of the said suit at Law commenced by your Oratrix as aforesaid - and that the said Nancy & William stand to and abide by such order and decree as your honor shall make in the premises and to that end that the Sheriff of Burke County be commanded by a writ of sequestration to seize and detain them untill such bond & security be given by said defendants - and may it please your Honor to grant unto your Oratrix such other and further relief as in Equity and good Conscience is right and proper - and your Oratrix as in duty bound will ever pray &c.
Wm. J. Alexander
Nat. W. Alexander
John [?]

State of North Carolina }
Rutherford County }
    James Money agent and attorney in fact of complainant Patsy Williams Vs. Nancy & William Presswood swears that the several matters of fact set forth in this Bill of Complaint of the said Patsy Williams as of his own knowledge are true and those as not of his own knowledge he believes to be true.
James Money
Sworn to before me at the County Court Clerks Office the 22nd April 1833
T. F. Birchett Clk

Subpoena
Patsy Williams
Vs.
Nancy Presswood

Burke County

for return
A Coppy of the within delivered Acompanyed with a Bill
John Boon Shff
March the 25 1833   By P. Ballew DShff

State of North Carolina
To the Sheriff of Burke County - Greeting:

We command you to Summon Nancy Presswood if to be found in your county, that all excuses aside, and that under the penalty of £100, she personally be and appear before the Judge of the Court of Equity to be held for the County of Burke at the Court-House in Morganton on the 4th Monday in September then and there, upon oath, to answer the Bill of Complaint of Patsey Williams now filed in said Court, a copy of which accompanies this writ of subpoena; and this you shall in no wise omit, at your peril; and have you then and there this writ.

Witness Sidney S. Erwin Clerk and Master of said Court of Equity, at Office, the 4th Monday in March Anno Domini, 1833 and of our Independence, the **[Left Blank]**
Issued the 23d day of Apl. 1833

S.S. Erwin CME Subpoena
Patsy Williams
Vs.
William Presswood
for return

A Coppy of the within delivered Acompanyed with a Bill
John Boon Shff
March the 25 1833 By   P. Ballew DShff

State of North Carolina

To the Sheriff of Burke County - Greeting:

We command you to Summon Wm. Presswood if to be found in your county, that all excuses aside, and that under the penalty of £100, he personally be and appear before the Judge of the Court of Equity to be held for the County of Burke at the Court-House in Morganton the 4th Monday in Sept. then and there, upon oath, to answer the Bill of Complaint of Patsey Williams now filed in said Court, a copy of which

Burke County

accompanies this writ of subpoena; and thisyou shall in no wise omit, at your peril; and have you then and there this writ.
  Witness S.S. Erwin Clerk and Master of said Court of Equity, at Office, the 4th Monday in March Anno Domini, 1833 and of our Independence, the [Left blank].
  Issued the 23d day of Apl. 1833.
S.S. Erwin CME

Patsy Williams
Vs.
Nancy Presswood
&
William Presswood
Writ of Sequestration
To Burke C. Equity
September 1833

Executed as to all except the negro Willis - him not found after diligent Search & Defendant William Presswood has refused to tell him This 24 Sept. 1833
Jn. Boon Shff

State of North Carolina
  To the Sheriff of Burke County Greeting
You are hereby commanded to arrest and take into your possession the following Negroes named Willis, Silvia, Eliza, Harriet, Mira [Ira marked thru] & John now said to be in the possession of Nancy Presswood & William Presswood & hold them untill the said Nancy Presswood & William Presswood enter into bond with sufficient security for the sum of twenty five hundred dollars condition that the said Nancy Presswood & William Presswood answer the bill in Equity for said County filed by Patsey Williams Complaint against them as defendants and that they stand to & abide by & perform whatever decree the said Court may make in the final hearing of the same. This writ issued by order of decree of the Judge of the Court of Equity for said County made in the suit of Patsey Williams Complainant against Nancy Presswood & William Presswood defendants. Herein fail not under the penalties by law enjoined & make due return how you have executed this writ to the next court of Equity to be held for said County at the court house in Morganton on the fourth Monday of September next. The aforesaid bond payable to Patsy Williams

Burke County

& conditioned for the delivery of said negroes at the final hearing of the aforesaid suit of Patsy Williams Complainant against Nancy Presswood & William Presswood defendants. Witness Sidney S. Erwin Clerk & Master in Equity at office the 4th Monday of March 1833 & 57 years of American Independence -
Issued 23d day of April 1833
S.S. Erwin C.M.E.

Patsey Williams
Vs.
Wm. T. Presswood & others

Answer
Nancy Presswood
filed Sept. 1833

State of North Carolina	} Superior Court
	}
Burke County	} September Term 1833 Patsey Williams
	}
Vs.	} In Equity
William T. Prestwood	}
Nancy Prestwood	

To the Honl. the Judge of Equity for said County

    The Separate answer of Nancy Prestwood to the complainants bill. The defendant answering saith: That she does not admit the right of the complainant to the slaves in her bill mentioned; She has not set up claim to the same in her own right , but altogether disclaims any title thereunto. Her possession of the slaves which were in her service at the commencement of the the complainants Suit against her & the other defendant was under the right of the sd William T. This defendant never did attempt to remove the slaves that was in her possession as then claimed by the complainant beyond the jurisdiction of this superior Court of this County nor did she ever entertain such an intention. This defendant [?] in abatement & for cause of Plea saith that at the time of the exhibiting of complainants Bill she was and still is a Feme Covert that she was married to one Thomas Prestwood Who is Still living in Darlington District in the State of South Carolina & wherefore because the said Thomas Prestwood is not named in the Bill aforesaid, she prays Judgment

Burke County

of the Court, whether she ought to be held to answer further the said Bill - This defendant having answered &c prays to be hence dismissed &c

Caldwell & Mitchell
sol. for plff

N. Carolina   } The defendant maketh
Burke County   } oath that the several notions
& things set forth in her forgoing answer a plea as of her Knowledge are true & those not of her own knowledge she believes to be true.
Nancy Prestwood
Sworn to & Subscribed
before me 28th Sept. 1833
S.S. Erwin CME

                    Patsey Williams
                           Vs.
          Wm. T. Prestwood & others
          Answer of Deft.Wm. T. Presswood
                  filed Sept. 1833

No. Carolina   }
                    } In Equity September Term 1833
Burke County   }

Patsey Williams   } To the Honourable the Judge
      Vs.   } of the Court of Equity for
William T. Prestwood   } Burke County
Nancy Prestwood

The separate answer of William T. Prestwood to the Bill of Complainant, of Patsey Williams this defendant answering &c Saith, that the action at law of Complainant against this defendant & the sd Nancy is by a writ on the [?] & not in detinue. He further answering Saith that he never did attempt to remove the slaves mentioned in the Complainants bill beyond the Jurisdiction of the Superior Court of Burke County. And since the Suit was instituted by the Complainant for the slaves that were in his possession before the exhibiting of her bill, this defendant has not at any time since attempted to conceal or remove them beyond the limits of this

Burke County

State nor has he at any time [**Rest of the line is marked thru.**] Defendant for further answer saith that the Negroes in Suit are his property, that their ancestor was conveyed to him in the year 1805 & that he hath had possession of her and her increase as they came in esse claiming & having them as his own property ever since, being a period of near twenty eight years - Defendant for further answer Saith that Negro Byner died something over two years ago, & that Negro Silvey died in this month of June last. Defendant for further answer Saith that the Ancestor of the Negroes which were in his possession (& which have been taken from him by an order of this Court) was given to the father of this defendant in 1796 or 7 & by him had as his property until 1805 when she was by him given to this defendant & hath been held by him as above stated. Defendant for further answer Saith that the fact of his residing in Burke County must have been [?] was well known to Complainant, as her father who lives in this neighborhood, has been to this County three or four times within the last nineteen years years & Defendant for further Saith that he is protected by the Statute of Limitations on which he insists, even supprising that Compl ever had Title which is [?]. Defendant having answered &c prays to be hence dismissed &c.
Mitchell & Caldwell
Sol

No. Carolina
  Defendant maketh oath that the several matters & things set forth in the forgoing answer which are of his own knowledge are true & those not of his own knowledge he believes to be true.
Sworn & subscribed   W.T. Prestwood
before me 28th Sept. 1833
S.S. Erwin CME

****

J.T. Avery
Vs.
J.B. Allison

To the Sheriff of Haywood County--Greeting:

Burke County

We command you, That of the goods and chattels, lands and Tenements of J B Allison J R Love & R V Welch if to be found in your bailiwick, you cause to be made the sum of nine hundred and sixty eight 54/100 Dollars nine hundred dollars is principal to beare intrest from the 22nd of May 1855 - Subject to various endorced Credits which J T Avery Costr in our Superior Court of Law, Held for Burke County, at the Court-House in Morganton recovered against them together with the sum of $1.43 for costs and charges in the said suit expended, whereof the defendants are liable, as appears to us of record. And have you the said moneys, besides your fees for this service, before our said Court at Morganton aforesaid, on the eighth Monday after the 4th Monday in March 1857, then and there to render the moneys aforesaid. Herein fail not, and have you the and there this writ.
 WITNESS, JOSEPH D. FERREE, Clerk of said Court, Office, the eighth Monday after the fourth Monday in Sept A.D. 1856
JD Ferree Clerk

J T Avery the Plaintiff in this Case Maketh oath that he is informed and believes that the Sheriff of Jackson County is a relative of one of the Defendants and he believes that he will not discharge his duty in executing and Collecting this fifa if the same is placed in his hands
J T Avery Costr
Sworn to before me this 13th Apl 1857
J D Ferree Clk

To the Sheriff of Haywood County Greeting: We command you, that of the goods and chattels, lands and tenements of J B Allison J R Love & Dillard Love if to be found in your bailiwick, you cause to be made the sum of Seven Hundred and Sixteen 72/100 Dollars Six Hundred and Sixty Six Dollars is principal to beare intrest from the 22nd of May 1855 subject to various endorsed Credits which J T Avery Cost in our Superior Court of Law, held for Burke County, at the Court-House in Morganton recovered against them together with the further sum of $1.43 for costs and charges in the said suit expended, whereof the said defendants are liable, as appears to us of record. And have you the said moneys, besides your fees for this service, before the said Court at Morganton aforesaid, on the eighth Monday after the fourth Monday in March 1857, then and there to render the moneys aforesaid. Herein fail not, and have you then and there this writ.

Burke County

WITNESS, JOSEPH D. FERREE, Clerk of Court, Office, the eighth Monday after fourth Monday in Sept A.D. 1856 and in the year of our Independence.
Issued the 13 day of Sept 1857
J D Ferree Clerk

J T Avery the Plaintiff in this Case Maketh oath that he is informed & believes that the Sheriff of Jackson County is the relative of one of the defendants and he believes that he will not discharge his duty in executing and Collecting this fifa if placed in his hands
J T Avery Costr
Sworn to before me this 13th Apl 1857
J D Ferree Clerk

To the Sheriff of Haywood County--Greeting
We command, That of the goods and chattels, lands and tenements of J W Davis Walter Brown & Wm Thattearn[?] if to be found in your bailiwick, you cause to be made the sum of Six Hundred and forty five Dollars is pl to bear intrest from 22nd May 1855 Subject to various endorsed Credits which J T Avery Costr in our Superior Court of Law, held for Burke County, at the Court House in Morganton recovered against them together with the further sum of $1.43 for costs and charges in the said suit expended, whereof the said defendants are liable, as appears to us of record. And have you the said moneys, besides your fees for this service, before our said Court at Morganton aforesaid, on the eighth Monday after the fourth Monday in March 1857, then and there to render the moneys aforesaid. Herein fail not, and have you then and there this writ.

WITNESS, JOSEPH D. FERREE, Clerk of said Court, at Office, the eighth Monday after the fourth Monday in Sept A.D. 1856 and in the year of our Independence.
Issued the 13th day of Apl 1857
J D Ferree Clerk

J T Avery the Plaintiff in this Case Maketh oath that he is informed & believes that the Sheriff of Jackson County is the Relative of one of the

Burke County

defendants and he believes that he will not discharge his duty in executing and Collecting this fifa if the Same is placed in his hands
J T Avery Costr
Sworn to before me this 13th of April 1857
J D Ferree Clk

STATE OF NORTH CAROLINA
To the Sheriff of Haywood County--Greeting:

You are hereby commanded to expose to sale One Negro boy 16 years old one Woman 40 years old nine mules one Wagon & Harness for 6 - three oxen and two wagons and one house and lot in the Town of Webster Heretofore served on by Wm Green Sheriff of Haywood as the property of J B Allison to satisfy the sum of nine hundred and Sixty eight 54/100 dollars $900 beares intrest from 22 May 1855 which Superior Court of Law for the County of Burke at the Court House in Morganton recovered against J B Allison together with the further sum of $1.43 for costs and charges in suit expended, whereof the said J B Allison J R Love & R V Welch are liable as appears to us of record. And have you the said monies besides your fees for this service before our said Court at Morganton on the 8th Monday after the 4th Monday in March 1857, then and there to render the said Debt, costs and charges aforesaid.
Herein fail not, and have you then and there this writ:

Witness J D Ferree Clerk of said Court at Office the 8 Monday after the 4 Monday in Sept and in the year of our Independence **[Blank]**.
Issued the 13 day of Apl A.D., 1857.
J D Ferree Clk

STATE OF NORTH CAROLINA
To the Sheriff of Haywood County--Greeting:

You are hereby commanded to expose to sale One Negro boy 16 years old one negro Woman 40 years old nine mules one Wagon and Harness for 6 three oxen two wagons and one house & lot in the Town of Webster Heretofore served on by Wm Green Sheriff of Haywood as the property of J B Allison to satisfy the sum of seven hundred and sixteen 72/100 Dollars $666.00 is pl to bear intrest from 22 May 1855 which Superior Court of Law for the County of Burke at the Court House in Morganton recovered against said Dfts together with the further sum of **[Blank]** for costs and charges in the said suit expended, whereof the said J B Allison J R Love & Dillard Love are liable as appears to us of record. And have you the said monies besides your fees for this service before our

Burke County

Court at Morganton on the 8th Monday after the 4th Monday in March 1857, then and there to render the said Debt, costs and charges aforesaid.
Herein fail not, and have you then and there this writ
    Witness J D Ferree Clerk of said Court at Office the 8th Monday after the 4th Monday in Sept and in the **[Blank]** year of our Independence.
    Issued the 13 day of Apl A.D. 1857
J D Ferree Clerk

           STATE OF NORTH CAROLINA
To the Sheriff of Haywood County--Greeting:
You are hereby commanded to expose to sale One negro boy sixteen years old 1 negro Woman 40 years old nine mules one Wagon and Harness for six three oxen & two wagons and one House & Lot in the Town of Webster Heretofore served upon as the property of J B Allison by Wm Green Sheriff to satisfy the sum of Six hundred and forty five dollars $600 is principal to bear int. from 22d of May 1855 which Superior Court of Law for the County of Burke at the Court House in Morganton recovered against said Allison & others together with the further sum of $1.43 for costs and charges in said suit expended, whereof the said J B Allison W Brown & Wm Hattern[?] are liable as appears to us of record. And have you the said monies besides your fees for this service at our said court at Morganton on the 8 Monday after the 4 Monday in March 1857, then and there to render the said Debt, costs and charges aforesaid.
Herein fail not, and have you then and there this writ:
    Witness J D Ferree Clerk of said Court at Office the 8 Monday after the 4 Monday in Sept and in the **[Blank]** year of our Independence.
    Issued the 13 day of Spt A.D., 1857.
J D Ferree Clk

228	46
J T Avery Costr	J T Avery Costr
Vs	Vs.
J B Allison et al	J B Allison
Fifa	J R Love
Burke Supr Court	R V Welch
Spring Term 1857	Judgement $968.54
Received of J B Allison	of which $900.00

Burke County

the Defendent Twenty
Eight 76/100 on this
20th May 1857
$100.00
      J T Avery Costr
30.27
Bal. principle 858 dolls
125.30
May 20th /57.
$255.57

is pl to beare intrest
from the 22nd may 1855
Cr 22d Nov   1855

" 20th of May 1856

" 29th oct   1856

J D Ferree fifa annexed
Seal [?] on $1.43

North Carolina }
Burke County   } Supr Court office 13th Apl 1857
    It is considered in this case an affidavit of plaintiff that the Sheriff of Haywood County proceed to the County of Jackson and Execute and Collect the annexed fifas according to act of Assembly
J D Ferree Clerk

229
J T Avery Costr
   Vs
J B Allison et al
   Fifa
Burke Supr Court
Spring Term 1857
$716.72
Received of Defendant
   666.00
J B Allison Eighteen 10/100
Dollars 20th May 1857
   J T Avery Costr
   $60.54
Balance of principle 540
21.18
20th May /57
   154.94

   45
J T Avery Costr
   Vs
J B Allison
J R Love
Dillard Love
Judgement

of which

is pl to beare intrest
from 22d of May 1855
Cr 22nd Nov 1855

" 20th May 1856

" 19th Oct 1856

fifa annex & Seals

Burke County

                     & [?]

$1.43

                               J D Ferree

Ck

North Carolina }
Burke County }Superior Court office 13th Apl 1857.
    It is considered in this case upon affidavit of Plaintiff that the Sheriff of Haywood County proceede to the County Jackson and Execute & Collect the annexed fifas According to act of Assembly
J.D. Ferree Clerk

230	44
J.T. Avery Costr	J T Avery Costr
Vs	Vs
J W Davis et al	John W Davis
Fifa	Walter Brown &
Burke Supr Court	Wm Thattearn[?]
Spring Term 1857	Judgement $645.00
Credit on the Within	of which 600.00
By two hundred & Eighty	is pl to beare int
six 38/100 Dollars Paid by	from 22nd of May 1855
John B Allison 20th May	Cr 22d Nov 1855
$35.54	
1857 J T Avery Costr	20th May 1856
19.55	
Balance on the 20 May /57	29th Oct 1856
119.60	
is 230 28/100 Dollars	
$174.69	
	J D Ferree Clerk
	fifa anex & seal [?]
	$1.43

North Carolina }
Burke County   } Supr Court office 13th Apl 1857

Burke County

It is considered an affidavit of the Plaintiff in this Case that the Sheriff of Haywood County proceede to the County of Jackson and Execute & Collect the annexed fifa according to act of Assembly
J D Ferree Clerk
Ballance due on 29th Oct 1856 $500
five Hundred Dollars
Came to hand April 17th 1857
   W. Green shff

****

No 165
Wm F McKisson
Vs
Wm F Gibbs
Complaint

North Caroilna } Superior Court
Burke County } Spring Term 1869
William F McKisson
  Vs
William F Gibbs
The plaintiff Complains of the Deft in the above Case and alledges
1. That in Consideration that the Plaintiff would hire to the Deft a certain negro slave from the nineteenth of January AD 1865 - until the Twenty fifth of December AD 1865 the said Deft undertook and promised to deliver to the said Plaintiff Ninety bushels of Good sound corn at Plaintiffs mill on Linville River in the Fall of 1865
2. That Plaintiff delivered to Deft the negro slave aforesaid in performance of his part of the Contract aforesaid
3. That Deft did not deliver the Corn aforesaid at the time and place aforesaid or at any other time and place
Wherefore PQ demands judgment of the sum of One hundred and fifty dollars and cost of suit
G Folk Atto
    165
   W F McKisson
    Vs

Burke County

Wm F. Gibbs
Answer

W F McKisson   } Superior Court
    against   } Spring Term 1869

Wm F Gibbs
Defendant answering the complaint of the plaintiff says
1st. That it is true that he hired from plaintiff a negro slave on or about the 19th of January 1865.
2nd. That it is true he was to pay for the hire of said slave in corn at the rate of ninety bushells of corn from the said 19 of July to the 25th of December 1865 for the time the said slave was in his service.
3rd. That said corn was to be delivered as stated in complainants as to time & place but as to quantity.
4th. That plaintiff obligated himself to defendant that he, plaintiff, would lose all the time in which said slave might be absent from the service of defendant, and would not exact payment for said lost time.
5th. That said slave was absent from defendant's service from the 15th of Apl 1865 or thereabouts until the end of the term for which she had been hired, without defendants privity or consent.
6th. Defendant alleges that Plaintiff became indebted to him in February 1863 in the sum of two hundred & seven dollars payable in North Carolina Bank bills & executed therefor his promissory note payable one day after date with one N.C. O'Neill as surety thereto and that said note nor any part thereof has ever been paid to him but that all and every part thereof is still due and owing which he asks may be allowed him as a counter claim so far as may be necessary to satisfy the claim set up by plaintiff against this defendant, and asks Judgments against plaintiff for the residue of said Counter claim which may be found to be due him and costs.

Caldwell & Tate for
Defendant
Plaintiff denies allegations on five and six of the Complaint
G Folk atto for Plaintiff
165
Wm F. McKisson
Vs

Burke County

Wm. F. Gibbs
Sub for
George Ledbetter
Instanter

Subpoena-Civil Action-Printed and for sale by Nichols & Gorman, Raleigh N.C.

Burke County: - In the Superior Court
State of North Carolina:
To The Sheriff of Burke County Greeting:
You are Commanded To Summonds George Ledbetter to appear before Judge Mitchell at Morganton Instanter on the [Blank] to give evidence in a Civil action the and there to be tried, wherein Wm. F. McKisson is Plaintiff and Wm. F. Gibbs is Defendant, on the part of the Defendent.
Hereof fail not at your peril.
This 31st day of May 1869.
F.D. Irvin
Clerk of the Superior Court of
Burke County.

Not found said to have left the County J.T. Patterson shff
By J Powell D.S.

Wm F McKisson
Vs
Wm F Gibbs
Writ Case
To Burke Co Court
Spring Term 1867
On a New Contract
G. Folk
Dorsy Clk $2.80 Att fees
I Depute Thos. R. James to Execute the Within Writ March the 22d 1867 B.A. Berry shff
Executed the Within March the 22 1867 B.A. Berry shff
T.R. James D.S. Cost to B.A.Berry shff

Burke County

STATE OF NORTH CAROLINA
TO THE SHERIFF OF Burke County, Greeting:
You are hereby commanded to Summons Wm F Gibbs if to be found in your County, to Appear before the Justices of our Court of Pleas and Quarter Sessions, at the next Court to be held for the County of Burke at Court-House in Morganton on the [Blank] Monday in [Blank] next, then and there to answer Wm F McKisson of a Plea of Tresspass on the Case to his damage Two Hundred Dollars.
    Herein fail not, and have you then and there this Writ.
               Witness, E.W. Dorsey Clerk of our said Court, at Office, the 5th Monday in December, 1866, and in the 91st year of American Independence.
Issued 15th March 1867   E.W. Dorsey Clerk.
Superior Court } Spring Term 1869
Burke County   }

W. F. McKisson
    Vs
W.F. Gibbs

Defendant swears that he cannot come safely to trial without the benefit of the testimony of George Ledbetter who is a material witness under subpoena & absent without the consent of affiant. He expects to prove by the witness that he held a written obligation on plaintiff by which he covenanted to be responsible for all lost time during which said negro was to serve him; that said written obligation is lost or mislaid or that affiant cannot find it and that said witness knows the contents of said obligation. This affiant is not made for delay, but to insure justice.
Sworn & Subscribed
in open Court 1st June 1869   Wm. F. Gibbs
     F.D. Irvin Clk

                   McKisson
                      Vs
                   Gibbs
                   Reply
North Carolina } Superior Court
Burke County   } Fall Term 1869

Burke County

The Plaintiff by way of reply to the said Counter Claim of Deft alledges

1. That one George Greenlee was indebted to Deft who has recovered Judgment against the said Greenlee and placed the Execution in the hands of one [Faded] a Constable for Collection
2. Amount of said Debt was seventy Eight Dollars.
3. That Plf paid the said debt to [?]
4. Afterwards the plf by mistake paid the said debt to Deft.
5. That before payment of the Plaintiff he had [?] to Greenlee to pay said debt
That said $78 is more than the value of the note claimed by Debt as a Counter Claim

	G Folk Att for plf
E.W. Dorsey	2.80
Co. Tax	1.00
Stamp	.50
B A Berry Shff	.60
G.A. Folk atto	4.00
F.D. Irvin	3.80
	$12.70

****

State
Vs
David (a Slave)
Sub. for Deft

Executed
J H Pearson Shff

STATE OF NORTH CAROLINA
To the Sheriff of Burke County--Greeting:

You are hereby commanded To summon Minty and Jane (Slaves of Charity Pearsons) and Matilda (a Slave of Tom Crawley's)

personally to be and appear before the Judge of our Superior Court of Law, at the next Court to be held for the County of Burke, at the Court House in Morganton, on the fourth Monday after the Fourth Monday in September, then and there to testify and the truth to say, in behalf of David (a Slave) in a matter of controversy before said Court

Burke County

depending and then and there to be tried, wherein The State is plaintiff and David (a Slave) is defendant. And this you shall in no wise omit, under the penalty prescribed by law.

    WITNESS, W.S. Pearson, Clerk of said Court, at Office, the Third Monday after the Fourth Monday in September A.D. 1845 and in the 70th year of our Independence.

    Issued the [Blank] day of [Blank] 184[Blank]
                W.S. Pearson C.S.C.

State
Vs
David (a Slave)
Sub.
Executed
J H Pearson Shff

                STATE OF NORTH CAROLINA
To the Sheriff of Burke County--Greeting:

    You are hereby commanded To summon Jacob Keller personally to be and appear before the Judge of our Superior Court of Law, at the next Court to be held for the County of Burke, at the Court House in Morganton, instanter; then and there to testify and the truth to say, in behalf of The State in a certain matter of controversy before said Court depending and then and there to be tried, wherein The State is plaintiff and David a negro slave property of A Harshaw defendant. And this you shall in no wise omit, under the penalty prescribed by law.

    WITNESS, W.S. Pearson, Clerk of said Court, at office, the 4th Monday after the Fourth Monday in Sept A.D. 1845 and in the 70th year of our Independence.

    Issued the 23 day of Octob 1845
                W.S. Pearson C.S.C.

State
Vs
David (a Slave)
Sub. for Def.

Executed on Wm Deal
Executed on W L McRee

Burke County

J H Pearson Shff
STATE OF NORTH CAROLINA
To the Sheriff of Burke County--Greeting:

You are hereby commanded To summon W.L. McRee and William Deal personally to be and appear before the Judge of our Superior Court of Law, at the next Court to be held for the County of Burke, at the Court House in Morganton, on the fourth Monday after the Fourth Monday in September, then and there to testify and the truth to say in behalf of (David a Slave) in a certain matter of controversy before said Court depending and then and there to be tried, wherein, The State is plaintiff and (David a Slave) is defendant. And this you shall in no wise omit, under the penalty prescribed by law.

WITNESS, W.S. Pearson, Clerk of said Court, at office, the Third Monday after the Fourth Monday in September A.D. 1845 and in the 70th year of our Independence.   Issued the [Blank] day of [Blank] 184[Blank]

W.S. Pearson C.S.C.

State
Vs
David (a Slave)
Sub. for Def.
Executed as to Kellers Betsey
Abr Harshaw

I Deputy Abraham Harshaw to Execute this Supoena on John Boyce & Wife & Betsey a Slave of Jacob Kellers this 23 Oct 1845
J H Pearson Shff

Executed on John Boyce & Isaac Boyce
J H Pearson Shff

STATE OF NORTH CAROLINA
To the Sheriff of Burke County--Greeting:

You are hereby commanded To summon John Boyce & Wife and Isaac Boyce (free persons of color) & Betsey (a Slave of Jacob Kellers)personally to be and appear before the Judge of our Superior Court of Law, at the next Court to be held for the County of Burke, at the Court House in Morganton, on the fourth Monday after the Fourth Monday in

Burke County

September Instanter; then and there to testify and the truth to say, in behalf of David (a Slave) in a certain matter of controversy before said Court depending and then and there to be tried, wherein The State is plaintiff and David (a Slave) is defendant. And this you shall in no wise omit, under the penalty prescribed by law.
      WITNESS, W.S. Pearson, Clerk of said Court, at office, the 4th Monday after the Fourth Monday in September A.D. 1845 and in the 70th year of our Independence.   Issued the [Blank] day of [Blank] 184[Blank]
                        W.S. Pearson C.S.C.

State
Vs
David (a Slave)
Sub for Def

Executed
J H Pearson Shff
STATE OF NORTH CAROLINA
To the Sheriff of [Blank] County--Greeting:
      You are hereby commanded To summon Judy Scott (a free woman of Color) and Isaac (a Slave of Charity Pearson) personally to be and appear before the Judge of our Superior Court of Law, at the next Court to be held for the County of Burke, at the Court House in Morganton, instanter; then and there to testify and the truth to say, in behalf of David (a Slave) in a matter of controversy before said Court depending and then and there to be tried, wherein The State is plaintiff and David (a Slave) is defendant. And this you shall in no wise omit, under the penalty prescribed by law.
      WITNESS, W.S. Pearson, Clerk of said Court, at office, the 4th Monday after the Fourth Monday in Sept A.D. 1845 and in the 70th year of our Independence.
      Issued the [Blank] day of [Blank] 184[Blank]
                W.S. Pearson C.S.C.

State
Vs
David (a Slave)
Subp

Burke County

I acknowledge the Service of this Subpoena
J H Pearson

STATE OF NORTH CAROLINA
To the Sheriff of Burke County--Greeting:

You are hereby commanded To summon John H Pearson to produce his negro Slave Emsey personally to be and appear before the Judge of our Superior Court of Law, at the next Court to be held for the County of Burke, at the Court House in Morganton, on the Fourth Monday in Sept Instanter; then and there to testify and the truth to say in behalf of The State in a certain matter of controversy before said Court depending and then and there to be tried, wherein The State is plaintiff and David (a Slave) is defendant. And this you shall in no wise omit, under the penalty prescribed by law.

WITNESS, W.S. Pearson, Clerk of said Court, at office, the 4th Monday after the Fourth Monday in Sept A.D. 1845 and in the 70th year of our Independence.

Issued the 24 day of Oct 1845
W.S. Pearson C.S.C.

State
Vs
David a Slave
Subp
To Oct 1845

Executed
J H Pearson Shff

STATE OF NORTH CAROLINA
To the Sheriff of Burke County--Greeting:

You are hereby commanded To summon Mary Pearson & Benjamin Ross personally to be and appear before the Judge of our Superior Court of Law, at the next Court to be held for the County of Burke, at the Court House in Morganton, on the 4th Monday after the Fourth Monday in September next; then and there to testify and the truth to say, in behalf of The State in a certain matter of controversy before said Court depending and then and there to be tried, wherein The State is

Burke County

plaintiff and David the property of A Harshaw is defendant. And this you shall in no wise omit, under the penalty prescribed by law.

    WITNESS, W.S. Pearson, Clerk of said Court, at office, the 4th Monday after the Fourth Monday in September A.D. 1845 and in the 70th year of our Independence.
    Issued the 20th day of Oct 1845
        W.S. Pearson C.S.C.

State
Vs
David a Slave
Subpoena
To Fall Term 1845

Executed
J H Pearson Shff

STATE OF NORTH CAROLINA

To the Sheriff of Burke County--Greeting:
    You are hereby commanded To summon Clark M Avery to produce his negroes Alfred & Hanible personally to be and appear before the Judge of our Superior Court of Law, at the next Court to be held for the County of Burke, at the Court House in Morganton, on the 4th Monday after the Fourth Monday in Sept next; then and there to testify and the truth to say, in behalf of the State in a certain matter of controversy before said Court depending and then and there to be tried, wherein The State is plaintiff and David a negro the property of A Harshaw is defendant. And this you shall in no wise omit, under the penalty prescribed by law.
    WITNESS, W.S. Pearson, Clerk of said Court, at office, the 4th Monday after the Fourth Monday in September A.D. 1845 and in the 70th year of our Independence.
    Issued the 20th day of Oct 1845
        W.S. Pearson C.S.C.

State	} Indictment--
Vs	} assault - Battery
Dave - a Slave, property	} with intent to kill
of Abr. Harshaw	} Madison a servant
	} Of Mrs. Vanhorn

Burke County

Judah Scott a Free Woman of Colour Sworn - Says the night of the affray whilst Madison (the Dec'd) was eating his supper in her house he said he would have his Watch - that he would hurt Dave - and that he didn't care about Keeping it a secret - that after Dec'd finished supper went down in the direction of the Cabin where Prisoner was at the time - was gone over 10 min: and returned - took the shot-bag off the Gun and threw it in the loft - took down the Gun and was about going out when she caught the Gun and tried to get it from him - told him it was loaded - in the scuffle gun swapped - Dec'd got out of doors and fixed the lock again and started towards the Cabin where Pris: was - Witness told Martha to go tell pris. Madison had the Gun and would Shoot him - Witness Called M. back and made her come in - Witness was not at the other Cabin where affray took place with Dec'd and Betsey--Isaac Boyce Free man of Colour Sworn - was with Dec'd friday evening - Did not leave Kellars Mine in company with him but met near McKissons Store -- Went to the Store, had some liquor, did not consider the Dec'd drunk -- when witness left about sun down or perhaps before (it was cloudy) Dec'd said to witness and others that were present - "Boys Dave or me one or other" will be killed - Wit. replied, have no fuss for one or the others say get killed if you get drunk - Dec'd said Well you will hear of it in the morning - Wit. left Dec'd at the Store - had a glass of liquor when he (witness) left.

John Boyce Free negro Sworn - was with Dec'd near Mike[?] Kellars friday evening - heard him say that if he didn't get his Watch he would kill Dave - Wit replied dont talk to me about none of yr negro scrapes

Tilly a female slave the property of Tom Crawly - Sworn - Went from old Mrs Pearsons down to where Dave and dec'd were on the Ck near the Pitts - Deal and Jane in company - also Miss Polly - heard Pris: holler to Mr. Deal and say "here he is Mr. Deal" Pris standing over dec'd one hand on his shoulder - Dec'd sitting on the ground - Pris: had stick in his hand - shovel handle - Pris. told Wife of Dec'd not to touch him - she the (dec'ds) Wife stepped towards him when Pris draw back as tho he intended to strike her - Heard a noise before she reached the parties like some persons fighting - like some one beating another - Dec'd did not speak or say a word after she went up ----------

Burke County

Jane Servt. of old Mrs Pearson - Sworn - went down to the swamp with Deal and Tilly where the parties were - started up to dec'd - Pris: threatened to strike her as stated by Tilly - Says Dec'd was very drunk - found his clothes very bloody next morning - mostly about the neck and shoulders - Dec'd staggered as he went from the field to the House - Dec'd complained of his head hurting him "mighty bad" and would put his hand to it

Isaac a slave of Charity Pearson - Sworn says Dec'd came to the kitchen where he was and told him to ask Dave to come out - Deal, Dave, Betsey, Cy Scott in the kitchen - Scott playing fiddle - told Dave dec'd wished to see him - Dave went out - Heard them talking - Heard Dec'd say "Dave do you want to put your life against mine" Dave said no I don't - Wit saw Madison pass the door with a Gun - Dave in the House when he (Wit) was -Deal went out and called [?] - Wit: saw Dec'd go round the Chimney and polk the gun thru a crack - thinks Dave was there sitting on the bed - Daves Wife came out and Caught hold of dec'd - deal was then at the other Cabin - Deal soon came back - Pris: knocked Betsey down or pushed her down twice - Dave ran out and knocked Dec'd down with a stick - handle of shovel - Dec'd run off

George slave of Abr. Harshaw Sworn - Says he was not out of his House during the affray between parties - Heard Pris: Call to Deal that he had found him - Heard licks like some one striking another - Dec'd compld. of sickness next morning - Wit dressed Dec'd head - Dec'd had puked thro' the night as appeared from the floor in the House

George slave of Isaac Pearson - Sworn Says he knows but little about the affray - was not at Kellars that night - a week or more before the occurrence heard Pris say that he intended to kill some person

State of north Carolina }
Burke County }
    Whereas it has been represented to me that within the last four days an affray has taken place between Madison a Servant of John Vanhorn and Dave a man Servant of Abr. Harshaw in which said affray Madison has been seriously injured and his life endangered.
    These are therefore to command the Shff of Burke County or any other lawful officer forthwith to apprehend the Sd. Dave (Servant as

Burke County

aforesd. of Abr. Harshaw) and also his wife Betsey a negro Woman belonging to Jacob Kellar who was also engaged in said affray as well as any and all other negro slaves suspected or charged with being engaged or Concerned in the affray which took place at Kellars Gold Mine between the sd. Madison and Dave and them bring before me or some other acting Magistrate for said County to be examined and their Conduct on said occasion legally investigated and disposed of as the law directs, and peace and good order of Society requires
Herein fail not - Given under my hand & seal this 15th day of Oct 1845
                         R Pearson (JP)Summons for the State
Isaac Boyce & John Boyce & Juda Scott Free Negroes
Jane & Isaac Slaves of Charity Pearson
Tilly a Slave of Thomas Crawley
George a Slave of Isaac Pearsons
Benj. a Slave of John Kincaid
George a Slave of Abram Harshaw
Minty a Slave of Charity Pearson
Wm R Deal

North Carolina }
Burke County   } After our examination of this caseIt is adjudged by us that the Dft. Dave be held in custody and that he be fully committed to the jail of this County to answer this Indictment at the next Supr. Court - to be held for this County
    The Dft. Betsey may be discharged
Given under our hands & seals 14th Oct 1845
                     R.C. Pearson J.P. (Seal)
W R Deal   } Tho Walton J.P. (Seal)
Judah Scott   } Ea Bound in $200 -
Isaac Boyce   } for their app: as Wit
John Boyce   } on part of the State

J H Pearson bound in like sum for the app. of Pearsons George & Crawleys Girl Tilly
Jacob Kellar in like sum for the app. (Harshaws Geo:) Pearsons Isaac Minty and Jane servants of Charity Pearson all Wit. in behalf State

                     State
                       Vs

Burke County

Dave a Slave
of A Harshaw
& Betsey his Wife
owned by Jacob Kellar
Warrant
AB

Executed
J H Pearson Shff

Minty a slave of Charity Pearson, Sworn -
 Says she was at house night of the affray - Pris: came over to her Mothers went in the House - remained but a little time - said I dont want to make any of you mad Polly but Dave has drawed a gun on me - went off in the direction of the Pitts - Heard Dave holler to Mr Deal - Heard licks as if they were fighting - Dave was cursing - gives the same account of Daves Conduct after they went up as is given by the other Witnesses

Deal (the Overseer) Sworn - Says on friday night it rained - Went to work after breakfast - when at the Pitts Dec'd dropped his Watch, in attempting to put it in his coat pocket which he had taken off and hung up - Pris: took the Watch and when asked for it at the House said he had it & if Dec'd would give up his money that he would give him the watch - Pris: said to Dec'd that he had ackd. to taking the money and had promised to pay it back, if he would make no more fuss about it - Dec'd left during the day - saw no more of him untill after night when he came to the door, and Dave went out to where he was - Dave came in and soon after dec'd again came passing by the door - Saw that Dec'd had either a stick or a Gun, went out and was satisfied that it was a Gun - Dec'd went around the house in the Chimney Corner - Witness called to him to give up the Gun - Did not go around the House but went up to see if it was his (Witnesses) Gun - found his gun gone retd. saw Dec'd and Bets scuffling - Dec'd pushed or knocked Bets down twice - was cloudy, but the moon gave light - could see pretty well - saw Dave come out and run towards dec'd and knock him down - took the Gun and gave to this Wit - Dec'd jumped into the Pitts and run off - Wit & Pris. pursued - Went to acquaint Mr Kellar of the circumstances - Heard Dave say he had him - then went (run) to the spot - heard [?] licks - told Dave if he found him not to strike him - took Pris and confined him - Kept him chained that night and brot him to town next day - Dec'd said but little - had been drinking -----

Burke County

Chapter Ten

Burke County

WEAPON PERMIT

Know all men by these presents that we John McDowell and Robert McElrath are Justly and indebted unto Frederick Sho[?] or his Successors in office in the sum of one hundred pounds good money and to be Void on Condition that whereas the County Court of Burke has Granted and Signed a permit to the above bound John McDowell for his Negro Slave Ben to carry Gun on his said McDowells plantation or land. Now provided the said John McDowell shall and well and truly imdemnify the County of Burke and all the good Citizens of the State from all harm and damages that may be sustained in consequence of the said Negro Carrying by permission a Gun as aforesaid Then the above obligation to be Void but otherwise to remain in full force and Virtue the 28th day of July 1818.

test	J. McDowell	(seal)
J. Erwin	Robt. McElrath	(seal)

Burke County

Chapter Eleven

Burke County

BASTARDY BONDS

Bond of Indemnity
E. Vanderpool

We Elyas Vanderpool and Reuben Coffey do acknowledge Ourselves Justly indebted unto James Grant Esqr and the rest of the Justices for Burke County in the Sum of One hundred pounds. And to be Void on Condition that the above bounden Elyas Vanderpool Shall well and truly indemnify the Court of Burke for the maintenance of a base born child begotten on the body of Vire Pearce of Whom the above said Elyas Vanderpool is the reputed father otherwise to remain in full force and Virtue Given Under our hands and Seals this 30th January 1812

	his	
Test	Elyas Vanderpool	(Seal)
J. Erwin Clk	mark	
	Ruben Coffey	(Seal)

Burke County

Chapter Twelve

Burke County

TRADING WITH SLAVES

State
Vs.
Reuben Throgmorton
Trading with Slaves

Presentment
John Goff
Jacob Powell [Marked thru]
Hall Butler
Sworn to & Sent
J.S. Ferrer Clk

not a true bill
J.H. Pearson
Foreman

Burke County, to wit:
Superior Court of Law, Fall Term A.D. 1851

The Jurors for the State, on their oath present, that Reuben Throgmorton late of the County Burke at and in said County, on the the first day of November in the year 1851, certain goods and merchandize to wit, One Gal. of spiritous Liquors to a Slave named Hiram the property of Robert McElrath unlawfully did sell and deliver - the said goods and merchandize not being then and there sold and delivered to said Slave, in exchange for, or in payment of money due for, any article or articles which the said slave had then and there by written permission of his owner or manager been authorized to sell; Contrary to the form of the

Burke County

Statute in such case made and provided, and against the peace and dignity of the State.
B.S. Gaither Solicitor

Rowan County

Chapter Thirteen

Rowan County

CRIMINAL AND CIVIL ACTIONS

Harris
VS
Nicholas Drury

Copies of the Depositions
of Robert Green, Fady Christian, Mary Jennings
& John McLemore

State of No. Carolina } In obedience to the Commission
Montgomery County } to us directed we have Caused

Robert Green to appear before us Thomas Ursery and Alexander Beard Esquires, Justices, And being duly Sworn deposeth and saith. The complainant asked Robert Green the question, what did you hear pass between my self and Nicholas Drury - The answer was, some time in December in the year one thousand seven hundred and ninty three he heard the Complainant say here I will give you up every thing, Satisfy me for the trouble I have been at, and go and Collect your money your self, for I would wish to be done with it. - Drury's answer was you have undertaken it, I shant have any thing to do with it. - And the deponent Sayeth that the Negro Girl it was said had a rising Cancer on Her thumb. - And Drury asked the Complainant what he must do. - The answer was take her immediately to a Doctor and have it cured, and I will pay all Cost, or else give her up to me and I will get my Son in law to take her to a doctor and have her Cured. - The answer from Drury was I will have it Cured my self. - Mr. Harris's reply was, If the negro Girl should Come to any misfortune by his neglect, Drury should pay the damage on account of that rising, and says take notice. - and further this deponent Saith not. Robert Green

Rowan County

Test
Alexander Beard (Seal)
Thos. Ursery (Seal)
November 12th 1798

State of No. Carolina } In obedience to a Commission
Montgomery County } to us directed we have Caused

Fady Christian to appear before us Thomas Urssary and Alexander Beard Esquire Justices for the said County and being duly Sworn deposeth and saith, that some time in the year one thousand Seven hundred and ninty One, she then lived with her Father Joshua Harris, she understood that he made a Contract or agreement with Nicholas Drury, for money due him in Virginia, and that Mr. Drury Carried away a Small negro Girl but what was the agreement she did not know at that time, But some Considerable time after, in the beginning of the next year the Said Drury came to her father's house again and she heard Mr. Drury say to her Father, I am glad you are not gone to Virginia, for he was not Satisfied with their former contract, for he did not want him to distress his Brother by suing him for he did not want him Sued at any rate. - Mr. Drury said I had rather loose his money, than for his Brother to be Distressed or said she saith her father then asked Mr. Drury what he must do. Drury said if his Brother Could not pay it take his Bond for the money, and give it for any good trade such as he Could Bring away with him or exchange it for any persons Bond, who her father might suppose to be as good as his Brothers. And she further saith from the whole of this Conversation she understood that Mr. Drury was disatisfied at the Contract they first made. Then her father told him it would not answer his purpose to be Concerned with it, If he could not get it in money. She then understood the first bargain they had made was for a sum of money, Mr. Drury was to lend her Father what was due him in Virginia from his Brother, and that the little negroe he Carried away at the first time they made the agreement was to be given for the Interest. Her Father told Drury that if he Could not get as much as Fifty pounds Virginia Money in Cash at that time he was going in, the first bargain was to be void, and that her father was to take back the negro again which was the agreement between them both. Mr. Drury told her father to get the best he could to get it paid or Settled in the best manner he could and to do for him as was it for himself, and he would pay him for his trouble, that he would have it his own hands after paying him for his

Rowan County

trouble and expences he was to return him the ballance. The deponent further Saith, that this Second Contract took place before ever her father went to Virginia, after the first between him and Mr. Drury at the time he Carried away the negro Girl. The deponent saith that Mr. Drury told her further to do for him as he would for himself and whatever he might do Mr. Drury would oblige himself to stand to. Further this Deponent Sayeth not.

                              her
Test   Fady   X   Christian
Alexr. Beard   mark
Thos. Ursery   November the 12th 1798

State of No. Carolina   } In obedience to a
Montgomery County   } Commission to us directed

we have caused Mary Jennings to appear before us two of the Justices for the said County and after being duly Sworn on the Holy Evangelists of Almighty God was asked by the Complainant what did you hear Drury say, and the deponent Saith some time in the year 1797 she heard Complainant ask the defendant why did he not give up the negro when I wanted you. And the Answer was of the defendant my work was at a distance from the House and I wanted her for Company for my wife.
Mary Jennings
Test
Alexr. Beard
Thos. Ussery   November 12th 1798

State of No. Carolina   } In obedience to a
Montgomery County   } Commission to us directed

we have Caused John McLemore to appear before us Thomas Ussery and Alexander Beard Esquires Justices for the said County and being duly Sworn deposeth and saith that some time in the year one thousand Seven hundred and ninty Two, the deponant then being at the House of Joshua Harris where he then lived in the month of January that Nicholas Drury Came to the House of Said Harris and in his hearing said I am glad you are not gone to Virginia for that he was not Satisfied with the bargain or agreement he had with him. - that he was afraid he would Sue his brother

Rowan County

for the money he lent him, and he did not want his brother Sued or Distressed at any rate, that it would make a difference between them and that he wanted to make another bargain with him for he would rather loose it altogether than that his Brother should be hurt by being Sued. - The deponant further saith that Harris then said to Drury. If that is the Case and your Brother knows it that I am not to Sue him for the money I shall not get the actual Cash and without it will answer no purpose, I had rather have nothing to do with it, Mr. Drury then said you must Keep Secret from him that you are not to Sue him untill you get the Estate Settled with him and then if you Cannot the money in Cash, from him the first Bargain they had made must be void and the deponant saith further that Mr. Drury said then to Mr. Harris you must do the best for me with my Brother in the best way you Can and get it out of his hands to take it in Negroes or Horses or take his Bonds for it and exchange them for any other bonds on persons that you think good pay. That Mr. Harris replied & said if it was his own Debt he would know what to do, but if he should take negroes or Horses for him, and they were to be lost or die he could lay himself liable for such accidents as might happen it being a great Distance, they then both Called this Deponant Witness what they then agreed upon and Saith that Drury told Harris to Act and do for him as he would for himself, And he would stand to it or be satisfied. The deponant further saith that Harris then said to Drury that if he Could not get fifty pounds of the Sum Virginia money in Cash when I now go in the bargain we had made is intirely void and I will take back the negro, he understood it was a small Girl and heard her name Called Violet. - The deponant saith that this was agreed to by both parties, Harris then asked Drury how he should get paid for the trouble and expence of going backwards and forwards and the expence he should be at for it might be Several years before it might be done with as his Brother was not to be sued. - Drury's answer to this was to be shure there will be as much in my brother's hands to pay you for all the trouble and expences you will be at, and you will have it in your own hands make use of the or return as much as will satisfy here for your expences and then return me the ballance when the whole is Collected & settled with my brother as he understood. - This deponant further Saith that since this Suit has Commenced Harris Called on him to go with him to Drury's House, he heard Harris then offer to settle with him & take the debt on himself and pay him his money

Rowan County

agreeable to [?] this Mr. Drury refused to do and further this deponant saith not.
John McLemore
Test
Alexr. Beard   (Seal)
Thos. Ussery   (Seal) November 12th 1798

State of No. Carolina   } I do hereby Certify that the
Salisbury District   } aforegoing Depositions to wit.

Robert Green's, Fady Christian's, Mary Jenning's and John McLemore's are all true Copies of the Originals now in the office Certified at office the 17th day of December 1799.
Max Chambers C.M. Eq

The Depositions were taken at the Dwelling House of Thos. Jennings on the First Day of February on Saturday agreeable to Notis 1800.

****

State
Vs } Murder
Charles (a Slave)
Examinations

The undersigned Justices on the 2nd day of December 1831 caused to be arrested the body of a negro man Charles the property of Alexander Neely upon suspicion of having murdered and wounded a Boy Child of Alexander Neely and Margaret Neely aged two years and two months. - The examination taken before us and witnesses sworn before us as follows at house of Alexander Neely.

1st   Duncan Sworn and says. - he was sowing wheat in the field. He saw this child Richard which is missing with another Called Julius and two of Charle's children going to the field about 10 or eleven Oclock And he was back and forward at the house he thinks twice afterwards, and does not remember of taking notice of the Children from that time untill it was mentioned by some of the boys that were plowing in the field that Richy

Rowan County

was gone. He says he does not recollect which of the boys mentioned it. He said he reckoned not and looked towards the house and said that yonder was Julius going up the hill towards the house. He Duncan says he went on to the end, towards the house, and went out of the field at the gap. - As he went on to the house he saw his mystress coming. She asked him was Ricky out at the field. He says he answered he was not. His Mistress turned back he discovered she did not understand him. - He Duncan went on to the house, and asked his mistress if Ricky was there? She said I thought you said he was out at the field. He told her he said no he then looked round the house and started with his Mistress out to the field to look for the child as they went down the branch towards the Creek they saw Charles coming from towards the pond. - His Mistress asked him where he had been. He said he had been looking for Ricky. His Mistress then asked him if he had been at the Creek. He said not quite. They Duncan and his Mistress went on towards the Creek to look for the child and could not find it. Duncan being asked where the rest of the boys were when he left the field. He says Charles Webb started down the branch and Dave took a different course towards the head of the field. He was then asked by his Master if Charles's little girl did not tell them that Ricky was lost. - He said that he did not hear her say any thing about it. His Master then asked Duncan if he did not see Charles's little girl in the field. He answered and says he did. Duncan was then asked if he had heard Charles make any threats against his Mistress. - He answered and said that he never heard Charles make any but he heard from other Negroes. He was then asked what negroes. He answered that Charles himself told him that one of Mr Barbers negroe Girls had told it but it was not true. His Master, Alexander Neely answered and said no, Neither he Duncan nor nobody else ever heard it.

2ndly Dave sworn And says upon Oath that in the evening about two hours by sun they were all plowing and hurrying to get done to go to the husking, he says they were all at the side of the field next to the house where they had come out at the end of the rows, the children was all there Ricky with the rest. - He says he called Julius to give him Dave parsimmons; Julius went to him and gave him one, He Dave told Julius his Mamma would whip him for having parsimmons in his eats & Julius said Ricky has some too. He then called Ricky to give him some simons. Ricky started to come, and a briar hung in his hair, and Charles told his little Girl to take it off. - He Dave did not wait for the Child Ricky to come

Rowan County

to him but turned his horse round to go to the other end as he turned his horse round the child scared and run off a little piece, they all three Dave, Charles Webb & old Charles went on to the other end, and Charles Webb foremost. They went on to the other end stade no time, turned and come back, as they came back they met the little Girl Charles Webbs child, and she said to Charles Webb Ricky was lost. - And Charles asked which way he went. - She said he went towards the old tantrough. They went on to the end Charles foremost nothing said Charles bound his horse first, and started down the branch He Dave started after him a short distance, and turned back and went towards the other end of the field, and waited up there till He saw his Mistress coming. - He went down the branch where his Mistress and Duncan came down the branch to hunt for the child. The Question was then asked Dave if he believed the little child Ricky went down the branch, why he started to go that way & then turned and went up to the head of the field and wait there till he saw his Mistress. - He stood as if at a loss to answer and his Master answered for him, and said he supposed to let them know that the child was lost. - As soon as his Master had said this Dave followed and said the same as his Master had said. - The Question was then asked Dave how long it was after that before he saw Charles. - He answered and said he could not tell how long. - Dave was then asked if he heard Charles make any threats against his Mistress. - He answered and said no. - Old Charles or Dad Charles sworn. - And said that at the time they were all at the side next the house he was not nearer than twenty yards. - They all three saw him there at that time they all three turned the child scared at their turning he Old Charles was the last one that turned, and after he had went some little distance he heard the child Cry he looked back, and saw it sitting on the fence. - they went on to the end and turned to come back, as we came along we saw Charles Webbs little Girl coming meeting us. And Charles Webb asked her where Ricky was, She said he was gone. - They all went on to the end Charles Webb foremost. - Charles Webb bound out his horse and took right down the branch without saying any thing. He old Charles continued, and said Dave started to go and went as far as the Hog-pen which was 50 yds. - and then turned and went up to the head of the field and staid there till he saw his Mistress coming. - And he old Charles staid at his plow till he saw his Mistress coming, he then went on to the glade that was in the field they were plowing in.

Rowan County

4thly   Mrs. Margaret Neely sworn and says the curses and abuses that Charles Webb put upon her in her presence, would be in vain to attempt. One day she attempted or was whipping one of Charles Webbs children. He Charles come in put his hands upon her shoulders, and pushed her back, and jerked the Child from her, and swore she would not whip his child, and swore by God if she did not let him alone he Charles would lay her aside. - And at another time he abused her by oaths rashly and she says that she picked up a rock and struck him. He turned round, and swore that before six months he would give her something that she would not get over for six months.

5th   James Cline Sworn. - and says, One day they working in the field He Cline and Charles Webb fell out. - and Cline says because Charles did not do his work right. - And he Cline Pickt up a stick and told him if he did not do better he would strike him. And if he get hold of him that he would not find his Mistress to park about. He Charles damned if he did not take care that he would put him and his Mistress both where they would not trouble him. - Cline was then asked why he did not whip him? He answered and said knowing that his Master would never have him whipped for any of his abuse to his Mistress. He let him alone.

6th   Washington Neely sworn Says he saw the two Childs traks at the edge of the Creek one in the water and one at the edge. - And that he did believe if it was a childs tracts it could not have got there unless it had been put there.

The foregoing is the evidence taken before us upon the Examination of Negro Charles Webb upon the Murder of an infant child Richard Neely, - Child of Alexander & Margaret Neely

Given under our hands and seals
Will Barber JP   (Seal)
Solomon Hall JP   (Seal)
Abel Cowan JP   (Seal)
Wm. Wood JP   (Seal)

****

Rowan County

Tho. Spraggins
Vs
Jno Brevard jr
Detinue
To May 1787

State of North Carolina

To the Sheriff of Rowan County, Greeting.

We Command you to take the body of John Brevard junr. Gentleman (if to be found in your bailiwick) and him safely keep so that you have him before our Justices of our County Court of Pleas and Quarter Sessions to be held for our County of Rowan at the Court-House in Salisbury on the first Monday in May next; then and there to answer Thomas Spraggins of a plea wherefore he detains a female negro slave named Hannah alias Minder of the price of one hundred & fifty pounds.Damage fifty pounds.
Herein fail not, and have you then and there this writ.Witness Adlai Osborne - Clerk of our said Court, at office, the fifth day of February Anno Dom 1787 and in the XI year of our Independence
A: Osborne CC

Thomas Haggins
Vs
John Brevard jr.
Nar. Detinue May 1787
filed 7th May 1787

Rowan Ss. May Sessions 1787.
Thomas Haggins complains of John Brevard junior for that he unjustly detains a negro girl slave named Hannah alias Minder the property of the said Thomas of the price of one hundred and fifty pounds, to the damage of the said Thomas fifty pounds for which he brings suit &c.
Jno Stokes   atto. for pltff.

[Editor: Name shown as Spraggins on one document and Haggins on the other.]

Rowan County

****

State
Vs
Negro Man Slave Jacob

State of North Carolina }
Rowan County   }

Be it remembered that at a Special Court called and held by the Sheriff of said County at the Court House in Salisbury on the fifth day of September Anno Domini (1812) one thousand eight hundred and twelve, for the purpose of trying Negroe Man Slave Jacob the property of Jane Phelps Charged with a Misdemeanor to wit, with confederating and conspiring with others to Kill and injure the good citizens of the County of Rowan, Present the worshipful Justices (to wit)

John Steele   }
Lewis Beard   }
John March   } Esquires
Mack Crump   }

State   }
Vs   } Misdemeanor
Negro Man Slave Jacob   } Not Guilty
(the property of Jane Phelps}

The owner having admitted notice according to act of the General Assembly. The following good and lawfull men sworn & charged to try the above issue of trans[?]

1. Samuel Lemly   4. John Beard
2. John Murphy   5. Joseph Kincade
3. Harrod B. Pruett   6. Henry Crider
7. Albert Torrence   10. Jeremiah Brown
8. Thomas L. Cowan   11. Thomas Craig
9. George Bitz   12. John Fulton

Rowan County

Find the defendant Guilty in Manner and form as stated in the charge exhibited.

Ordered that the Sheriff take him to some convenient place and give him one hundred lashes, on his bare back and that he be committed to prison, six weeks with irons and to be fed with bread and water only for that time, and at the expiration of said time that he receive fifty lashes more; then to be delivered to the owner on payment of costs.

I John Giles clerk of the Court of Pleas and quarter Sessions of Rowan County do hereby certify the foregoing to all the proceedings of the Special Court
John Giles CC

****

Absalom Taylor
Against
John Hanglighter
To the Clerk of Supr. Court
Salisbury

Sepr. 1786
South Carolina   } Before me thomas Knight one of the
Winton County   } Justices of the peace for said County

Persuant to this Writ to me Directed I have this Day caused to appear before me William Buford a Witness for the Defence the plantiff being Sighted to appear Made Default - Who being Duly sworn According to Law Decleared that about the first of May 1780 he the Deponent Was present at the taking of a Number of Negroes - among which was a negroe man named Sampson which negroe was he said in possession of William Allbrook and that Said negroes taken Within the Posts Maintained by the British army at that time and Sold at Public Sale in South Carolina agreeable to a Proclamation of Govrnr Howley to the Best of his Knowledge.
William Buford
then Capt.
Sworn to before me this 28th August 1786
Thos. Knight JP

Rowan County

****

Isaac (Free man)
Vs
Benjamin Abbit

State of No. Carolina } To Any Lawfull officer to Execute
Rowan County } Whereas Benja. Abbett of Said

County Complaines To me one of the Justices of said County that Free Isaac of Said County Stands Justly Indebted to him the sum of three Pounds twelve shillings Speacie and Delayeth payment these are therefore to Command you to Summonds Free Isaac to Appear Before me or Sum other Justices of said County to answer the Above Complaint Given Under my hand and seal this twentey Ninth Day of March 1783.
Robert Mackie JP
summond Solomon Wallon as a Witness for the Plantif
Executed and Returned by me   Henry Wells

Summond   Samuel Freeman
             Benjamine Howard
             for the Defendant
Benja. Abbets his Warrant
The Plantif and Defendant both appearing before me and After Hearing the Complaint my Judgment is that the Defendant free Isaack Pay the Plantif £ 3-12-0   Given under my Hand and Seale This 26 Day of April 1783.
Free Isaac Dr. to me Benja Abett
To Cash Due me for Eighteen Bushels Corn   £ 3-12-3
April 26 1783
Sworn To before me   Robert Mackie

Appeal
Recognizance
Benjamine Abbott
Bound

Rowan County

the State of North　　　　} Memorandum of Recognizance
Carolina Rowan County　} an appeal
Benjamine Abbitt of Said County bound to the Next Quarter Sessions in May to appear and Prousecute Free Isack a Negro man so Called in the Sum of £20 in Specie.
Free Isack of the County of Rowan Planter bound To Appare at the Next May County Court of Please and Quarter Sessions of the Peace To be Held at Salsbury for Said County of Rowan and not Depart the sd Court with out Leave In the Sum of £40 in Specie.
John Howard as Security bound in the Sum of £20.
Acknoledg before me This 26 Day of May 1783
Robert Mackie JP

****

James Bowman
Vs
Wade Hampton

No Carolina　　} to the sheriff of Rowan County
Rowan County　} or any sworn Constable

Whereas James Boman hath Complained on oath to me Dav. Caldwell one of the Justise of the County Court of Rowan that Waid Hamton an Inhabitant of South Carolina is Justly Indeted to Him thirty Eight Dolars & a half pence which is fifteen pound for shillings worth Curancy Dolars at Eight shillings and sd James Boman having given Bond & security according to the Direction of the act of the general Assembly in Such Case made and provided I Therefore Command you to attach the Estate of the said Waid Hamton if to Be found in your County or so much thereof Replenable on Security as shall Be of value sufficient to satisfy the said Debt and costs according to the Complaint and such Estate so attached in yours to Secure or so to Provide that the same may Be liable to further Proceedings thereupon to be Had at the County Court to Be Held for said County at Salisbery the first monday agust Next so as to Compell the said Hamton to appear and answer the above Complaint of the said James Boman When and Whear you shall make known to said Court how you

Rowan County

shall Have Executed this Writ given under my Hand and seal this 18th of May 1782
Dav. Caldwell JP (Seal)
VI year of american Independence

Attach'd two Negro Children Named Will & Samson in behalf of James Boman the property of Waid Hamton. By me
John Baley   Const
May ye 31st 1782

****

Burton Craige
Vs
R.H. & H.G. Burton

Beaties Ford Oct-12th
Mr B Craig Salesbury N.C.

Whereas Burton Craige purchased of Hutchins G. Burton a lot of negroes in August last, which will appear from a bill of sale from the said Hutchins G. Burton to Burton Craig bearing date the 27th September 1834, and whereas the said Burton Craig alleges that some of the aforesaid negroes are unsound and whereas they are both willing to have the matter amicably adjusted, this instrument therefore witnesseth, that they agree each to select a man to whom the subject shall be referred, who are to be governed by the notes of Law, equity & evidence and who are to determine, what allowance is to be made to the aforesaid Burton Craig for the unsoundness of the aforesaid negroes, and whatever allowance they shall make is to be deducted from the amount of a note of five thousand dollars given by the aforesaid Craig to the aforesaid Burton for five thousand dollars and due the first day of May 1835 which note is now in the possession of Robt. H. Burton - It is also understood that if the arbitrators chosen cannot agree they shall have power to select a third person by whose decision we both bond ourselves in the penalty of one thousand dollars to abide all [?] made before signing and sealing - this 10th February 1835.
Copy signed by Burton Craige

Rowan County

Witnessed by R.A. Burton   H.G. Burton
a copy by A M B

Dear Friend. Being very much engaged I asked my Father to copy the above & have read it over & found it correct. My goods are now Scattered in cry Auction must be my Excuse for this short line.
Your friend with much Respect
R. H. Burton

Writ of Injunction
To April Term 1836

Made Known to H G Burton this 3rd day of Feby 1836
Jas Simmons Shff

State of North Carolina
Court of Equity }
Rowan County   } Sp-to Robert H. Burton of Lincoln County, Hutchins G. Burton of Hallifax County their Counsellors, Attorneys, Solicitors, Agents, and to the Clerk of Rowan Superior Court of Law, - the Sheriff of Rowan County and all others whom it may concern Greeting Whereas it hath been presented unto us in our Court of Equity that the said Robert H. Burton at a Superior Court of Law held for the County of Rowan at October Term thereof 1835 obtained a fraudulent Judgment as assigned of H.G. Burton against Burton Craige of Rowan County for the sum of Five thousand dollars with interest and costs of suit. And whereas the said Burton Craige hat exhibited his Bill of complaint against said H.G. Burton and R.H. Burton before the Honourable William Norwood one of the Judges of the Superior Courts of Law and Equity for the State of North Carolina praying that the complainant might have an injunction for stay of your the said Defendants proceeding at Law until the hearing of the cause; whereupon the said Honourable Judge hath by his fiat signified his assent to the said prayer.
    We therefore in consideration of the promises aforesaid do strictly enjoin you the said Robert H. Burton and the said H.G. Burton and all and every persons before mentioned under the penalty of five hundred dollars, to be levied of your goods and chattles, lands and tenements, to our use, that you forbear and absolutely desist from carrying the said

Rowan County

Judgement into effect, or taking any other proceedings thereon, until this Hearing of this Case by our said Court of Equity.
Witness Samuel Silliman Clerk and Master in said Court of Equity at office and under seal of office the 21st day of November Anno Domini 1835 and of the Independence of the United States the 60th years
Sam. Silliman C.M.E.

Burton Craige
Vs
H.G Burton and R.H. Burton
Fiori Facias against Complainant
To October Term 1836
Principal & Interest Paid to Robert H. Burton
and cost Paid to office
Satisfied
Jas: W. Hampton   Cor

Came to hand 10th June 1836 F. Slater Shff
Came to my hands 29th Sept. 1836 J.W. Hampton coroner

State of North Carolina

Rowan County}
To the Sheriff of Rowan County -- Greeting:
    We command you, that of the goods and chattles, lands and tenements of Burton Craige, Robert N. Craige & Robert Huie if to be found in your County, you cause to be made the sum of Five thousand four hundred & Ninety five dollars with interest on $5000 from 16th April 1836 until paid; and the sum of Ninety one dollars 67 1/2 cents which was lately in our Court of Equity, held for the county of Rowan decreed to H.G. & Robert H. Burton for costs and charges in this suit expended, whereof the said Burton Craige & others is liable, as appears to us of record. And have you the said moneys, besides your fees for this service, before the Judge of said Court, at Salisbury on the 2nd Monday after the 4th Monday in September next, then and there to render and make known how you have executed this writ. Witness Samuel Silliman Clerk and Master in said Court of Equity, at Office the 2nd Monday after the 4th Monday in March Anno Domini 1836 and in the 60th year of the Independence of the United States.

Rowan County

Saml. Silliman C.M.E.

Specification
Judgment on the Injunction Bond 16th April 1836 $5495.00
1805 Decr.   Enrolling Bill for Injunction   880
        2 copies thereof for Defendants   1760
        2 Writs of Injunction   200
        2 Writs of Subpoena   200
        4 Seals to the 4 Writs 25   100
        State Tax   200
        Sheriff of Lincoln 2 Writs   200
        Sheriff of Halifax 2 Writs   200
        Postage from Halifax   37 1/2
        Enrolling Defendants Answers   1260
        2 Affidavits to Answers   80
        Attorneys fees for 2 Answers   4000
        This Writ of Execution   100
                                           $91.67 1/2

****

State
Vs
Jesse a negro Slave

Charity Jones, Mary Downs, Jno. McNeely, John Graham, Alfd, Lawrence, Jude, negro girl.

Sworn & Sent 8th April 1825   Hy Giles

A True Bill
John Andrews, Foreman
North Carolina   } Superior Court of Law. 1st Monday
Rowan County   } after the 4th Monday of March A.D. 1825
      The jurors for the State upon their oaths present that Negroe Jesse a man slave the property of James Jemison of the county of Rowan on the 15th day of October about the hour of one oclock of the night of the same day withe force and arms in the county aforesaid the dwelling house of Charity Jones there situate feloniously and burglariously did break and

Rowan County

enter with intent the said Charity Jones then and there being to Kill and Murder against the peace and dignity of the State.

And the Jurors aforesaid upon their oaths aforesaid do further present that the said Jesse a negro man Slave the property of Alexander Jemison of said county on the said fifteenth day of October in the year of our Lord 1824 in the county aforesaid about the one of the night of the same day with force and Arms the dwelling house of Charity Jones there situate feloniously and burglariously did break and enter with intent her the said Charity Jones to kill and murder against the peace and dignity of the State.

[Editor's Note: This next paragraph has been struck through with cross marks in the original document.]

And the Jurors aforesaid upon their oaths aforesaid do further present that negro Jesse a man slave the property James Jemison of said County on the fifteenth day of October in the year of our Lord 1824 in the night time about the hour of one of the same day in the county aforesaid the dwelling house of Elizabeth McNeely there situate feloniously and Burglariously did break and enter with intent her the said Elizabeth McNeely to ravish and Carnally know - against the peace and dignity of the state.

And the Jurors aforesaid upon their oaths aforesaid do further present that Jesse a negro man slave the property of James Jemison of the county of Rowan on the 15th day of October about the hour of one of the night the same day in the year of our Lord 1824 in the County aforesaid the dwelling house of Charity Jones there situate feloniously and burglariously did break and enter with intent Mary Downs then and there being to ravish and carnally to know against the peace and dignity of the state.

And the Jurors aforesaid upon their oaths aforesaid do further present that Jesse a negro man Slave the property Alexander Jemison late of said County on the 15th day of October about the hour of one of the night of the same day in the year of our Lord 1824 in the County aforesaid the dwelling house of Charity Jones there situate did feloniously and burglariously break and enter with intent Mary Downs then & there being to ravish and Carnally to know against the peace and dignity of the State. E. Jones S.C.

Rowan County

And the Jurors for the state aforesaid upon their oaths present that Jesse a negro man Slave the property of James Jemison late of said county on the 15th day of October in the year of our Lord 1824 in the county of Rowan with force and arms in and upon the bodies of Charity Jones and Mary Downs then and there being an assault did make with intent then and there feloniously to ravish and Carnally to know the said Charity Jones and Mary Downs the said Charity Jones and Mary Downs being white females Contrary to the act of Assembly in such case made and provided and against the peace and dignity of the State.

And the Jurors aforesaid upon their oaths aforesaid do further present that Jesse a negro slave the property of Alexander Jemison late of the county of Rowan on the 15th day of October in the year of our Lord 1824 with force and arms in the county aforesaid an assault did make in and upon the bodies of Charity Jones and Mary Downs then and there being with intent then and there feloniously to ravish and Carnally to know the said Charity Jones and Mary Downs being white females contrary to the act of Assembly in such cases provided and against the peace and dignity of the State.
E. Jones S.C.

****

Elizabeth Helton
Vs
Josephus Helton

Elizabeth Helton Take Notice that on the 23rd Inst at the Dwelling House of John Snider I Shall take the Deposition of Lucy Snider to be red as evidence in a suit Depending in the County Court of Rowan wherein the said Elizabeth Hilton is ptf & my self Defendant where you may attend & Cros examine if you think proper. July 23rd 1823
J. Hilton

Wiley Jones maid Oath that he deliver A true Coppy of the Will[?] to Elizabeth Helton on the 23 of July 1823.
Test M. Hanes, J. Berryman
Executed the 23 of July 1823 by Wilie Jones

State of North Carolina Rowan County

Rowan County

Pursuant to an order of Court to us Delivered we Michael Hanes & Gilson Berryman two of the Justices of the peace for the County & State aforesaid proceeded on the 23rd of July 1823 to take the Deposition of Lucy Snider at the Dwelling House of John Snider to be red as evidence in a Suit Depending in the County Court of Rowan Wherein - Elizabeth Hilton is ptf & Josephus Hilton Deft. the Said Lucy Snider being in a low state of health & after being Sworn on the holy avengilus of almighty God Deposeth & Saith that she heard Elizabeth Helton say that Josephus Hilton went out to whip the said Elizabeth Heltons Negro Girl & She said She would try & prevent him from whipping said Negro & when She got to the Door the Negro had a Crock in her hand & she said She thought she would go in & take the Crock out of the Negroes hand that it might not get broke & she said as she went to take the Crock the said Josephus Struck at the Negro & struck her the said Elizabeth Hilton on the arm & hurt her Very much & two or three more times & she further said that she did not think that he struck her Designedly but in Striking at the Negro he hit her & broke the Crock this Deponent further saith that Elizabeth Hilton said that Josephus Hilton ordered her not to Come in & She thought she would go in to Save the Crock this Deponent further Saith not.

         her
Test   Lucy X Snider
M. Hanes J.P., G. Berryman J.P.   mark

This is to Certify that we Michael Hanes & Gilson Berryman did attend at the house of John Snider on the 23 of July 1823 & took the Deposition of Lucy Snider in the presence of the plt & Deft. the day & Date above.
M. Hanes J.P.
G. Berryman J.P.

****

State
Vs
Joel Shaver
Indict
Trading with a negro

A true bill

Rowan County

Michael Brown
North Carolina } Court of Pleas and
Rowan County   } Quarter Sess. 1832

The Jurors for the state upon their oaths present - that Joel Shaver - late of the County of Rowan and State of North Carolina - being an evil disposed person - did on the tenth day of February in the year of our Lord one thousand eight hundred and thirty two - a negro woman - by the name of Milly - the property of George Millar - two pieces of pork contrary to an act of Assembly - and against the peace and dignity of the State.

R. W. Alexander

****

State
Vs
William Swink

Supr. Court   Rowan County

Fall Term 1844

The Grand Jurors for the state, upon their oaths present William Swink, for selling & delivering spirituous liquor to a Slave.

Witness } Ann Bird
E.A. Austin For

****

Ezra Allemong
Vs
Elizabeth Parker

Allemong
Vs
Parker} Award
Filed Octr. 1830
Motgomery

Rowan County

fine for costs only

We William Harriss of Montgomery County No. Ca. and Samuel Reeves of Salisbury No. Ca. having been called by Mrs. Elisabeth Parker & her Son John Parker of Montgomery County and Ezra Allemong of Salisbury to determine and say what damages the said Allemong shall receive for the unsoundness which he alleges he has sustained in a certain negro Girle he purchased from said Elisabeth Parker do agree & Say that he shall receive the Sum of one Hundred & fifty Dollars and that Mrs. Parker shall pay all costs that may have accrued in consequence of said Allemongs having to bring Suit for the Same.

Witness our hands & Seals this 21st Day of August AD 1830
Wm. Harris
Saml. Reeves

****

William B. Atrell
Vs
David H. Patterson

State Of North Carolina
To David R. Bradshaw Esqr.
Justice assigned to keep the Peace in and for the County of Rowan -- Greeting:

Know Ye, that we in confidence of your prudence and fidelity, have appointed, and by these presents do give unto you full power and authority, in pursuance of an order of our Superior Court of Law, made in a cause wherein Wm. B. Atrell is Plaintiff against David H. Patterson Defendant, at such time and place as you shall think fit, to take, upon oath, the deposition of Rebecca Patterson touching and concerning what she may know in and about the said controversy: And that you take such deposition in writing, and return the same closed up, under your hand and seal, to our said Court, to be held for the County of Rowan on the 13th Monday after the 4th Monday in August next, together with this Writ.

Rowan County

Witness, H.H. Helper Clerk of our said Court at Office, the 8th Monday after the 4th Monday in March A.D. 1855, and in the 79th Year of our Independence.
H.H. Helper C.S.C.
By virtue of the annexed commission to me directed from the Superior Court of Law for the County of Rowan, I proceeded on this the 17th day of November, 1855, at the residence of David H. Patterson in the County aforesaid, to take the deposition of Rebecca Patterson to be read in evidence in a suit now pending in said Superior Court, wherein William B. Atrell is plaintiff and David H. Patterson is defendant, where said witness being duly sworn according to law deposeth and saith as follows:

Int 1st by plaintiff,
Did you know a negro slave named Nancy formerly owned by James Owens and sold by defendant to plaintiff; if so, state how long you knew said slave and your opportunity of knowing her?
Answer I have known the Slave Nancy for some six or eight years, from the time Mrs. Owins died which is now some eight years. I was in the habit of being at Mr Owens, and frequently stayed there two & three months at a time during all which time the girl Nancy lived with Mr Owing.

Int 2 Do you know the age of the girl Nancy, if so state what it was, state also what was the appearance of Nancy, whether healthy or unhealthy
Ans. I do not know the age of the girl, her appearance was tolerably healthy

Int 3d Do you know what was the condition of Nancy as to health during the time before spoken of, if so, state all that you may know about it?
Ans. She was as healthy as common, tolarbly so, I never knew her to have a bad spell of Sickness - She cooked and don the house worke, and in a common way was able to do it.

Int 4th Who had charge of the girl Nancy after the death of Owens up to the time of the sale, where did she stay, and what white person was with her?

Rowan County

Ans.   My sister Evalina, and myself, stayed at the house of Mr Owins after his death, untill the sale - no white male stayed thare during that time, my brother David H. Patterson was there occasionally

Int 5th   What was Nancy's condition of health from the death of Mr Owens until the time of the sale, did you discover at any thing peculiar about her, any nervousness, any affection of the head and eyes or any sudden suspension of her power of motion?
Ans.   After Mr Owens Death, and before the sale Nancy had two or three light chills, but was not confined to bed, during the day while she had the chills, I never saw any thing peculiar about Nancy, I never saw any thing wrong about her head or eyes, she complained some times that she could not see well, but I suposed that that was from her age. I never saw her deprived of her powers of motion

Int 6th   Did you ever have any conversation with the defendant about the health of the girl Nancy; if so, state when it was and what he said to you about her health?
Ans.   I never heard him say any thing about her health, further she saith not.
Rebecca Patterson

I hereby certify that the foregoing deposition was taken down by me, read over to the witnesses, sworn to and subscribed by her the date above written - In witness whereof I have hereto subscribed my name and affixed my seal
D.R. Bradshaw J.P.

****

State
Vs
Jesse Valintine

Subpa.
To Rowan Supr. Court Fall Term 1842
Executed   R.N. Long Shff
Came to hand June 10, 1842

Rowan County

R.N. Long Shff

State Of North Carolina

To the Sheriff of Rowan County -- Greeting:
    You are hereby commanded to summon Thomas Hillard and Hezekiah Turner personally to be and appear before the Judge of our Superior Court of Law, at the next Court to be held for our said County, at the Court House in Salisbury on the 4th Monday after the 3rd Monday in August next; then and there to testify, and the truth to say in behalf of the State, on a Presentment against Jesse Valintine a free man of color for intermarrying and cohabiting with Hannah, a Negro woman Slave the property of Catherine Hillard. And this you shall in no wise omit, under the penalty prescribed by Law.
    Witness, [?] Sneed Clerk of our said Court at Office, the 4th Monday after the 3d Monday of February A.D. 1842, and in the 65th year of our Independence..
F.[?] Sneed
Issued 30th May

North Carolina } Superior Court of Law
Rowan County   } Fall Term 1842

    The Jurors for the state on their oaths present Jesse Volentine late of said County a free man of Color on the 10th day of April in the year of our Lord 1842 and on divers other times both before and since that day in the said County Unlawfully did cohabit and live together as Man and Wife with Catharine a negro woman slave the property of Catharine Hillard against the form of the statute on such case made and provided and against the peace and dignity of the State.
H.C. Jones
Solicitor

****

State
Vs.
Wilson Sides

Rowan County

J.S. Johnson
Joel Jenkins
H.S. Miller

Acted on
Superior Court Rowan Cty.
Fall Term 1844
The Grand Jurors upon their Oaths present Wilson Sides a free Man of Color for intermarrying and Cohabiting with a Slave named Suckey, slave of William Chambers.
Witness John S. Johnson
Joel Jenkins   E.A. Austin
Henry S. Miller

****

State
Vs
William Shavers

State of North Carolina   } March Term
Rowan County   } 1845

The Jurors upon their Oaths present William Shavers for Stabing a Negro Man (Slave) of George Vogler name Aleck with a knife or Sharp pointed instrument about the last of Feby or 1st March
W. Chambers Forman

****

Margaret West by
Next Friend
Michael Filhous
Vs.
Joseph West

State of North Carolina   }
Rowan County   } SS.

Rowan County

To the Sheriff of Burke County - Greeting For certain causes offered before us in our Court of Equity We command you to Make known to Joseph West; That he is hereby commanded and strictly enjoined from selling or otherwise disposing of a Certain Negroe Woman slave named Jane, lately taken into his possession, and removed from Rowan County and claimed as his property in right of his wife Margaret West Alias Margaret Filhous under the penalty arising from a contempt of Court and have you this Writ before the Judge of said Court of Equity at Salisbury on the third Monday after the fourth Monday in February next. Witness Samuel Silliman Clerk and Master in said Court of Equity under seal of office the 3rd Monday after the fourth Monday in August Anno Domini 1844 and of American Independence the 69th year.
Issued the 29th day of January 1845.
Samuel Silliman C.M.E.

Writ of Injunction
To Spring Term 1845

Executed by making the within Known to Joseph S. West

5 Feby 1845   J.H. Pearson Shff

Know all men by these presents that we Joseph West & E.B. Reeves & E.P. Jones are held & firmly bound unto Saml. Sillimam Clerk & Master in the Court of Equity for Rowan County or his Successors in Office in the Penal Sum of Four hundred Dollars for the payment of which we bind ourselves our heirs Exr or Adms firmly by these presents given under our hands & Seals this 17 Feby 1845.
The Condition of the above obligation is Such that whereas Margaret West otherwise Called Margaret Filhous, has filed a Bill of complaint against the above bounden Joseph West in the Court of Equity of Rowan County and has obtained a writ of Sequestration to the sheriff of Burke County Commanding him to seize and take into possession and custody a negro woman named Jane, now in case the said negro woman Jane shall be forthcoming and delivered to answer such order and decree as said Court of Equity shall make in this behalf, then and in that case the above bond to be void, otherwise to remain in full force and effect. J.S. West (S), E.B. Reeves (S), E.P. Jones (S).

Rowan County

****

**State
Vs.
Thomas Kelly
(Freedman)**

Not sustained
Presentment

North Carolina }
Rowan County   }

Superior Court May Session 1866 The Grand Jurors on their Oaths present Tom Kelly a freedman for getting a Gun through false pretences from Danl. Hoffman and trading it away

           Summon for the State
           Margaret L. Hoffman
           Danl. Hoffman
           Alfred Kluttz
           William Weant

Issued   Thos. Barber Foreman

           Subpa. for State
           Margaret L. Hoffman
           Daniel Hoffman
           To Fall Term 1866
           Rowan Supr. Court
           Executed

        Nov 14 1866 W.A. Walton shff
        By M.A. Smith D.S.

State of North Carolina,
    To The Sheriff Of Rowan County--Greeting:
You are hereby commanded to summon Margaret L. Hoffman, Daniel Hoffman, Alfred Kluttz **[Alfred Kluttz marked through]**, personally to

Rowan County

be and appear before the Judge of the Superior Court of Law, at the next Court to be held for our said County, at the Court House in Salisbury on the 12th Monday after the last Monday in August next, then and there to testify and the truth to say, in behalf of the State of North Carolina in a certain matter of controversy before said Court depending, and then and there to be tried, wherein the State of North Carolina is Plaintiff, and Thomas Kelly, (a Freedman) is Defendant. And this you shall in no wise omit, under the penalty prescribed by law.
  Witness, A. Judson Mason Clerk of our said Court at Salisbury the 12th Monday after the last Monday in February and the 90th year of our Independence, Anno Domini 1866
A. Judson Mason C.S.C.

       Subpa. for State
       Alfred Klutts
       To Fall Term 1866
       Rowan Supr. Court
       Executed
       Nov 16 1866
       WA Walton Shff
       By MA Smith DS

State of North Carolina,
  To The Sheriff Of Rowan County--Greeting:
You are hereby commanded to summon Alfred Klutts personally to be and appear before the Judge of the Superior Court of Law at the next Court to be held for our said County, at the Court House in Salisbury on the 12th Monday after the last Monday in August next, then and there to testify and the truth to say, in behalf of the State of North Carolina, in a certain matter of controversy before said Court depending, and then and there to be tried, wherein The State of North Carolina is Plaintiff, and Tom Kelly (Freedman) is Defendant. And this you shall in no wise omit, under the penalty prescribed by law.
  Witness, A. Judson Mason Clerk of our said Court, at Salisbury the 12th Monday after the last Monday in February and the 90th year of our Independence, Anno Domini 1866.
A. Judson Mason C.S.C.

     Subpa. for State William Weant
     To Fall Term 1866, Rowan Supr. Court

Rowan County

Executed WA Walton Shff
By MA Smith D.S.

State of North Carolina,
To The Sheriff Of Rowan County--Greeting:
You are hereby commanded to summon William Weant personally to be and appear before the Judge of the Superior Court of Law at the next Court to be held for our said county, at the Court House in Salisbury on the 12th Monday after the last Monday in August next, then and there to testify and the truth to say, in behalf of the State of North Carolina in a certain matter of controversy before said Court depending, and then and there to be tried, wherein the State of North Carolina is Plaintiff, and Tom Kelly (Freedman) is Defendant. And this you shall in no wise omit, under the penalty prescribed by law.

Witness, A. Judson Mason Clerk of our said Court at Salisbury the 12th Monday after the last Monday in February and the 90th year of our Independence, Anno Domini 1866.
A. Judson Mason C.S.C.

****

State
Vs.
Tony & Jacob (Slaves)

| State of No Carolina | } The prisoners brought |
| Rowan County | } before us three Justices |

Of the peace of the said County & Witnesses a negro Belonging to Sqr. D. Pool[?] of the name of Bob After being duly Sworn deposeth & sayeth Ephraim Hampton's Anthony told sd Bob to procure all The powder he could in order to Kill white people Also states that Mrs. Phelp's boy Jacob asked him if he would not help to Kill the Whites & states that sd Jacob Intimated that he Would have a Certain Miss Polley Claunch to wife after accomplishing their Design Also the sd Jacob Desir'd him to get as much powder as he could & to Carry the same to meeting which was to be the Sunday after & then at that time & place he would Inform him of his Intention Also states that the sd Jacob told Capt. Philips Negro boy

Rowan County

Dennis to get as many blacks to attend the sd Meeting as possible the Examination of Samuel Harriss's Vincent on oath Sayeth that Mr. Hamptons Anthony in the time of harvest told him not to be in a hurry to marry that War Was Coming on & then they Would have Choice of the White Girls for Wives
The Confession of sd. Anthony he states that he Asked bob Which side he Was for the Americans or the British.
Giles   Craunch

State of North Carolina
Rowan County August Session 1812

State
Vs.
A Negro Slave Tony the property of Ephraim Hampton's and a Negro Slave Jacob the property of Jane Felps.

The aforesaid Negro slaves Tony and Jacob are Charged with having consulted Advised and conspired to rebel and make insurrection. And have ploted and conspired to murder the good Citizens of the county of Rowan Contrary to an act of Assembly in that case made and provided and against the peace and dignity of the State.
WL Henderson
Atto for the State

State
Vs.
Negro Man Tony

State of North Carolina Be it Remembered that
Rowan County at a Special Court called
and held by the Shariff of said County at the Court house in Salisbury on the Twentieth day of September One thousand eight hundred and Twelve for the purpose of trying negroe man slave Tony (the property of Ephraim Hampton) charged with a misdemeanor, to wit, with confederating & conspiring with others to Kill the good citizens of the County of Rowan, Present

Worshipfull Justices owners of Slaves to wit
John Steele   }

151

Rowan County

Lewis Beard } Esquires
John March }

State Vs
Negroe Man Slave Tony   } Misdemeanor
property of Ephraim Hampton }

The following good and lawful men owners of slaves, were sworne and charged on the above issue of [?] to wit

Wm Pinkston	Wm Crider	Henry Sleighter
Saml Lemly	John Smith	Wilie Yarbrough
David Craig	Thos. Craig	Geotge Betz
H.B. Pruitt	John Utzman	Danl. Cress

Names of Witnesses Examined in behalf of the State to wit
Vincent negroe man Slave the property of Saml. Harris
Bob negroe man Slave the property of Daniel Corill Esqr
James Pelly, Daniel Corill Esqr, John Armsworthy

and the said Jury having retired under a charge of the court after some time returned and delivered in a verdict, that the Said Negroe Slave Tony is guilty of conspiring and misdemeanor as chargeable in the above accusation.

    Whereupon the Court ordered and adjudged that the said negroe man Tony be punished by fifty lashes well laid on his bare back at the present time five weeks imprisonment In Irons from this day to be fed on bread and water only; and Fifty lashes more at the expiration of said term of imprisonment After which he may be delivered to his owner or payment of Costs
Test Ezra All[?]
for John Giles Clk

****

State
Vs.
Bett a Slave

Rowan County

State of No Carolina }
Rowan County   }

Be it remembered that on the thirteenth day of May In the Year of our Lord one thousand Eight Hundred and eighteen Thomas Maxwell of the County and State aforsaid and Benjamin Maxwell of Said County came before John H. Fauling one of the Justices of the peace for said County and Severally acknowledged Themselves to owe to the State of North Carolina that is to Say Each of them In Three Hundred Pounds Each to be respectively Levied of their Lands and Tenements Goods and Chattles If the Said Thomas Maxwell Shall make Default In the performance of the Conditions underneath.
Jno H Fauling (JP)   Thos. Maxwell

The Condition of this recognizance Is such that If the above Bounden Thomas Maxwell Shall personally present to the County Court of pleas and quarter Sessions In and for the said County at Salisbury at the next Court of pleas and quarter sessions on the third Monday In May Instant or before the Judges of the Superior Court of Law to be held for this Said County of Rowan at the Court House In Salisbury on the Second Monday of October next then and a Certain Negroe woman the property of Said Thomas Maxwell named Bett, Said Negroe Bet then and there to Answer the Said State for and Concerning the Fellonious taking and Stealing of a Hundred Dollar Bill supposed to be the property of Said Thomas Maxwell with the suspicion whereof the Said Bet stands Charged before one of the Said Justices and to do and to Receive what Shall by the Court be then and there [?] on her and shall not Depart the Court without Leave then the above written recognizance shall be Void.
Test   Thomas Maxwell (Seal)
John H. Fauling   his
                    Benja X Maxwell (Seal)
                        mark

State
Vs.
Bett (a Negro Slave)

Rowan County

State of North Carolina:
To the Sheriff of Rowan County, Greeting;
You are hereby commanded to summon Milly Renshaw personally to appear before the Judge of our Superior Court of Law, at the next Court to be held for the County of Rowan at the Court House in Salisbury on the Second Monday after the 4th Monday in September next; then and there to testify and the truth to say in behalf of Bett (a Negroe) in a certain cause then & there depending, & to be tried; between The State -- plantiff, and Bett (a Negroe) -- defendant. And this you shall in no wise omit under the penalty prescribed by law. Herein fail not, and have you then and there this writ.
Witness H.M. Stokes Clerk of our said court at Office the 2nd Monday after the 4th Monday in March 1818 and in the XXXX2d year of our Independence.
H.M. Stokes

****

Inst. poisoning
Afftin Worsham
Tabitha Worsham
Eliza Vick

Ann, Sally, Captain
Sworn & sent   H.M. Stokes
True Bill
A. Frohock, Foreman

State of North Carolina   } Superior Court of Law begun and held
County of Rowan   } the 2d Monday after the 4th Monday in
                           } September AD 1818

The Jurors for the State upon their oath present that a certain negroe woman Slave called **Bett** owned by One Elizebeth **[Torn]** contriving and intending to hurt and damage the body of one Tabitha Worsham on the tenth day of June AD 1818 with force and arms in the county Aforesaid unlawfully wickedly and knowingly did prepare and mix certain poison to wit Hillibore with Water and the same poison mixed as aforesaid in the

Rowan County

County aforesaid unlawfully and knowingly with intent to poison the said Tabitha Worsham then and there did give to the said Tabitha Worsham not knowing the said drink to be poisin did drink the same by Which She the said Tabitha Worsham of the poison aforesaid then and Afterwards became distempered and weak in her body to her great Injury and against the peace and dignity of the state.
Ed Jones SCL

****

State
Vs.
Barbara Treffinger
Mdr [Misdemeanor]
Richard Harris
M. Mckenzie Wit
Sworn & Sent J.E. Kerr Clk

A True Bill Wm. Heatleman Foreman

State of N Carolina   } August Sessions
Rowan County   } 1849

The Jurors for the State on their oath present that on the 1st day of August AD 1869 that Barbara Treffinger late of Rowan County did in the sd County unlawfully and with force and arms receive from certain slaves Hope the property of Richard Harris and Levi the property of William Smith in the night time a certain hog of the lawful goods and chattels of the sd Richard Harris against the form of the statute in such case made and provided and against the peace and dignity of the state.
Robert E. Love Sol.

Misd.
Capias
To Nov. 1849
Executed and bail bond filed C. Klutts Shff
Came to hand the 1st day of Sept. C. Klutts Shff

State of North Carolina, Rowan County

Rowan County

To the Sheriff of Rowan County----Greeting;
You are hereby commanded to take the body of Barbara Treffinger if to be found in your County, and her safely keep, so that you have her before the Justices of our Court of Pleas and Quarter Sessions, at the next Court to be held for the County of Rowan at the Court House in Salisbury on 1st Monday in November next then and there to answer the State upon a Bill of Indictment for trading with a slave. Herein fail not, and have you then and there this writ.
   Witness, James E. Kerr Clerk of our said Court, at Office, the 1st Monday in August A.D. 1849, and in the 74th Year of our Independence.
Issued the 31st day of August 1849
James E. Kerr Clk

     A True Bill Allen Peale Foreman
     Indct Trading with Slaves
     Richard Harris
     [?]
     M.S. Mckenzie
     Wit
     Sworn & Sent

James E. Kerr Clk
North Carolina } Court of Pleas & Quarter
Rowan County   } session November term AD 1849
   The jurors for the State upon their oath present that Barbara Treffinger late of said County spenster, with force & arms in the county aforesaid, on the first day of August 1849 did buy of, traffic with & receive from two slaves to wit Hope the property of Richard Harris & Levi the property of William Smith, one hog of the value of one doller, without any permission in writing from the owner or in such case made & provided & against the peace & dignity of the State.
Robert E. Love

****

State
Vs.
Mary Myers

State of NC } To the Sheriff of the County
Rowan County } or other Lawful officer Greeting

Rowan County

Whereas information has this day been made to me David Barringer one of the acting Justices of the Peace by Eve Eller that on one Sunday in March last that Harry a Slave the Property of Peter Kerns of this County did bring one half or about one half Bushel of Corn to Mary Myers of this County and the said Mary Myers did there and then buy of and receive of the said Harry a Slave the said Corn and did for that give the said Harry, a Slave one quart of ground Peas and some dried apples against the Peace and dignity of the State.

You are therefore commanded to take the Body of said Mary Myers if to be found in your County and have you her before some justice of the Peace to answer the above charge and to be further dealt with as the Law directs. Herein fail not. Given under my hand and Seal and have there and then this [?]

Octbr the 2nd day 1850 David Barringer JP
Summon for the State Eve Eller

N. Carolina   } Judgment against the
R. County   } defendant for cost $40

Oct. 4th 1850   R.H. Halton JP

State of NC   }
Rowan County   }

The Defendant pleads an [?] to our Next County Court and gives for Security Jacob Myers. Oct 4th 1850
Jacob S. Myers
Fredk Shaver JP

The State Against Mary Myers Executed by G.H. Peeler Const.

****

John Cook
Vs.

Rowan County

Solomon Hall
Runaway from the Subscriber on the 28th of June A Negroe man Named Charles formerly was the property of William Shaw any Person apprehending Said Negroe and brings him to Me shall receive the Reward of Twenty Dollars.

Solomon Hall
Rowan County
October 6th 1810

No Carolina } To any lawful Officer of Said County
Rowan County } You are hereby commanded to take the body of Solomon Hall if to be found in your County and cause him to appear before some Justice of the peace for said County within 30 days from the date hereof Sundays excepted To Answer John Cook in a plea of debt due By reward offered for taking up a certain Negro Man Charles by Which sum he delays the payment of herein fail not given under my hand & seal this 28th day of June 1811
R. Powell JP (Seal)

20th of July 1811, Witness examined
Judgment in behalf of the plantiff
for the sum of   5.0.0
Cost   0.6.0
Amt   5.6.0
R. Powell JP
from which Judgment the defendant appeals to Court & gives John Little Senr. security for the same.
John Little
Test } R. Powell Jp
Executed By Beal Jianes[?]

****

State
Vs.
Tom Bailey
A Negro

Rowan County

To any Lawful officer to Execute & return fourthwith whereas information has been maid to me Enos Shavers an Acting Justice of Said County David Hoffan & maid oath in due form of Law that he has had a gun stolen from him & he has reason to beleave a Negro Man named Tom Bailey Stole it, this is therefore to command you to arrest the said Tom Baley & have him before me or some other Justice of said County & be delt with according to Law & have you then & there this Warrent given under my hand & seal this 23d of May 1866[?]
Enos Shavers (JP)

****

**R.J. West
Vs.
J.W. Hall
et. al.**

North Carolina }
Supreme Court }   January 1870
235 Rowan

R.J. West   }
Vs.   }   Opinion
J.W. Hall   }
et. al.   }

Pearson, Ch. J:

    There is no error. It is settled that a contract for the purchase of a slave is not illegal even when made after the Proclamation of the President, the slave not being under the control of the Military forces of the United States. Harrell Vs. Watson, 63 N.S.R. 454.
    In our case the contract was made in 1859, so the matter is to plain for discussion.
    The evidence in regard to the warranty of Title was properly rejected. It did not tend to support any of the pleas. Indeed there was no breach of the warranty. The negro was a "slave for life", and the contract

Rowan County

could not in any way be affected by the events of the late war, and the abolition of the institution of Slavery. Judgment affirmed

A true copy--
Test: W.H. Bagley Clerk
for Johnston Jones[?] D.C.

****

Anne R. Robertson
Vs.
John Wright

State of Virginia
Halifax County to wit

    The Deposition of Stephen Jones of lawful age taken at the house of Henry Chandler of Halifax County on the 18th day of Jany 1802 Virginia to be read as evidence in a suit now depending in the County Court of Rowan & State of N. Carolina wherein Anne R. Robertson is plaintiff & John Wright Defendant.

    This Deponent being first sworn on the Holy Evangelist of Almighty God Deposeth & sayeth - that somewhere about the year 1792 & in the Spring of the said year John Brough boarded at the house of the sd. Jones a negro boy Child of the name of Bob & that the sd. Brough engaged to make him Compensation for the board of said Boy but whether he did or not this Deponent does not now recollect & further this Deponent sayeth not

Sworn to in due form   Stephen Jones
before us

Given under our hands & seals this 18th day of Jany 1802
William Thompson   (Seal)
Henry E. Coleman   (Seal)

State of Virginia
Halifax County to wit

Rowan County

The Deposition of Robert Rickman of lawful age taken on the 18th day of Jany 1802 at the house of Henry Chandler of sd. County to be read as evidence in a suit now depending in the County Court of Rowan & State of N. Carolina wherein Anne R. Robertson is Plaintiff & John Wright Defendant.

This Deponent being first sworn on the Holy Evangelist of Almighty God Deposeth & sayeth that some time after he heard that Anne R. Robertson had given a negro of the name of Bob to John Brough, he this Deponent asked the said Anne R. Robertson why she gave the sd. negro to the sd. Brough - she Anne R. Robertson replied that she gave the sd. boy to him (Brough) before he (the negro boy Bob) was born because he (Brough) was so good a boy to her.

quest 1st By R. Leach agent for Defendent - Was it not a general report in the neighborhood that Anne R. Robertson had given the negro boy Bob to John Brough & whether it was not in consequence of that report that he asked her the question as above stated? Ansr. By Robt. Rickman - Yes it was.

quest. by A.R. Robertson the plaintiff - Did you not believe from the Conversation that passed between us that I was in Jest when I made the above reply? Ansr. I cannot tell - And further this Deponent sayeth not.

Sworn to in due form
before us --
Given under our hands seals
this 18th day of Jany 1802
William Thompson (Seal)
Henry E. Coleman (Seal)

       his
    Robert X Rickman
       mark

State of Virginia   }
Halifax County to wit }

In obedience to a commission to us directed, from the county court of Roan & State of N. Carolina to take the Deposition of Saml. Annett & others, to be read as evidence in a suit now depending in the county court of Roan & State of N. Carolina We have caused the said Saml. Annett to come before us on the twenty second day of July 1802 at the house of Henry Chandler in the county & State above, who being first sworn upon the holy Evangelist of Almighty God Deposeth & Sayeth that

Rowan County

in the year 1793 in a conversation with A.R. Robertson the plaintiff he heard her say, that she had promised Bob a negro boy to John Brough whilst his mother Phillis was pregnant with him if a boy, upon condition he did not part with him & that at the time this conversation passed the sd. boy was at the house where John Brough lived & that in short time after, Anne R. Robertson moved to the same house - He further states that in the year 1794 and directly after John Brough had left this county, in a second conversation with Anne R. Robertson he heard her say Damn Joh Brough he has carried away my negro & I believe he is rogue enough to sell him & that she had never made him a right to the boy nor never would - He further states that since the commencement of the above Writ in a third conversation with A.R. Robertson he observed to her, now old woman give conscience fair play did you never give John Brough this negro - she answered I never did, but what I did was only to frell Doctor Brough - & further he sayeth not.

Sworn to in form	his Samuel X Annett mark

William Thompson
Henry E. Coleman

****

Samuel Edwards
Vs.
Meshack Gentry

State of Tennessee   }
Green County   }

Pursuant to a commition to us Directed from the Court of Equity held for the County of Rowan in Salisbery North Carolina dated the 2 Monday after the fourth Monday in March 1818 and which is hereunto annexed impowering of us to take the Deposition of Ruben Gentry Aged forty six years concerning what he may know of the matters in contreversy in a certain action depending in the Sd. Court Between Samuel Edwards Plantif & Meshack Gentry Defendant we have proceeded to take the Deposition of Ruben Gentry in that case in the Dwelling house of Robert

Rowan County

Hays in the County of Greene and State of Tennessee on the twenty Eighth of August in the year of our Lord one thousand and Eight Hundred and Eighteen and the Defendant being present and the plantif not.

We have caused the Sd. Ruben Gentry to come before us who being first Sworn on the holy Evangelist of Almighty God to speak the truth the whole truth and nothing but the truth concerning what he knoweth of the matter and thing in Controversy in the Sd. cause Deposeth and Saith as followeth, &C.

Ruben Gentry Some time about the year Eighteen Hundred and nine my wife Fanny Gentry went to See her people in Surry County North Carolina and after Staying Some Considerable time she returned in company with George Hudspeth & Allen D. Gentry and a Waggon Loaded with Brandy and a Negro girl called Alidia the girle my wife told me she for to give two hundred and fifty Dollars for her to Meshac Gentry if I was willing I very well knew that the Negro was a fair a nuff at that price but as my wife had bargoned for her and Meshac Gentry had sent her to me I thought I would give it therefore I went on Directly to Meshac Gentry and confirmed my bargon payed him one hundred and thirty three Dollers for Sd. Gurle Alidia and I agreed to pay the Ballence of the Negro about Six Mounths accordingly George Hudspeth came to my house about the time the money was Reddy and I sent to Meshac Gentry one hundred and Seventeen Dollers by him as the Last payment of Sd. Gurl & I wish it known to the Court and Jury before whome this deposition May be red that I did absolutely bye this Negro Gurl of Meshac Gentry before she had any Childe and did give unto Meshac Gentry two hundred and fifty Dollers as afforesaid but after She became my property she had three childring in the time I had her. About two years after I Bought her from Meshac Gentry John Hudspeth & Allen Gentry came from Tennessee to my house in Sparklingburg District South Carolina and after hearing a great praise of that Country I concluded to send my Wench and Childe to Tennessee for these men or one of them to Sell her for me to bye Small tract of Land accordingly I sent her to Tennessee by John Hudspeth & Allen Gentry the wentch remained at the House of Hudspeth in Tennessee Some time and I had no letter from Sd. Hudspeth at lenth I went according to my agreement to See after my Negroes & how I liked the Country and when I went the wench was not Sold nor I did not like the Cuntry one bit I directly discovered that I would not live in that part of the

Rowan County

world and accordingly I took my Negroes to South Carolina again sometime about the year 1815 Jordan Gentry and George Hudspeth came to my house so they say on there way to Georgia to see some part of that Cuntry myself and Jordan Gentry Struck a traid I sold Jurdon the Negro wench Lidia for a certain Sum & as he returned Called and payed me twenty five Dollars as a part of the price of Sd. Negrowes.

Question by the Defendant
was there any More Squire Brutons in Sparklingburg District than one.
Answer -- there was two.

Question by the commitioners
was there any intended fraud in the purchase of this Negro.
Answer -- I do not know that there was any and this deponent further Sayeth not.
Sworn to and Subscribed this 28th of August 1818

	his
Test	Rubin Gentry
Saml. Caldwell	mark
Justice of the peace	
Cornelius Heserman[?]	
Justis of the Peace	

****

**State
Vs.
Mack Rankin
Free Negro**

Recognizance of
JP Revis, Wm J Willis
Witnesses
Attend Tuesday

State of North Carolina } Be it remembered that
Rowan County } JP Revis, EB Smith

Rowan County

& Wm J Willis Severally acknowledged themselves indebted to the State of No Carolina in the sum of forty dollars each To be void on conditions they respectively make their personal appearance at our next Court of Pleas & Quarter Sessions to be held for said County in the town of Salisbury on the 1st Monday of Feby next (They the Witness to attend on Tuesday). And then and there to give evidence in behalf of the State Vs. M. Rankin (a free negro) in two several cases drunkeness &C &C And do not depart the same without leave.
Acknowledged before me Jany 1858.
Jas. C. Barnhardt JP

State Vs. M. Rankin (a free negroe)

Dr. To EB Smith deft Coust for Conveyance to bring prisoner to jail.

Dr. To EB Smith deft Coust Mileage, 14 Miles.
Dr. To William Jackson assistant do.
State Vs. Mack Rankin
Misdemeanor
Warrant
W.J. Willis, J.P. Reavis, E.B. Smith, Wits.
Sworn & Sent, James E. Kerr Clk.
A True Bill
John Shuman Jr. forman

State of North Carolina   } Court of Pleas &
Rowan County   } Quarter Sessions
    The Jurors for the State on their oath present that Mack Rankin a free person of color late of said County in the County aforesaid on the 1st day of January AD 1858 and on divers days and times afterward and before the finding of this inquisition unlawfully and with force & arms did wear and carry about his person a pistol not having obtained a license therefore from the court of Pleas and Quarter sessions of his County within one year next preceeding the time of the wearing and carrying thereof against the form of the statute in such case made and provided and against the peace and dignity of the State.
Robt. E. Love

Rowan County

****

State
Vs.
Young Harris

Rowan

North Carolina
Supreme Court   June Term 1868
The State Vs. Young Harriss
Reade

In considering the legal questions involved, we have not allowed ourselves to be unduly influenced by the cruel and inhuman facts detailed in the evidence.

I. In considering the first exception on the part of the defendant, it is to be explained that the theory of the prosecution was that the deceased came to his death by severe Whippings on the part of the defendant, repeated every day for a week And the Whippings were testified to by a girl who was an inmate of the family. The defendant attempted to show that the deceased did not come to his death by the Whippings, but by reason of a severe burn on the abdomen. And then Dr. Fraly was introduced by the State, and gave it as his opinion that the burn was put upon the body after death. The testimony of Dr. Fraly was left to the Jury by His Honor, as Ending to Corroborate the evidence of the girl, and the theory of the prosecution. And this was excepted to by the defendant. We see no force in the exception. The opinion of the Doctor as an Expert was clearly admissible, and if his opinions was well founded, it proved the defendant's theory, that the deceased came to his death by the burn, to be false, and it tended to corroborate the Testimony of the girl.

II. After the evidence was closed on both sides, the defendant's counsel asked leave to recall a witness to make an explanation of some point in his testimony. He was permitted to do so. And after the explanation was made, the Counsel attempted to extend the examination to new matter. This was refused by the Court, and the defendant excepted. It was clearly within his Honor's discretion whether he would allow the witness to be recalled and it was as clearly within his discretion to present the terms, and to limit the examination. It might be unjust to

Rowan County

the Counsel to suppose that there was any attempt to entrap the Court by proposing to recall the witness for a simple explanation, when the real purpose was to open the evidence anew; and therefore, we suppose that the only purpose in recalling the witness was to explain. And therefore as soon as the explanation was given, it was legitimate for his Honor to stop the examination.

III. The defendant offered Jane Harriss as a witness. The defendant while slaves, lived and co-habited as man and wife. After their emancipation they observed the ceremonies prescribed by the Statute of 1866. Chap. 40. L. 5. That Statute provides that the parties shall be deemed "To have been lawfully married as man and wife at the time of the commencement of such co-habitation, altho, they may not have been married in due form of law". The competency of Jane as a witness was objected to by the State, and she was ruled out. And the defendant excepted. Whether Jane was a competent depends upon the question whether she was the defendant's wife. And whether she was his wife depends upon the force of the said Statute. Marriage is a civil contract. It is more than that: or at least the status which marriage creates is a divine, as well as a civil institution. But our Courts deal with it only as a civil contract. And, therefore, it is insisted that slaves have no power to contract, and that the status of marriage did not exist among them. **The State Vs. Samuel - 2 Dev. & Bat. 177** is the authority for that position. We have no purpose to controvert that position. It is true that during the existence of slavery our law did not provide for the solemnization of marriage among them. They were left in a state of nature. And being so it might be interesting to inquire how far in such a state, a marriage per verba de presenti affected their relations when their conditions were changed from slavery to freedom. For, in a state of nature, or where no solemnities of marriage are prescribed, a marriage per verba de presenti is valid. But we are relieved from the necessity of entering into the consideration of that question because of the wholesome statute, which we have cited. The substance of marriage, the consent of the parties, existing, it was as clearly within the power of the Legislature to dispense with any particular formality as it was in the power to prescribe formalities. It neither made nor impaired the contract but gave effect to it, with the parties consent recognized as a legal relation that which the parties had recognized as a natural one. So that by force of the original consent of the parties while they were slaves, and the received consent

Rowan County

after they were free, and the performance of what was required by the Statute, they became to all interests and purposes, man and wife. This would be so, upon the strictest construction to be given to a statute of great public necessity, affecting the domestic relations of one third of our people, and the morals of society as well. We conclude that Jane was the wife of the defendant, was incompetent to testify for him, and was therefore properly excluded.

IV. The defendant insisted that he was in loco parentis towards the deceased, and that in the absence of express malices, his crime would be manslaughter only. His Honor charged otherwise, and the defendant excepted. Conceeding for the sake of the argument that the defendant did stand in the place of parent to the deceased, still the exception cannot avail him. It is true that the law allows to parents the broadest latitude in governing and to that end, correcting their Children. But the facts detailed in this case, if true, were so cruel and inhuman, and so often repeated, and long continued, as to manifest, "a heart totally regardless of social duties and fatally bent on mischeif". They totally exclude the idea of passion, and fully prove malice as distinguished from passion. "Parents, masters, and other persons having authority in foro domestico, may give reasonable correction to those under their case; and if death ensueth without their fault, it will be no more than accidental death. But if the corrections exceedeth the bounds of due moderation either in the measure of it, or in the instrument made use of for that purpose, it will be either murder or manslaughter according to the Circumstances of the case". **Foster's Crown Law. p. 262. l. 4.** In the case before us, what was the "measure" of correction? The deceased was placed on his back, his feet tied up, he was stripped naked, and left in that position from morning until dinner for the space of a week and repeatedly whipped each day while in that position, and on the first day severely whipped. What were the "instruments" used? A [?] leather strap, a knotted cord four double, and an iron ram-rod. And with these he was beat day after day until he died. There was "due moderation" neither in the "measure", nor the "instrument". The provocation was a very slight one, and all the circumstances showed deliberation and malice. We are entirely satisfied with his Honor's ruling in this particular.

V. It being a question in dispute whether a severe injury, supposed to be a burn, was put upon the abdomen before or after death, the defendant offered to prove that the deceased said that he had a burn upon

Rowan County

his abdomen. The Solicitor for the state objected to the evidence, and his Honor ruled it out. In this we think his Honor erred. The declaration of the deceased as to the condition of his body and health, at the time when the declarations were made, fall under the head of natural evidence. Such declarations are in the very nature of things admissible. No physician would undertake to prescribe for a patient without enquiring of him "how he felt", "Where were his pains, and the like. What weight the physician would give to the patients declarations, would be for his consideration. And so, what weight the Jury would give, would be for their consideration. This question has been before this Court repeatedly, and need not be elaborated now. All that can be said upon the subject will be found in **Runebae[?] Vs. White. 9 Ired. 63. Riles Vs. Holmes 11 Ired. 16. Lusk Vs. McDaniel 13 Ired. 485. Bell Vs. Morrisett, 6 Jones 178. Henderson Vs. Crouse, 7 Jones 623.** For this error there must be a venire de novo. Let this be certified.

This Cause came on to be argued upon the transcript of the record from the Superior Court of Law of Rowan County - Upon Consideration whereof this Court is of opinion that there is error in the record and proceedings of the said Superior Court: therefore, it is ordered that the opinion of this Court, as delivered by the Honorable Edwin G. Reade, Judge, be certified to the said Superior Court to the intent that the said Judgement be reversed and a venire de novo be awarded. And it is directed by the Court here, that the County of Rowan pay the costs of the appeal in this Court, to wit, the sum of nine dollars and twenty five cents.
A True Copy
Test: C.B. Root, Clk,
per Johnston Jones, dep. Clk.

****

James Cowan
Vs.
Alexander Silliman

Interrogation to be administered to John M Ervin & David Cowan - also to Alexr Graham & John Cowan, Witnesses resident near Charlotte in No. Carolina -- to be Examined in the part of the Pltff

Rowan County

1st   Do you know the parties Plaintiff & Defendant in this case?

2nd   Were or were you not present on the 29th of July 1818 in the Store of the Defendant when the Plaintiff demanded of him a negro woman named Dorcas then in his possession, and did or not the Defendant refuse to give her up.

3rd   Did or not the Plaintiff offer to return the Defendant his note given for the negro which the Defendant refused to take: and did or not the Plaintiff then demand payment was also refused?

4th   Did or not the Defendant acknowledge that the negro Dorcas belonged to the Plaintiff, and that he knew it at the time he purchased and that he saw the Plaintiffs Bill of sale.

5th   Do you know anything further in this matter to the advantage of the Plaintiff's state is at large.

White & Deheefortive[?]
Pltffs Attys

James Cowan   } Cross interrogatories to be administered
    Ags   } to James Bell a Witness to be
Alexr. Silliman   } examined on the part of the plaintiff

1st   If to the second interrogatory you answer that you know whom the woman Dorcas belonged, state minutely the sources of your knowledge, and the precise time when she did belong to the person or persons whom you may state in your answer, and the length of time she remained in his, her or their possession.

2nd   If you were present, where the deft. purchased Dorcas, and the bill of sale to the plaintiff was produced, was it not at the same time admitted that the wench belonged to his mother who lived with John Silliman, and was not the bill of sale in the possession of John Silliman.

3d   To the 4th Interrogatory, state particularly the sources of your information if any you have.

Rowan County

4th   If the wench did not bonafide belong to the mother of John Silliman to whom did she belong?

5th   Are you acquainted with the result of a suit brought by the plaintiff against the defendant in No. Carolina for the present alleged cause of action? if yes, state the same, and particularly whether it was not discontinued on account of the death of Dorcas? and if she be dead, where did she die?

6th   Do you know any other matter or thing material to the defendant in this cause? if yes, disclose the same as fully as if particularly interrogated

Commissioners   MCall & Hayne
Geo. McCulloch   Defts Attys
Joseph Kerr
Alexr. Silliman } Interrogatories to be administered
         V   } to James Bell, a Witness, resident
James Cowan   } in Rowan County No Carolina 12 miles West of

Salisbiry - on the part of the Plaintiff.

1st   Do you know the Plaintiff and Defendant in this case?

2nd   Did you or not know a negro woman named Dorcas - if yes - To whom did she belong.

3rd   Were you or not present when the Defendant went and purchased the negro woman Dorcas - if yes - from whom? for what time? how to be paid? and was or not the right of the Plaintiff made known at the time to the Defendant as well by declarations as by shewing a Bill of sale of the Negro Dorcas.

4th   Did or not the Defendant well know that the seller had no right and did or not the Defendant get the negro into his possession without paying any thing for her

5th   Do you know any thing further in this matter to the advantage of the Plaintiff - State it at large

Rowan County

White & D E [?]
Plts Attys

Alexr Silliman   } Interrogatories to be administered
V   } to John Smith resident in Rowan
James Cowan   } County in N. Carolina on the part of the plaintiff.

1st   Do you know the Plaintiff and Defendant in this case.

2nd Did you or not know a Negro woman Dorcas? If yes were you not once her Master and did you not sell her on or about July 1815 to Dr. Alexander Silliman, the Plaintiff in this case? If yes, Did not the said Dr. Silliman pay you her price in Money.

3rd   Was or was not the said Wench Dorcas after Silliman purchased her from you always considered & known in the Neighborhood as his property?

4th   Do you know any thing further in this Matter to the advantage of the pltff Dr. Silliman - If yes - state it.

White & D E [?]
Ptff Attys

We consent that a Commission do issue without cross interrogation
M Call & Hayne

Alexr Silliman   } Interrogatories to be administered
V   } to Samuel McCall a Witness
James Cowan   } Resident in Charlotte No. Carolina on the part of the
Plaintiff.

1st   Do you know the parties Plaintiff & Defendant in this case?

Rowan County

2nd   Do you know Any and what of a demand made by the Plaintiff of a negro woman belonging to him in the possession of the Defendant? If yes - What is her name.

3rd   Can you state, and if you can, do so fully, the particulars of what took place at the time of the demand, where and when it was, the name and value of the negro, who besides yourself were present, and what passed between the Plaintiff and Defendant.

4th   Do you recollect any thing of a paper now shewn you with these interrogatories, and marked (A) Were you not present when the Plaintiff read it to the Defendant and requested him to sign it, and did the Defendant not say that it was true, but refused to sign it - state the whole fully and particularly.

5th   Do you know any thing further in this Matter to the advantage of the Plaintiff - State it at Large.

Alexr Silliman } Interrogatories to be administered
V } to Joseph McConneaughy, John
James Cowan } Erwin & James Torrants, Witnesses, resident in Charlotte N. Carolina

1st   Do you know the parties, Plaintiff & Defendant in this case?
2nd   Do you recollect any thing of a paper now shown you with these interrogatories & marked (A) Were you not present when the Plaintiff read it to the Defendant and requested him to sign it & did the Defendant not say that it was true, but refuse to sign it. State the whole fully and particularly?
5th   Do you know any thing further in this matter to the advantage of the Plaintiff - State it at large.
White & D E [?]
Pltff Attys
Cross Interrogatory
If the defendant refused to sign the paper referred to in the 2d. Interrogatory, state the reasons which he assigned.
McCall & Haynes

Rowan County

Defts. Attys

Alexr Silliman }
    Vs   } No. A
James Cowan }
Sir,
I acknowledged you yesterday demanded of me a negro woman Dorcas, & I refused to deliver her - I value her now at $750 you estimate her at $900, I also acknowledge I saw your Bill of sale of that negro at the time I purchased her.
Charlotte
30 July 1818
To A. Silliman

****

William R. Darby
William Murdoch &
William Reeder
Vs.
Joseph W. Hall

State of North Carolina }
Rowan County   }

William R. Darby for himself and as agent for William Murdoch and William Raeder makes oath before me James E. Kerr clerk of the Court of Pleas and Quarter Sessions for the county of Rowan that William Murdoch William Raider and himself have been in lawful possession of a negro slave by name Andy, of a light complexion and about the age of thirty two years within three years next preceeding this time and that they have been deprived of the possession of said slave by Joseph W. Hall without their permission or consent The said William R. Darby further makes oath that the said slave is of the value of fifteen hundred dollars.

W.R. Darby
Sworn to and subscribed before me this 26th January 1859.
James E. Kerr Clerk

Rowan County

State of North Carolina
To the Sheriff of Rowan County: Greeting:

Whereas William R. Darby for himself as one of the Plaintiffs in this writ has made oath that Andy a negro boy of light complexion and of the age of thirty two years has been in the lawful possession of the plaintiffs within three years next preceeding the date hereof and that they have been deprived of the possession of said slave by the defendant Joseph W. Hall without their consent or permission and whereas the said William R. Darby has further made oath as aforesaid that the said slave is of the value of fifteen hundred dollars and whereas the plaintiffs have given bond with approved security in the sum of three thousand dollars payable to the said Joseph W. Hall and conditioned to perform the final judgment which may rendered on this writ of replevin and have also given bond with security for the prosecution of this suit You are therefore commanded forthwith to take said slave into your custody if to be found in your county and to deliver him to the said plaintiffs unless the said defendant shall execute and deliver to you a bond with approved security in the sum of three thousand dollars payable to the said plaintiffs and conditioned to perform the final judgment which shall be rendered upon this writ and if the said defendant shall execute and deliver to you a bond as aforesaid you are commanded to return said bond with this writ You are further commanded to summon the said defendant Joseph W. Hall if to be found in your county To be and appear before the Justices of our Court of Pleas and Quarter Sessions to be held for the county of Rowan at the Court House in Salisbury on the first Monday in February next Then and there to answer the said William Murdoch William R. Darby and William Raider of a plea of taking and unjustly detaining the said slave to their damage five hundred dollars when and where you shall make known how you shall have executed this writ.

Witness James E. Kerr clerk of our said Court at office in Salisbury the first Monday in November A.D. 1858 and in the 83rd year of the independence of said state.

Issued 26th day of January A.D. 1859
James E. Kerr Clerk

Rowan County

We and each of us bind ourselves, our heirs, executors and administrators to pay to Joseph W. Hall all such costs and damages as may accrue in account of the above named suit not being prosecuted with effect.
                  W.R. Darby   (Seal)
                  W.   Raider   (Seal)
                  W.L. Saunders (Seal)
                  To hand January 28th 1859

                  W.W. Walton

Executed
Bonds filed
January 29th 1859
W.W. Walton SF

State of N. Carolina
Rowan County

    Know all men by these presents that we Joseph W. Hall and Nathaniel Boyden are held and firmly bound unto William R. Darby William Murdoch and William Reeder in the sum of three thousand dollars for which payment we do hereby bind ourselves our heirs executors and administrators, Jointly and severally, sealed with our seals and dated the 29 day of January 1859.

    The condition of the above obligation is such, that whereas, William R. Darby William Murdoch and W. Reeder hath sued out a writ of replevin against the said Joseph W. Hall for a certain slave by name Andy and hath placed the same in the hands of the sheriff of Rowan County and the said Joseph W. Hall hath determined to reclaim the possession of said slave and to give bond with approved security according to Act of assembly: now if the said Joseph W. Hall shall well and truly perform the final Judgment of said Court upon said writ of replevin then this obligation is to be void otherwise to remain in full force and effect.
J.W. Hall   (Seal)
Signed and sealed   Nathaniel Boyden (Seal)

State of North Carolina
Rowan County

Rowan County

Know all men by these presents that we William Murdoch William R. Darby William Raeder and A.J. Mock are held and firmly bound unto Joseph W. Hall in the sum of three thousand dollars for the payment of which we do well and truly bind ourselves our heirs, our executors and administrators and dated this 26th January A.D. 1859.

    The condition of the above obligation is such that whereas the said William Murdoch William R. Darby and William Raeder have this day applied to the Clerk of the court of Pleas and Quarter sessions for the county of Rowan, To issue a writ of replevin in their favor and against the said Joseph W. Hall for a slave by name Andy, returnable to the next term of the said Court and have obtained the same. Now if the said William Murdoch William R. Darby and William Raeder shall well and truly perform the final judgment of said Court upon said writ of replevin then the above obligation is to be void otherwise to remain in full force and effect.

W.R. Darby	(Seal)
W. Raeder	(Seal)
A.J. Mock	(Seal)

****

M.F. Nesbitt
Vs.
Isaac A. Witherspoon

Mr. McNeely
    Will you if you please fill up the blanks in the enclosed writ - and sign A - & hand A to your Sheriff & request him to serve it as soon as he can conveniently.

& oblige yours truly
F H Caldwell

No. 38
Summons for Plaintiff
O.P. Huston
to appear on Wednesday
at first week of Rowan Superior Court Fall Term

Rowan County

1860
I Acknowledge Service of the within Subpa.
O.P. Huston

State of North Carolina
To the Sheriff of Rowan County--Greeting:
You are hereby Commanded to Summon Dr. O.P. Huston personally to be and appear before the Judge of our Superior Court of Law, at the next Court, to be held for our said County, at the Court House in Salisbury, on the 13th Monday after the 4th Monday in August next; then and there to testify, and the truth to say in behalf of I.A. Witherspoon in a certain matter of controversy before said Court depending, and then and there to be tried, wherein M.F. Nesbitt is Plaintiff and I.A. Witherspoon is Defendant And this you shall in no wise omit, under the penalty prescribed by Law. Witness, Thomas McNeely, Clerk of our said Court, at Office, the 13th Monday after the 4th Monday in February, 1860, and in the 84th year of our Independence.
Thomas McNeely C.S.C.

Subpo. for Defendt to Rowan Superior Court
Fall Term 1859 Executed Nov. 7th, 1859
W A Walton Shff by T. Cranford DS
Came to hand Oct 8th 1859
W A Walton Shff by T. Cranford Ds

State of North Carolina
To the Sheriff of Rowan County--Greetings:
You are hereby Commanded to Summon Drs. D.B. Wood and M.A. Locke and have them personally to be and appear before the Judge of our Superior Court of Law, at the next Court, to be held for our said County, at the Court House in Salisbury, on the 13th Monday after the 4th Monday in August next; then and there to testify, and the truth to say in behalf of the Defendant in a certain matter of controversy before said Court depending, and then and there to be tried, wherein M.F. Nesbitt is Plaintiff and I.A. Witherspoon is Defendant And this you shall in no wise omit, under the penalty prescribed by Law. Witness, Thomas McNeely, Clerk of our said Court, at Office, the 13th Monday after the 4th Monday in February, 1859, and in the 83rd year of our Independence.Thomas McNeely C.S.C.

Rowan County

Summons for Defendt.
Margaret McNeely
To Rowan Superior Court Instanter
Fall Term 1862
Service Acknowledged
I Acknowledge the Service of the within Subpoena
Margaret McNeely

State of North Carolina,
    To the Sheriff of Rowan County--Greeting:
You are Hereby Commanded to Summon Margaret McNeely (wife of Jesse) personally to be and appear before the Judge of our Superior Court of Law, at the next Court to be held for our said County, at the Court House in Salisbury, on the 13th Monday after the 4th Monday in August next; then and there to testify, and the truth to say in behalf of I.A. Witherspoon, in a certain matter of controversy before said Court depending, and then and there to be tried, wherein M.F. Nesbitt is Plaintiff, and Issac A. Witherspoon is Defendant. And this you shall in no wise omit, under the penalty prescribed by Law. Witness, Thomas McNeely, Clerk of our said Court, at Office, the 13th Monday after the 4th Monday in August A.D. 1861, and in the **[Blank]** year of our Independence.
Thomas McNeely C.S.C.

Subpoena
To Fall Term 1859 for Plaintiff
Executed on Wood & sent Thos. Weather Spoon
a Written Summons on 31st day of October 1859
W.A. Walton Shf by T. Cranford DS
Wood & Witherspoon
Came to hand Oct 20th 1859
W.A. Walton Shf by T. Cranford Ds

State of North Carolina.
    To the Sheriff of Rowan County--Greeting:
You are hereby Commanded to Summon Dr. D.B. Wood and Dr. Thomas Witherspoon personally to be and appear before the Judge of our Superior of our Superior Court of Law, at the next Court to be held for our said

Rowan County

County, at the Court House in Salisbury, on the 13th Monday after the 4th Monday in August next; then and there to testify, and the truth to say in behalf of M.F. Nesbitt in a certain matter of controversy before said Court depending, and then and there to be tried, wherein M.F. Nesbitt is Plaintiff, and Isaac Witherspoon is Defendant. And this you shall in no wise omit, under the penalty prescribed by Law.Witness, Thomas McNeely, Clerk of our said Court, at Office, the 13th Monday after the 4th Monday in February, 1859, and in the 85th year of our Independence.
Thomas McNeely C.S.C.

Bond

State of North Carolina }
Rowan County }

We, the Subscribers, do jointly and severally bind ourselves, our Heirs, Executors and Administrators, in the sum of Two hundred dollars to be paid to Isaac Witherspoon his Heirs, Executors, Administrators or Assigns.
    The above Obligation to be void on Condition that M.F. Nesbitt do prosecute a certain suit brought in the Superior Court of Law for the County aforesaid, wherein the said M.F. Nesbitt is Plaintiff, against Isaac Witherspoon Defendant, and in case of failure, shall pay the said Witherspoon all such costs and damages as may be awarded against the said Nesbit by the Court having cognizance thereof. Witness our hands and seals, the 2nd day of September A.D. 1859.
Witness,
F.H. Caldwell   C.A. Carlton (Seal)

Notice to Rowan Superior Court
Spring Term 1860
Executed May 21 By Delivering a Coppy of the saim
W.F. Wasson[?] & W.T. Watts DS
Postage 3 cts.

North Carolina }
Rowan County } Superior Court of Law. Fall Term 1859

To the Sheriif of Iredell County

Rowan County

Mr. Jacob Parker, Agent of Plaintiff, You are hereby Notified to produce on the trial of the above suit the bill of Sale from defendant to Plaintiff, for the Girl Adaline, otherwise [?] evidence will be given of its Contents, May 11th 1860.
Kerr & Fleming Attos.
for Defendant
Subpoena
To Spring Term 1861
I acknowledge the service of this subpoena
James M. McKay

State of North Carolina.
To the Sheriff of Iredell County--Greeting:
You are Hereby Commanded to Summon James M. McKay personally to be and appear before the Judge of our Superior Court of Law, at the next Court to be held for our said County, at the Court House in Salisbury on the 13th Monday after the 4th Monday in February next; then and there to testify, and the truth to say in behalf of M.F. Nesbit in a certain matter of controversy before said Court depending, and then and there to be tried, wherein M.F. Nesbit is Plaintiff and Isaac Witherspoon is Defendant. And this you shall in no wise omit, under the penalty prescribed by Law. Witness, Thomas McNeely, Clerk of our said Court, at Office, the 13th Monday after the 4th Monday in Aug., 1860, and in the 85th year of our Independence.
Thomas McNeely C.S.C.
Subpoena for pltff
Executed Nov. 27th, 1860
W.W. Walton Shf

This is the day
    4.00
    2.00
    2.00
    8.00
   $16.00

State of North Carolina.
To the Sheriff of Rowan County--Greeting:

Rowan County

You are Hereby Commanded to Summon Jacob Parker personally to be and appear before the Judge of our Superior Court of Law, at the next Court to be held for our said County, at the Court House in Salisbury on the 13th Monday after the 4th Monday in August next; then and there to testify, and the truth to say in behalf of M.F. Nesbit in a certain matter of controversy before said Court depending, and then and there to be tried, wherein M.F. Nesbit is Plaintiff and I.A. Witherspoon is Defendant. And this you shall in no wise omit, under the penalty prescribed by Law. Witness, Thomas McNeely, Clerk of our said Court, at Office, the 13th Monday after the 4th Monday in February, 1860, and in the 84th year of our Independence.
Thomas McNeely C.S.C.

Subpoena
To Fall 1861
Executed Oct. the 16th By Leaving a Copy of the
Saime at her residence
W.F. Wasson Shff By W.T. Watts DS
Postage 5 cts.

State of North Carolina.
To the Sheriff of Rowan County--Greeting:
You are hereby Commanded to Summon Margaret McNeely - wife of Jesse McNeely personally to be and appear before the Judge of our Superior Court of Law, at the next Court to be held for our said County, at the Court House in Salisbury, on the 13th Monday after the 4th Monday in August next; then and there to testify, and the truth to say in behalf of M.F. Nesbit in a certain matter of controversy before said Court depending, and then and there to be tried, wherein M.F. Nesbit is Plaintiff, and I.A. Witherspoon is Defendant. And this you shall in no wise omit, under the penalty prescribed by Law. Witness, Thomas McNeely, Clerk of our said Court, at Office, the 13th Monday after the 4th Monday in February, 1861, and in the [Blank] year of our Independence.
Thomas McNeely C.S.C.

Subpoena
To Rowan
To Spring 1860
Executed April 9th 1860
W.F. Wasson Shff

State of North Carolina.

Rowan County

To the Sheriff of Iredell County--Greeting:
You are hereby Commanded to Summon A.M. Walker and Reuben Reynolds personally to be and appear before the Judge of our Superior Court of Law, at the next Court, to be held for our said County, at the Court House in Salisbury, on the 13th Monday after the 4th Monday in August next; then and there to restify, and the truth to say in behalf of M.F. Nesbit in a certain matter of controversy before said Court depending, and then and there to be tried, wherein M.F. Nesbit is Plaintiff and Isaac A. Witherspoon is Defendant And this you shall in no wise omit, under the penalty prescribed by Law. Witness, Thomas McNeely, Clerk of our said Court, at Office, the 13th Monday after the 4th Monday in March, 1859, and in the 83rd year of our Independence. Thomas McNeely C.S.C.

Subp for Pltff
To Fall 1859
Executed on A.M. Walker & Reuben Reynolds
October 4, 1859
WF Wasson Shff by W. Watts DS

State of North Carolina.
To the Sheriff of Iredell County--Greeting:
You are hereby Commanded to Summon Hugh Reynolds, Reuben Reynolds, A.M. Walker and George H. White personally to be and appear before the Judge of our Superior Court of Law, at the next Court, to be held for our said County, at the Court House in Salisbury, on the 13th Monday after the 4th Monday in August next; then and there to testify, and the truth to say in behalf of the defendant in a certain matter of controversy before said Court depending, and then and there to be tried, wherein M.F. Nesbitt is Plaintiff and I.A. Witherspoon is Defendant And this you shall in no wise omit, under the penalty prescribed by Law. Witness, Thomas McNeely, Clerk of our said Court, at Office, the 13th Monday after the 4th Monday in February, 1859, and in the 83rd year of our Independence.
Thomas McNeely C.S.C.

Subpa. for Defendt.
To Rowan Superior Court Fall Term 1859
Executed Oct. 28, 1859
W.F. Wasson Shff By WT Watt DS

State of North Carolina.

Rowan County

To the Sheriff of Iredell County--Greeting:
You are hereby Commanded to Summon Hugh Reynolds personally to be and appear before the Judge of our Superior Court of Law, at the next Court to be held for our said County, at the Court House in Salisbury on the 13th Monday after the 4th Monday in February next; then and there to testify, and the truth to say in behalf of M.F. Nesbit in a certain matter of controversy before said Court depending, and then and there to be tried, wherein M.F. Nesbit is Plaintiff and I.A. Witherspoon is Defendant And this you shall in no wise omit, under the penalty prescribed by Law. Witness, Thomas McNeely Clerk of our said Court at Office, the 13th Monday after the 4th Monday in August 1859 and in the 84th year of our Independence.
Thomas McNeely C.S.C.

      Wnt (Warrant)
      Case
     To Fall Term 1858
   Executed Bond filed October 2nd 1858
     W.[?] Walton Shf
      WB & WH

State of North Carolina,
  To the Sheriff of Rowan County--Greeting:
You are hereby commanded to take the body of Isaac Witherspoon if to be found in your County, and him safely keep, so that you have him before the Judge of our Superior Court of Law, at the next Court to be held for the County of Rowan at the Court House in Salisbury on the 13th Monday after the 4th Monday in August next, then and there to answer M.F. Nesbit of a plea of Trespass on the Case to his damage Twelve hundred Dollars. Herein fail not, and have you then and there this Writ. Witness Thomas McNeely Clerk of our said Court at Office, the 13th Monday after the 4th Monday in February A.D. 1858, and in the 82 year of our Independence.Issued the 3d day of September 1858.
Thomas McNeely C.S.C.

    Summon for Defendt.
     John L. Lyon
  To Rowan Superior Court Spring Term 1861
   Executed Novr. the 19, 1860
   WF Wasson Shf by WT Watt DS
     Postage 3 cts.

Rowan County

State of North Carolina.
   To the Sheriff of Iredell County--Greeting:
You are Hereby Commanded to Summon John L. Lyon personally to be and appear before the Judge of our Superior Court of Law, at the next Court to be held for our said County, at the Court House in Salisbury on the 13th Monday after the 4th Monday in February next; then and there to testify, and the truth to say in behalf of I.A. Witherspoon in a certain matter of controversy before said Court depending, and then and there to be tried, wherein M.F. Nesbitt is Plaintiff and Isaac A. Witherspoon is Defendant And this you shall in no wise omit, under the penalty prescribed by Law. Witness, Thomas McNeely, Clerk of our said Court, at Office, the 13th Monday after the 4th Monday in August, 1860, and in the 85 year of our Independence.
Thomas McNeely C.S.C.
   State of North Carolina
To Otho Gillespie Esqr., Justice assigned to keep the Peace in and for the County of Iredell, Greeting:
   Know Ye, That we in confidence of your Prudence and Fidelity, have appointed, and by these presents do give unto you full power and authority, in pursuance of an Order of our Superior Court of Law, made in a cause wherein M.F. Nesbitt is Plaintiff, and I.A. Witherspoon is Defendant, at such time and place as you shall think fit, take, upon Oath, the deposition of Hugh Reynolds touching and concerning what [Blank] may know in the said controversy And that you may take such deposition in writing, and return the same closed up, under your hand and seal, to our said Court, to be held for the County of Rowan on the 13th Monday after the 4th Monday in Febt next, together with this writ. Witness, Thomas McNeely, Clerk of our said Court at Office, the 13th Monday after the 4th Monday in August 1859, and in the 84 year of our Independence.
Thomas McNeely C.S.C.

Statesville Decbr. 5th 1859
Mr. Jacob Parker
   Sir you will hereby take Notice that on Saturday the 10th Inst at the Office of the County Court Clerk of Iredell at the Court House in Statesville I shall proceed to take the deposition of Hugh Reynolds to be read as evidence in a suit now pending in Rowan Superior Court Whereas

Rowan County

M.F. Nesbit is plaintiff & I.A. Witherspoon is defendant when & where you can attend & Cross examine if you see proper.

You are further notified to produce the bill of sale made for the negro now in suit, at the same time & place. I.A. Witherspoon

State of North Carolina
To William A. Drennan, Esquire, Justice assigned to keep the Peace in and for the County of Holmes, Mississippi, Greeting:
Know Ye, That we in confidence of your Prudence and Fidelity, have appointed, and by these presents do give unto you full power and authority, in pursuance of an Order of our Superior Court of Law, made in cause wherein M.F. Nesbit is Plaintiff, and Isaac Witherspoon is Defendant, at such time and place as you shall think fit, take, upon Oath, the deposition of J.M. Stewart & others touching and concerning what they may know in and about the said controversy And that you may take such deposition in writing, and return the same closed up, under your hand and seal, to our said Court, to be held for the County of Rowan on the 13th Monday after the 4th Monday in August next, together with this writ. Witness, Thomas McNeely, Clerk of our said Court at Office, the 13th Monday after the 4th Monday in March 1859, and in the 83d year of our Independence.
Thomas McNeely C.S.C.
Mr. Issac Witherspoon

You are hereby notified that on the twelth day of November next at the Court House in Lexington Holmes County, Mississippi I will proceed to take the depositions of J.M. Stewart and others to be read in evidences in a suit now pending in Rowan County Superior Court wherein M.F. Nesbit is Plantiff and you are defendant - when and where you can attend a cross examine. September the 10th 1859

Yours -
M.F. Nesbit
By W.P. Caldwell

State of Mississippi }
Holmes County }

Deposition of John M. Stuart - E.S. McGehee and I.W. Grace taken before William A. Drennan An acting Justice of the Peace in and for the County and State aforesaid on the 12th day of November A.D. 1859 (pursuant to

Rowan County

the annexed Commission to him directed by Thomas McNeely C.S.C.) at his office in the Town of Lexington in said County and State Said Deposition to be read as evidence on the part of the Plaintiff in a certain Suit - now pending the Superior Court - of Law for Rowan County State of North Carolina wherein M.F. Nesbit is Plaintiff and Issac Witherspoon is Defendant.

John M. Stuart - being of lawful age and duly sworn Says to

Interrogatory - Are you acquainted with M.F. Nesbit - one of the parties to this Suit?
Answer I am.
Interrogatory 2nd Did M.F. Nesbit ever sell to you in the year of 1858 a dark Copper colored Girl named Adeline?
Answer They did.
Interrogatory 3rd What were the conditions of the bill of sale in regard to Soundness of said girl Adeline?
Objected to by Defts Counsel.
Answer She was warranted to be Sound in the bill of sale - but proved after two months trial to be unsound And I returned her to Nesbit.
Objected to by Dfts Counsel
Interrogatory 4th In what manner was the girl Adaline afflicted and State - how long was she in the afflicted State when attacked?
Answer She was afflicted with fits - She had several fits - while at my place and she appeared As dead for three or four hours on the first attack. As she was recovering the fits grew lighter until she would apparently get well. She was going to work on the plantations and Stepped into a Cabin and dropped down in the first fit - and remained in a Stupor for three or four hours.
Interrogatory 5th Was the girl Adaline at the time you returned her to Nesbits laboring under an attack of Fits.
Answer She had not recovered from a previous attack though had not had a fit in the day when she left my house.

Cross Examined

Interrogatory 1st How long did you know the said girl?
Ans - About two months.
Interrogatory 2nd What time did you buy said negro Girl?
Ans - In March 1858.
Int. 3rd How long did she remain at your house before she had a Fit?

Rowan County

Ans - About two months - and she remained at my house a week or more after having a Fit.

Interrg. 4th   You have stated in answer to Int 4th that the girl dropped down in a Fit - did you know this of your own knowledge?

Ans - I did not - but she was crying on the bed when I got to her.

Int. 5th   State whether or not the said girl at the time you found her lying on the bed might not have Received some blow - which caused her to be thus Prostrated.

Answer   I Cannot Say positively but I do not think she received any blow.

Int. 6th   State whether Mr. Nesbit ever said anything about the Complaint of this girl to you at any time?

Ans - On the way from North Carolina - Nesbit told me the girl had something like a fit - but as it was in the night and raining in the swamp - he did not attach much importance to it as he thought it was from fear - and she soon got over it.

Re Examined

Int 1st   What did you do with Nesbits bill of sale?

Ans - I do not recollect what but I think I destroyed it yet I have made no search for it.

Int 2nd   What is the Girl Adeline Worth?

Ans - I would not buy such a negro - she is not worth anything to me.

John M. Stewart

E.S. McGeehee being duly sworn and of lawful age

Int 1st   Are you a practicing Physician in your neighborhood?

Ans - I am - And have been for Twenty one years.

Int 2nd   Were you ever at Mr John M Stuarts request called out to attend in a professional capacity?

Ans - I was in the Month of April 1858 sent for by Mr Stuart to attend upon the Girl Adeline.

Int 3rd   Where was the place you attended upon the Girl Adeline?

Ans - In Holmes County Mississippi.

Int 4th   What was her condition when you reached her?

Ans - She was in a state of [?] Stupor - Caused from An Attack of Epilepsy.

Int 5th   What was the Character of the disease?

Ans - Ideopathetic Epilepsy.

Rowan County

Int 6th   From the symptoms of the girl how long do you think she had been laboring under the above disease?
Ans - From the marks of local Treatment Upon her body I think the disease has existed from childhood - The mark consisted of an issue of long standing upon her dorsal spine and evidences of Cuffing & Scarrifying from the issue to her cervical region.
Int 7th   From your knowledge of the disease do you think it dangerous?
Ans - It rarely produces death immediately - but gradually incapacitates the subject from profitable Employment.
Int 8th   Have you ever known any permanent cures effected in that disease?
Ans - I have not.
Int 9th   Does not the disease as it advances become more malignant?
Ans - It does.
Int 10   Do you think a permanent Cure can ever be effected in Adelines Case?
Ans - I do not and advised Mr Stuart to return her.
Int 11   Do you Consider Adeline as worth anything?
Ans - I do not.

Cross Examination

Int 1st   In your Answer to the 6th Int. in your direct examination you Speak of an issue of long Standing - will you
describe it?
Ans - It was a scar produced by a long standing ulcer made for the purpose of derivation.
Int 2nd   In what sense do you use the word derivation?
Ans - I use it in a Revulsive Sense.
Int 3rd   Are you fully satisfied that this [?] could not have been recently made?
Ans - I am.
Int 4th   Are you fully satisfied that this erclar[?] was made treating the disease of Epilepsy?
Ans - I am from that being one of the places of local treatment in the disease of Epilepsy.
Int 5th   Is it not an erchar? Sometimes made by physicians in the treatment of other diseases?
Ans - They are.
Int 6th   Will you state what those disease are.

Rowan County

Ans - Apoplexy is one - Coahreas - otherwise called St. Vitus' dance - Menningitis and all chronic disease might require an erchar in their treatment.
Int 7th Might not this erchar be produced from an accident?
Ans - It could not have been as it was too regular in its form.
Int 8th In your answer to the 6th Cross Interrogatory you mention certain diseases besides Ideopathetic Epilepsy in which physicians sometimes resort to such treatment as produces an erchar - now may it not have been that a physician in treating of some of these other diseases resorted to such treatment as usually produces an erchar and may not the girl Adeline have entirely Recovered from such disease?
Ans - I cannot positively say that it does not.
Int 9th Does not Ideopathetic Epilepsy sometimes attack Adults?
Ans - I cannot positively say that it does not.
Int 10 Did you not form your opinion that the disease under which Adeline was suffering was of long standing from the fact that it was Ideopathetic Epilepsy?
Ans - I did.

Re Examined

Int 1st Is it not the usual treatment in Epilepsy to use issues or counter irretants?
Ans - It is.
Int 2nd Are not the application applied to the spinal Column?
Ans - They are.
Int 3rd From seeing the girl was afflicted with Epilepsy and knowing that Counter irretants were used in the treatment of the disease were you not satisfied by seeing the erchar that it was the Result of a former treatment for the same disease?
Ans - it is my impression that the erchar was the result of former treatment for the Same disease - I cannot answer positively for I was not cognizant of the fact.
Int 4th Of what Temperament was the girl Adeline?
Ans - She was of a robust Sanguine Temperament.
Int 5th Is she not of that constitutional habit which would induce that disease?
Ans - She is of that habit - that is after attacked by the disease but I do not consider any habit would induce it as it as often attacks the fleshy as the lean.
E.S. McGeehee

Rowan County

James W. Grace being duly sworn says:

Int 1st Do you know the parties in this Suit?
Ans - I know Nesbit - but do not know Mr. Witherspoon.
Int 2nd Do you know the girl Adeline Sold by Nesbit to Stuart?
Ans - I do.
Int 3rd In whose possession did you know the girl?
Ans - I have known the girl in my own possession and in Nesbits and Stuarts.
Int 4th In whose possession was the girl when you first saw her? and where was it?
Ans - In Nesbits - and at Carrollton Miss. on her way from North Carolina.
Int 5th What was her condition when you first saw her?
Ans - She was helpless - and remained so for a week.
Int 6th Did the girl recover from that attack?
Ans - She did.
Int 7th In what month and year did you first see the girl in the above condition?
Ans - In November 1857.
Int 8th After she recovered fro the Attack in Nov./1857 did you ever know her to have a recurrence of the disease?
Ans - I have known her to have other attacks. She had another in May 1858 when Mr. Stuart sent her back to Nesbit.
Int 9th In whose possession has the girl been since Stuart returned her to Nesbit?
Ans - In my possession except about a month when she was returned to Nesbit on account of having Fits.
Int 10th How many paroxysms of the disease has she had since Stuart returned her to Nesbit and since she has been in your possession?
Ans - I cannot say how many though she has been afflicted frequently.
Int 11th Do you think the girl Sound or unsound?
Ans - I think her unsound.
Int 12th What do you consider the girl worth?
Ans - I do not think her worth anything.

Cross Examination

Int 1st In your answer to the 10th Interrogatory you say you think the girl Adeline unsound - Are you a physician?

Rowan County

Ans - I am not.

State of Mississippi }
Holmes County } I William

A. Drennan An acting Justice of the peace in and for said County & State do hereby certify that the foregoing depositions were by me taken at the time and place mentioned in the Caption, that said depositions were by me written & Read over to & understood by and subscribed by said witnesses in my presence and that the Counsel for Plaintiff & Defendant attended at Said time and place and examined & cross examined.

I further Certify that I am Related to neither party and am of Counsel for neither and am now about to sign seal and direct the within depositions to Thomas McNeely.

Cl. of S.C. of Rowan Co. North Carolina Given under my hand and seal this 14th day of November A.D. 1859
William A. Drennan J.P. (Seal)

****

**Myer Myers
Vs.
M.L. Bost**

STATE OF NORTH CAROLINA

To Richard D. Sanxay and Robert M. Burton Justices assigned to keep the Peace in and for the City of Richmond County of Henrico Virginia Esquires,

Greeting: Know ye, that in confidence of your prudence and fidelity, have appointed, and by these presents do give unto you full power and authority, in pursuance of an order of our Superior Court of Law, made in a cause wherein Myer Myer is Plantiff and M.L. Bost Defendant at such time and place as you shall think fit, to take, upon oath, the deposition of Benjamin Davis, Henry Davis & Doctr. Johnson and others touching and concerning what They may know in and about the said controversy: And that you take such deposition in writing, and return the same closed up,

Rowan County

under your hand and seal, to our said Court, to be held for the County of Rowan, on the 8th Monday after the 4th Monday in September next, together with this Writ.

Witness, Obadiah Woodson, Clerk of our said Court at Office, the 8th Monday after the 4th Monday in March A.D. 1853.
Obadiah Woodson, C.S.C.

Mr. M.L. Bost

Sir
You are hereby notified that I shall proceed on the 18th day of October next at the office of John M. Gregory in the City of Richmond, Virginia to take the deposition of Benjamin Davis and others to be read in evidence in a suit now pending in the Superior Court of law for the county of Rowan wherein I am plaintiff and you are defendant when and where you can attend and cross examine if you see proper. August 3rd 1853

Depositions of Benjamin Davis Doctor Carter J. Johnson Henry Davis, and Solomon Davis taken at the office of John M. Gregory in the City of Richmond and state of Virginia on Tuesday the 18th day of October, 1853 to be read as evidence in the trial of a suit now pending in the Superior Court of Law for the County of Rowan, in the State of North Carolina, wherein Myer Myers is Plaintiff and M.L. Bost is Defendant which Depositions are duly taken and subscribed before us Richard D. Sanxay and Robert M. Burton duly qualified Justices of the Peace for the City of Richmond, County of Henrico, Virginia in pursuance of notice and Commission hereto annexed.

Benjamin Davis a witness introduced by the plaintiff being first duly sworn deposes and answers as follows -

1 Question - By Plaintiff. Did you ever as auctioneer sell a negro man for Myer Myers of Salisbury in the state of North Carolina. If yes please state when you made the sale, who bought the negro and all you may know in relation to the said negro from the time you sold him to this day.
Answer - On the 8th of December 1852 I sold a negro man named John Young to Henry Davis, I sold him on account of Myer Myers of Salisbury, North Carolina, before I sold him, I discovered a large scar on one of his

Rowan County

largest Toes, it was also discovered by Henry Davis and Myer Myers. Henry Davis at first was unwilling to buy the negro man George Young, because he was apprehensive that there was something very serious to matter with his toe, but as Myer Myers assured me, and Henry Davis that he purchased the said negro man George Myers of a gentleman whom he had great confidence in and he having warranted the said negro to be healthy and sound, he Myers proposed to sell him, with a full warranty of soundness, and Henry Davis having full confidence in Mr. Myer Myers bought him at the price of one thousand & twenty five dollars, though at the time he bought him he thought his Toe was diseased, and he would not have bought him at any price but for the confidence he had in me as the agent and Myer Myers as the principle. Henry Davis sometime after he bought him complained that George Young was an unsound man, because the Toe which I have said had a scar on it proved to be unsound. Myer Myers being informed by Henry Davis that the negro was useless to him and Valueless because he was not able to do any work in consequence of his diseased Toe that he Myer Myers must take him back and refund to him his purchase money and his bill of expenses - Myer Myers being satisfied in his mind that at the time he sold the negro to Henry Davis, that his Toe was diseased authorized me as his agent to take back the said negro. I received him, back of Henry Davis, and returned him his one thousand & twenty five dollars, which he paid for the said negro. Mr. Myers paid to Henry Davis the bill of expenses himself. By request - of Myer Myers I sent the negro man George Young to the Richmond Medical College, his toe was then in a dreadful condition, his toe was examined by Doctor Carter P. Johnson one of the professors in said college and who I know to be a very Skillfull Surgeon, after Doctor Johnsons examination of it he was fully satisfied that his large toe was unsound, and that it was necessary to amputate the Toe, and he did take it off, the said negro remained at the Medical college nearly two months, he was discharged from the Medical College some four or five months ago, during the whole of the time since his discharge he has not been able to render any service whatever, it appears that although his to was cut off by Doctor Johnson, it did not have the effect to render him serviceable or fit for any kind of labour, the whole of the foot being very badly numbed from the bad effects of the diseased Toe. I have had some experience among negroes. I possess to know the value of negroes and how much defects, depreciates their value and I have no hesitation in saying, that his condition is such and has been such since he was returned by Henry Davis

Rowan County

as to make him valueless, and I am satisfied in my own mind that George Young's Toe had been diseased for a length of time previous to the date that I sold him to Henry Davis as the agent of Myer Myers. George is still in my hands, and I have had him ever since he was discharged from the Medical college, and condition has been and is such during all that time, that he is not fit for any kind of service. I have kept George by request and at the expense of Myer Myers - Mr. Myers would have sold him, but no one would give anything for him.

2 Question by the same Be pleased to State as nearly as you can all the expenses incurred by Mr. Myer Myers on account of the negro man George Young since Mr. Henry Davis returned him to you as the agent of Mr. Myers?

Answer - The bill paid for Keeping him at the Medical college paid by me, for Mr. Myers is thirty five Dollars and his board is since he came from the College is forty Dollars - making in all to this time seventy five dollars - And further this deponent saith not.

Benjamin Davis

Doctor Carter P. Johnson a witness introduced by the plaintiff, being first duly sworn and deposes and answers as follows--

1 Question by the plaintiff. Do you know a negro man by the name of George Young, if yes, please state how and when you became acquainted with him, what was his health and condition when you first saw him, what his health and condition is now, and any facts connected with him, which will show his present condition & value?

Answer - Mr: Benj: Davis entered a negro man named George in the Infirmary of the Medical College of this city on the 25 of March last. I was there in attendance upon the Surgical ward of the Infirmary and took charge of the patient. At that time, George was complaining of a severe pain in the big toe of one of his feet (I do not recollect which). He stated that some years previously he had received an injury of that toe, a cut I believe from an axe or some sharp instrument, that the wound had healed, but that he had never been able to use the foot well since, that if he used his foot much the part became swollen and painful. There was a scar across the toe just over the first [?], and when he entered the Infirmary the whole toe was very tender & much swollen.

    I tried for several weeks to cure the affection without resorting to any operation, but found all my efforts ineffectual. I then advised Mr:

Rowan County

Davis to have the toe amputated, hoping then by removing what appeared to be the principle source of his disease to cure him. Mr: Davis consented to the operation & I accordingly performed it.

    I was struck during the operation with the very bloodless state of the tissues and feared that the [?] would be long in healing up. Accordingly union took place between the edges of the wound very tardily. After the lapse of some weeks however the wound was perfectly healed, but the patient still complained of pain in the foot and of an inability to put it to the ground & bear his weight upon it. This state of thing continued until his discharge from the Infirmary which was about the middle of May, I don't recollect the exact date.

    I never saw the man but once after that, which was sometime after the date of his discharge from the Infirmary, when Mr: Davis asked me to go to a jail to see George. I found him with his foot swollen and very painful and I concluded that there was serious [?] of the tissues of the foot which would probably never be relieved except by the entire removal of the foot. And further the deponent saith not.
Carter P. Johnson

Henry Davis a Witness introduced by the plaintiff being first duly sworn deposes and says as follows,
1   Question by the plaintiff. Did you ever buy a negro man by the name of George Young of Mr. Benjamin Davis as the agent of Mr. Myer Myers of Salisbury North Carolina. If yes, be pleased to state about what time you bought him, what was his health and condition when you bought, and what did you do with him?
Answer. Yes I did buy of Benjamin Davis as the agent of Myer Myers of Salisbury North Carolina a negro man by the name of George Young, I bought him in December 1852 & I paid for him one thousand and twenty five dollars, he looked to be healthy, but he complained of his big toe which he complained very much of and said it had been diseases for several years. I should not have bought the negro but Mr. Myers told me he had bought him of a very correct - responsible man who had warranted the negro all sound and right, and that he Myers felt sure what the negro said about his toe was a lie. I know Mr. Myers intimately well and he warranted the said negro to be sound and healthy and promised if he proved not to be so he would take him back, which he did and returned me my money when it was ascertained that the negro was diseased. After

Rowan County

I bought the negro I carried him with me on the [?] to Petersburg where I reside a few days after I bought him. In about a week or ten days after that I sent him to New Orleans by railroad and steamboats, except about 16 or 20 miles; which distance in consequence of two railroads in Georgia not connecting, he walked, he never did anything whilst he was in my possession like work - He had not been at New Orleans many days before he complained so much of his toe that a doctor had to be called in to see him, and the doctor upon examining his Toe said it was an old disease, that he could do nothing with him and advised he should be sent back, and he was accordingly brought him back in the same manner that he had been Carried out except that he did not walk at all, he rode in the stage from one rail road in Georgia to the other.

2 Question by same. State if Mr. Myer Myers had to pay you for the expense you were at- about - the said negro whilst you had him, and if he did state as near as you can the amount he had to pay you for the said negro?

Answer. Mr. Myers had to pay me for the expense of the negro whilst I had him, the amount was about eighty five dollars it was certainly that much, if not more and further the deponent saith not.

his
Henry X Davis
Mark

Solomon Davis a witness introduced by the plaintiff being first duly sworn deposes and says --

1 Question by the plaintiff. Do you know a negro man by the name of George Young, if yes, how long have you known him, what has been his condition since you knew him, and what do you think he is now worth?

Answer. I do know a negro by the name of George Young, the property at this time of Myer Myers of Salisbury North Carolina. I have known him since last December when Mr. Myers brought him here, and he was sold by Benjamin Davis as the agent of Myers to Henry Davis, who sent him to New Orleans sometime in March 1853 he was brought back from New Orleans, when he got back here he staid at my jail a day or so, and was sent from there to Richmond Medical College where he staid about two months - after he was discharged from the college he returned to my house where he has been ever since. He has been all the time in a very bad condition entirely unable to do any work, I do not think he is worth a

Rowan County

cent - In fact - no person would take him, I presume as a gift - as he would be a tax to them. At least I would not take him. Mr. Myers is now and has been paying me for the board of George since he left the college twenty five cents a day, besides his washing and other expenses. And further this deponent saith not.
Solomon Davis

State of Virginia
City of Richmond in Henrico County to wit
We Richard D. Sanxay and Robert M. Burton justices of the peace in and for the city aforesaid do hereby certify that the foregoing depositions of Benjamin Davis, Carter P. Johnson, Henry Davis, and Solomon Davis were duly taken and sworn to and subscribed before us at the time and place mentioned in the caption.
      Given under our hands and seals this eighteenth day of October in the year one thousand eight hundred and fifty three.

                Richd. D. Sanxay   J.P.
                R.M. Burton   J.P.
Examined and allowed to be read in evidence
Obadiah Woodson, C.S.C.   October 28th 1853

Rowan County

Chapter Fourteen

Rowan County

SLAVE PATROL RECORDS

PATROL FOR 1862
CLASS NO. 3

James Clarke, John M. Coffin, Richard A. Caldwell, Julias A. Caldwell, Henry B. Casper, Thomas Chaffin, Burton Craige, John C. Correll, H.A. Correll, John Casper, B. Cody, William A. Cul[?], Pascall Callicot, Thomas M. Crawford, Joseph Pears

To James Clark, Capt. and in his absence to John M. Coffin, 2nd Captain.

Sir:- You are hereby appointed Captain for the 3d Class of Patrol for the year 1862. It is your duty to summon your Company, each armed with a loaded gun, to meet to-night, and on every thirteenth night hereafter, (until otherwise ordered,) at the Town Hall, in the Market House, at the hour of 10 o'clock, and perform patrol duty during the whole night. On all slaves found off their owners premises, without a written permission, you will inflict not more than fifteen lashes; no slave to be whipped except in the presence of the Captain. You will arrest and carry before the Intendant of Police, all free colored persons found associating with slaves in the night, or on the Sabbath day, in any kitchen, outhouse or place other than their own premises.

It is further your duty, to arrest and bring before the Intendant of Police, any and all persons whom you may know to be guilty of any breach of the peace, or disorderly conduct during the term of your service, whether in the day time or in the night. Your powers as patrol continue from the hour of meeting on your respective nights of duty, to the same hour of the succeeding night.

You will not resort to the use of fire-arms, except in cases of extreme emergency, such as to put down armed resistance to the execution

Rowan County

of the patrol laws, for the suppression of dangerous riots and mobs, for the arrest of persons engaged in treasonable outbreaks, or the arrest of Federal prisoners escaped, or attempting to escape from the garrison in this Town.

For neglect of duty, as Captain, you are liable to a fine of Five Dollars, and each one of your company for a similar neglect, to a fine of Two Dollars.

By order of the Board of Commissioners of Salisbury.

March 29th, 1862   John I. Shaver, Intendant.

Chapter Fifteen

Rowan County

DEPOSITIONS

[BADLY TORN AND FADED-IMPOSSIBLE TO READ]

State of North Carolina
[Torn] County

Thomas Dotson maketh Oath that on the 26th May last [Faded and Torn] James McCulloch [Faded and Torn] Negro

Sworn to before me at Salisbury this second day of July 1804.

[?] Macay   Thomas [?]

State of North Carolina
Rowan County

Moses Bell[?]
[Document torn and faded]

Thomas Dotson   James McCulloch

2nd day of July 1804

Rowan County

Chapter Sixteen

Rowan County

STEALING OF SLAVES

Rowan County   } this day Came William Dolton
North Carolina } Constable and [?] before me

James Dorchester one of his Magisties Justices of the peece for said County and brought Timmothy Terral and by Credeble information by Cornel William Callaway and Captain Gast[?] that that the Said Turrel hath stolen four negroes in South Carolina and is out Lawed there and now found Strowling in the hollow

(Seal)

to the Shireff & gole Keeper of Salzbery to witt I Command you to Receive into your gole the body of Timmothy Terral and him safely keep in your Said gole So that you have him at our next Superior Court to be held at Salsbery for the County of Rowan then & there to answer Such matters as shall be Lodged against him by our Sworn Lord the King giving under my hand and seal the Tweenty six day of December 1757[1767?]
James Dorchester

Rowan County

Chapter Seventeen

Rowan County

HIRE OF SLAVES

Sary Smith part of hiring of Negros and rent for land for the year 1806
Her part of hire of negros is Rent for land

```
     S    D
     25   4   0
     4    0   0
     29   4   0
```

We certify that on examining the possessors account we find a balance due Sarah Smith for the year [Faded] the sum of 1.10

Jany 21st 1808
                    J.A. Peasson JP
                    Daniel Orvell (S)

Sary Smith in account with Pleasant Chaffin	S	D
June the 2nd to 3yds of Calico at 7/6 per yd	1	2 6
1806 to 1 silk handkerchief	0	8 0
to 1 1/2 yds of Calico 7/6 per	0	11 3
July to 3 yds of durance 3/9 per yd	0	11 3
the 19th to 4 yds of tape 2 per yd	0	0 8

Rowan County

Sept to scain of silk & to scain thread 2d 8		0	0
the 8th to 4 yds of bumbaset 6/ per yd 0		1	4
October to 4 yds of planing 5/ per yd 0		1	0
the 10th to 1 Chex hankerchief 9		0	3
December to 1 Muscling hankerchief 0		0	4
the 19th to 3 yds of home [Torn] Cloth 5/per yd 0		0	15
to 3 yds of Callimanco 3/ per yd 0		0	9
to pair of shoes 10/ to pair fine slippers 3		1	1
January to 3 yds of Callico 4/4 per yd 2		0	15
the 12 to 2 scains of thread 2 each to making frock 4	3/	0	3
1807 to 3 yds of muscling 3/9 per yd to 1/4 yd Cambie 9	2/6	0	13
January to making 2 shifts 2/ 0		0	2
the 25th to 1 yd of silk to scain silk 1/ to yd of ribbon 6	2/6	0	11
March to 1 yd of lace 5/ makeing bonnet 3/ 0		0	8
the 18th April to scain silk 1/ to makeing 2 scirts 2/ 0		0	3
the 14th to speling book 1/10 1/2 to pair of shoes 10/ 10		0	11
to paing the Clark for entering her account 0		0	2

Rowan County

her part of tax for the land	0	3
2		
to twelve months bord	12	14
2		
	15	
	27	14
2		

****

Salisbury, N.C., January, 2 1865

$500 On or before the first day of January, 1866, we or either of us promise to pay to D.S. Pir[?]y or order, the sum of Five Hundred Dollars and **[Left Blank]** Cents, for the hire of Negro Boy Bill said Negro not to be worked out of this and the adjoining Counties. We further promise and bind ourselves to give said Negro Boy Bill one Winter and two Summer suits of clothing--Hat, Blanket or Quilt, two pair of Shoes and Stockings, pay Taxes and Doctor Bills, and return him at Salisbury, on the 1st day of January, 1866

                         his
                     B $ Cranford
                     mark
                     John L. [?]

Judgt. be compromised for $10 & costs rendered Decr. 28 1872

****

We promise to pay Maxwell Chambers admr. of Matthew Troy decd. One Dollar per week for the hire of Negro Girl Patience from this date (and it is understood that the contract is to end at any time by request of either of us the parties contracting) our hands & seals this 2d day of April 1822

Recd. Payt. of D.F. Caldwell[?] Robt. Mot[?]   (Seal)
Max Chambers admr.   }

of M. Troy   } J.E. Todd   (Seal)

Rowan County

Chapter Eighteen

Rowan County

DEED OF GIFT OF SLAVE

Sarah Rodgers To Noah Thompson

Know all men by these presents that I Sarah Rogers of the State of North Carolina and County of Stanley for and in consideration of the natural love and affection which I have and bear unto my daughter Tabbitha Thompson have given and granted and by these presents do give and grant unto my said daughter Tabbitha Thompson for her sole and separate use and benefit all my right title and interest in & to the tract of land on which I now live containing about forty acres also all my stock of cattle and hogs beds & bed clothes household and kitchen furniture and my negro girl Rachael reserving to myself the use and possession of such land and personal property and negro girl Rachael during my natural life to have and to hold said land and other personal property above named to her the said Tabbitha Thompson her heirs Executors and Administrators forever subject however to the reservation of my life interest as aforesaid, In testimony whereof I Sarah Rogers have hereunto set my hand & seal the 21st day of December 1849.

       her
    Sarah X Rogers (Seal)
       mark

Sealed & delivered
in the presence of
James L. Gaines

N. Carolina } May Sessions 1850
Stanly County } Then this deed of gift was proven in open Court by the Oath of James L. Gaines and ordered to be registered
R. Harris Clk.

Rowan County

Registered the 23rd day of May 1850 S.S. Stone Regr.

I certify the within to be a true copy from the registers.
Book No. 2 kept in my office   R. Harris Clk.

Rowan County

Chapter Nineteen

Rowan County

MORTGAGE OF SLAVES

[Top of page torn away]
January 17th 1812 Received of Allen Boughrous two hundred Dollars for which sum I have placed in his hands a Negroe Boy Named Dave to work for the Interest of said Money until paid. Witness my hand and seal
Test   Hugh Carson (Seal)
James C. Gamble
****

Settlement of			
Suit with			
Chs. Jones			
Fran. Locke			
To Chs. Jones	Dr.		
To price of negroe girl Kiss	162.10		
Cr.			
By your Mortgages notes [?] as also Todds	117	3	8
By your receipt at time of Purchase	25	10	
	142	13	8
Novbr. 16th 1811	142	13	8
Ballance due C. Jones	19	16	4
By Cash at this date	10		
	9	16	4

Chapter Twenty

Rowan County

LETTER OF INTENT REGARDING SLAVES

John T. Lomax   Oliver H. Prince
Lomax   Prince
Attorneys at Law,
Demopolis, Ala.
Will practice in Merengo, Green, Sumter and Choctaw Counties

N.V. Fleming Esq.   Ala. Sept. 29. 1859

Dear Sir
    Messrs. Lomax & Prince have shown me your letter of the 29 Aug. [?] to there in regard to my business.
    I want you to Commence proceedings forth with to recover of the admr., my wife's interest in her fathers Estate, and to claim all that by law she is entitled to---
    If the purchase of the negroes by the Admrs. is voidable, I want it set aside, and the negroes resold - They are now worth twice what he gave for them.
    You have all the information about the matter which it is in my power, now, to give you but if you know how I can materially help you by coming out I'll come.
    Dr. Sharpe has for my wife about 400 or $500 which he does not contest & I think more - I authorize to collect by suit or otherwise the amt. in his hands & hold as much as you deem necessary to indemnify you for standing my security for Costs of the suit you propose to bring. I wish you to become my security, if I shall be required to give security.
    You can proceed in any Amt. you think best. I leave that matter to you.

Rowan County

    As soon as you commence suit please inform me thro' Mssrs. Lomax & Prince and if you have to file a Bill in equity, if it does not cost too much, to copy it, send me a copy - & send me an abstract of Adams Answer - See if my wife's adult brothers will join me in the bill - If they will not, then make them defts. & go ahead.
John D. Crudup

J.D. Crudup
Sep. 29   1859
Amt. sent SC

Chapter Twenty-one

Rowan County

COHABITATION RECORDS

Rowan County Septr. 6th March Term 1842

The Grand Jury present Elijah Volentine a free man of colour for intermarrying & cohabitating with Nancy a slave of Sarah Brown, Witness Sarah Brown & Geo. Brown

Also Susan Volentine a free woman of colour for intermarrying and cohabiting with Isaac a man slave of Wm. Thomasons, Witness James Owen & Saml. Martin

Also Polly Hannon alias Casper & _____ Johnston formerly clerk of G.W. Brown for cohabiting together Witness Martin Clutz & wife Peggy Cluts

Also Betsey Wallis a free woman of colour for intermarrying & cohabiting with Angus a negro Slave the property of the late Nancy McCorkle Dec'd, Witness Jacob Correll & John C. Miller

Chapter Twenty-two

Rowan County

BILLS OF SALE

This article of Contract & agreement made and entered into this 9th day of August 1834 by & between H.G. Burton of the county of Halifax & State of North Carolina of the one part and Burton Craige of the County of Rowan & Said State of the other part, witnesseth, that the said H.G. Burton for and in Consideration of the money herein expressed & promised to be paid by said B. Craige, hath & by these presents doth bargain and sell unto the said B. Craige, the following negroes, to wit, Harry (Commonly Called Harry Scroggins) Clarissa, Caesar, Hannah, Ef[?], Mary, Eliza, Sam, Lucinda, & a child name not known, the last of eight Children of Clarrisa; - [?] & his wife Hopey & children, Moses, Wiley, Fil, Lucinda, Jane, Caroline, the last six children of Hopey, John, Jinny, Malissa, Alfred, Susan & a child name not known, the last four children of Jinny, Homer, Mary, peggy, Robin, Hagar, Edmund, Howell, Flora, Diana, Martha, Matthew, Rachel, Fed, Jim, Gustin, Pheby, Willis, a child name not known the last six children of Rachel, Betsey, Harriet, Simon, Jack, Nanny, Elick, which said negroes are to be delivered the said B. Craige on or before the 1st day of Oct. next, or by 15th Sept. if Convenient, at the Gullic[?] pine on Broad River in Rutherford County, but the said H.G. Burton has the privelege of retaining any of the negroes herein specified, and delivering others of equal value, and upon delivery, the said H.G. Burton is to execute to B. Craige, a bill of sale for said negroes, warranting the title and health of said negroes, and the said B. Craige is to pay the said H.G. Burton the sum of four thousand five hundred dollars in eight days from the date, and further sum of four thousand nine hundred dollars, on the 18th of Feb. next, with interest from the 9th of Oct., & the further sum of five thousand dollars on the first of May next, with interest from 1st Oct. next, and the said B. Craige covenants to give satisfactory security for the money herein contracted to

Rowan County

be paid, within eight days from this date, upon which this Contract is to be considered to be in full force and effect. It is understood between the parties, that in case any of said negroes should [Torn] the day of delivery, the loss is to be upon H.G. Burton.
Witness our hand & seals the date above written
H.G. Burton   (Seal)
Burton Craige   (Seal)
R.H. Burton
(Copy)
Salisbury No. Ca. aug 1834
I H.G. Burton thereby acknowledge the receipt of four thousand five hundred dollars from Burton Craige in accordance with the agreement above; and his notes for the two other payments, mentioned in the above agreement which are to be secured by a lien on these negroes
Given under our hands the day and date above written
Burton Craige
H.G. Burton

Those negroes in this schedule are to be conveyed to me with the privelege of on H.G.B.'s part to take any one of them out by replacing another of equal value; the negroes to be delivered by the middle of Sept if Convenient, if not by 1st Oct. next. 1st payment of $4,500 next week, another of equal amt. 1st Feb. next & one of $5,000 by 1st May 1835.

Family No. 1

Names	Ages	Value
Harry (Scrog)	33	450
Clarissa	30	300
Caesar	16	500
Hannah	14	275
Essex[?]	12	275
Mary	10	200
Eliza	8	150
Sam	6	150
Lucinda	4	100
1 Child	4 Ms.	50
	(10)	2,245

Rowan County

Family No. 2	Ages	
Samp[?]	36	350
Hopey	28	300
Moses	10	200
Wiley	9	175
Fil	6	150
Lucinda	5	125
Jane	3	100
Caroline	18 M.	75
	(8)	1,470

Names	Age	Value
John	38	300
Jinny	25	350
Malissa	6	150
Alfred	4	150
Susan	2	100
Child	--	50
	(6)	1,000

Homer	25	500
Mary	29	350
Peggy	3	150
	(3)	1,000

Robin	34	400	2245
Hagar	34	250	1470
Edmund	16	425	1000
	(3)	1,075	1000
		1075	
Howell	40	600	1300
Flora	53	---	8090
Dinah	18		350
Martha	14		350
	(4)		1,300

Names	Age	Value
Matthew	17	500

Rowan County

(His mother) Rachael	34	200
Fed	14	400
Jim	12	300
Gustin	10	250
Feba	15	300
Willis	4	175
1 child	--	50
	(8)	2175
Betsey x died	22	350
Harriet	19	350
	(2)	700
Cimon x	45	375
Jack x	40	375
Nanny (Sickly)	40	200
Elick [?]	19	500
		1075

4500 now	2175
4500 1st Feb next	700
	375
2500 - in 1 p	1075
2500 in 2 or $5,000	4320
with Int.	8090
in 2 p	12,410

****

For & in consideration of the sum of three hundred & sixty five dollars to me in hand paid the payment of which I hereby acknowledge I Allmand Hall of the State of No. Carolina do bargain sell & deliver to John Scott of the County of Rowan & State of N.C. one negro girl named Dinah which negro girl I do warrant to be sound & good to the said John Scott his heirs & assigns forever for which I bind myself my heirs & assigns to Warrant & defend against the Claim or Claims of all Person or Persons Whatever

Rowan County

In Witness I do hereunto set my hand & affix my seal this 13th day of Feby 1823.
Allmand Hall   (Seal)
Witness
Tho. Todd

****

Received of James W. Emmons Fourteen Hundred Dollars in full payment for a Certain Negro girl Named Lucy and her two Children, Named Bill and Jim, Lucy aged about Twenty Seven years, Bill aged about Four years & Jim aged about Two years. The right and title of said Negros I warrant and defend to be clear & free of all Lawfull incumbrance to the Said Jas W. Emmons his heirs & assigns for ever. I also warrant said Negroes to be Sound & Sensible & Slaves for life.
        Given under My hand & Seal This 17th Day of October 1855.
Test   Fountain Emmons   (seal)
C.A. Carlton Jurat   Agent for F A Emmons
State of North Carolina
Iredell County   } October 5th 1857
This Bill of sale Was duly registered
                     J.H. McLaughlin (Sol)
State of North Carolina   } County Court
Iredell County   } Clerk's Office
Oct 3rd 1857
The execution of the within Bill of Sale was duly proved before me by the oath of CA Carlton the subscribing Witness
Let it be registered   MF Freeland Clk

Rowan County

Chapter Twenty-three

Rowan County

PETITION EX PARTE

Hughe's & Randolph's Petition ex Parte

United States of America }   Exhibit A.
State of Louisiana   }

    Be it known that on this thirty first day of the month of March in the year of Our Lord one thousand eight hundred and fifty six, and of the Independence of the United States of America the Eightieth,
    Before me Theodore Guyol a Notary Public duly commissioned and sworn for the Parish and City of New Orleans, State of Louisiana and in the presence of the witnesses hereinafter named and undersigned.
    Personally appeared James W. Clark residing at Salisbury, in the State of North Carolina, who declared that he does by these presents, grant, bargain, sell, assign, convey, transfer and deliver with full warranty as to title only, Unto Emanuel Adler, and Mrs Hannah Rafel his wife, by him duly assisted and authorized, both residing in this City, present, accepting and acknowledging delivery and possession,
    A negro man named John, aged twenty three years, Slave for life and the lawful property of the said Vendor: This sale is made and accepted for and in consideration of the price and sum of Twelve Hundred Dollars, which the said Vendor acknowledges to have received in ready money from the said purchasers, and for which he grants acquittance,
    The said parties hereby dispense with the production of a Certificate from the Recorder of Mortgages for this City, to be annexed to this act as the law requires and exonerates the undersigned Notary from any liability in the premises,
    To have and to hold the said named Slave unto the said purchasers their heirs and assigns forever, And the said Vendor moreover transfers unto the said purchaser all the rights and actions of warranty to

Rowan County

which he himself is or may be entitled against all the former owners and proprietors of the Slave herein conveyed subrogating the said purchasers to the said rights and actions to be by them enjoyed and exercised in the same manner as they might have been by the said Vendor.

Done and passed in my Office at the City of New Orleans on the day, month and year first before written in the presence of William G. Latham and Gustave L. Garden Junr. competent witnesses who have signed with the parties and me Notary, after reading the whole.

Signed   Jas. W. Clark
"   E. Adler M.D.
"   H. Adler
"   W.G. Latham
"   G.L. Gardem Jr.
"   Theo. Guyol Not. Pub.

State of Louisiana   }
City of New Orleans   }

    I, William Shannon a Commissioner of the State of North Carolina in and for the City of New Orleans, State of Louisiana, do hereby certify that the above and foregoing is a true copy of an act of sale on file and of record in the Office of Theodore Guyol a duly appointed and Commissioned Notary Public in said City of New Orleans,

    In faith whereof I hereunto sign my name and affix an impress of my official seal at New Orleans this fifteenth day of January A.D. 1857.
William Shannon   Commr.

Depositions of witnesses taken before me William Shannon a Commissioner of the State of North Carolina, in and for the City of New Orleans, State of Louisiana, on the fifteenth day of January A.D. 1857, at the Office of Messr. Singleton & Clack, Attorneys and Counsellors at Law, in said City

    Emanuel Adler a witness of lawful age, being first duly cautioned and solemnly sworn, to tell the truth, the whole truth and nothing but the truth, deposed as follows,

    I am about Forty five years of age and have resided in the City of New Orleans, State of La. for the last fourteen years and am a practicing physician. -- Witness and his wife purchased jointly a Slave named John

Rowan County

as per copy of title hereto annexed marked Exhibit A. from James W. Clark, stating that he was of Salisbury, North Carolina, which said Slave was purchased on 31st day of March 1856 as will apear by said act of Sale above referred to; - I did not purchase any other Slave from said Clark than the boy John herein before referred to, and I bought this Slave through James White, that is out of his Slave yard in this City. During the Month of December last I placed said Slave in the yard of Mr. White for the purpose of being sold, and which said Slave was lately sequestered at the suit of Hughes & Randolph vs deponent, in this City, and in which suit the said Hughes & Randolph claim to be the Owners of said Slave. Further this Deponent saith not and signs his name.
E. Adler M.D.

Then also appeared James White who being in like manner by me Commissioner duly cautioned and solemnly sworn to tell the truth, the whole truth and nothing but the truth, deposed and said as follows, the said White being of Lawful age,

   I reside in Greenville Parish of Jefferson in this State, And do business in the City of New Orleans, where I have done business for the last five years, -- I am about Fifty four years old - During the year 1856 I kept a Slave yard in the City of New Orleans, and the Slave John referred to the annexed sale marked Exhibit A. and also referred to by the previous deponent was sold out of my yard to Dr. E. Adler on the 31st day of March 1856, - This same boy was placed in my yard for sale by Dr. E. Adler and was there during the Month of December last, and while he was in my yard in December last, Hughes & Randolph or two gentlemen calling themselves Hughes & Randolph came into my yard to look at some Slaves, and when the Slaves were all called up for them to examine, they immediately recognised the boy John above referred to as their Slave Tom which had run away from Mr. Randolph during the year 1854, from South Carolina, and the boy stated that Mr. Randolph was his master, that he had run away from Mr. Randolph in South Carolina, and went to North Carolina, where he was arrested and put in gaol, and there sold to James W. Clark and Wife - Hughes & Randolph brought a young Medical student to my yard by the name of Wilson, who recognised the boy the moment he seen him as the boy that had ran away from Mr. Randolph. This boy was Sequestered by Hughes & Randolph and taken out of my possession last Month.

Rowan County

Further deponent saith not and signs his name.
James White

  Also appeared James D. Wilson of lawful age who being by me Commissioner duly cautioned and solemnly sworn to tell the truth, the whole truth and nothing but the truth, deposed and said as follows,
  I have resided in Winnsboro, South Carolina up to the first of November last, and at present attending the Medical Lectures in New Orleans - I am twenty eight years old - I know Hughes & Randolph, and was with them in the Slave yard of James White in this City sometime last Month, say between the 20th and the last of the Month, and while there the said Hughes & Randolph discovered a Slave named Tom which belonged to them, and I know the said Slave to be their property in Winnsboro, South Carolina, I saw the boy there in 1854 and know that he ran away from Hughes & Randolph from Winnsboro, South Carolina, and never seen or heard of him from that time until the day I seen him in the yard of Mr. White as above stated - Hughes & Randolph seized the boy and I was present when the Sheriff took possession of him at the Slave yard of said White in December last - I am satisfied that this is the same boy that ran away from Hughes & Randolph in 1854, and the boy knew me when I went into the yard - The said boy was hired by Hughes & Randolph to Benjamin Ravenal of Winnsboro, S.C., when he ran away, the said Ravenal kept a Hotel in Winnsboro, where I boarded and where I became acquainted with the boy and knew him well from the fact of my boarding at the Hotel where he was employed - I knew said boy by the name of Tom, but I have heard that the boy says his name is John Thomas.
Further deponent saith not and signs his name.
J.D. Wilson

State of Louisiana   }
City of New Orleans   }

  I, William Shannon a Commissioner of the State of North Carolina, in and for the said City of New Orleans, State of Louisiana, duly commissioned and qualified: Do hereby Certify that, Emanuel Adler; James White, and James D. Wilson were by me severally Sworn to testify the truth, the whole truth and nothing but the truth, that the forgoing depositions were by me reduced to writing, sworn to and subscribed by

Rowan County

said witnesses in my presence, and taken at the time and place set forth in the caption hereof,
 In faith whereof I hereunto sign my name and affix an impress of my Official seal at the City of New Orleans this Fifteenth day of January in the year One thousand eight hundred and fifty seven.

(Seal)   William Shannon

For the Taking testimony and copy of act 10 00/100 paid by Messr. Singleton & Clack

State of North Carolina } Court of Pleas
          } & Quarter Sessions
Rowan County   } AD 1857 Febuary Term

To the worshipful Justices of the Court aforesaid. The petition of Jas. H. Hughes & E.S. Randolph: Your Petitioners Humbly praying represent unto your worships that they are the former true & lawful owners of a certain negroe Slave named Tom alias John or John Thomas that they purchased the said slave of J.S. Riggs from the residents of the City of [?] in the year of our Lord one thousand eight hundred and fifty four they brought the said Slave to the town of Winnsboro State of S.C. & that they hired him to one Benjamin Ravenal the keeper of a hotel that said negroe slave ran away from them on the 20th November 1854 & has heard nothing further from him till within the month of November 1856 they saw said slave in the [?] yard of Jas. White City of N. Orleans that they have been informed & believe that this said negroe was arrested in this County by some of your citizens & confined in the Jail of the County wherein he remained for the space of twelve months and after the expiration of the said term your worshipful body made an order for the sale of said negroe when after due advertisement the said negroe was duly sold, & purchased by Jas. W. Clark for the sum of seven hundred & ten dollars and that the sum of $430.38 was duly paid tp your county trustee that the residue to wit $279.62 was retained on account of expenses &c duly accrued in said sale & jail fee &c, that the said Clark sold the said negroe John to Dr. E. Adler of the City of New Orleans & the said Negroe was placed in the jail in yard of the said Jas. White again for sale by said Dr. E. Adler & that it was at this place your petitioners first discovered

Rowan County

him that they have by a writ of Sequestration taken the said boy into their possession but as they are adverse & admit the proceedings in the premise here are all duly [?] & in favor of law & that they can only recover the sum of four hundred & thirty dol 38 the amt paid by your Shff Caleb Klutts to your [?] Trustee Thomas Maxwell to wit the sum of $434. 38/100 as aforesaid, your Petitioners therefore pray that upon their proofs being filed & otherwise laid before you [?] this petition that you will make an order directing your County Trustee to pay over to your Petitioners or their true & lawful Attorney H.L. Roberts whose power they herewith present as a part of this petition the remainder of the proceeds of the sale of the said negroe slave John to wit $436.38 cts and your petitioners as in duty bound will ever pray &c--
     R.D. Gold[?] Atty for
      Petitioners
  James H. Hughes & Edward S. Randolph

Hughes & Randolph
Petition ex parte
To Nxt Court
Feby Term 1857 } Court of Pleas
       } & Quarter Sessions

  Upon hearing of the petition & the proofs filed together with the testimony of Jas Clark the court is satisfied that the rightful ownership in said Slave was in the Petitioners the [?] order according to act of Assembly in such case made & provided that the county Trustie pay to the petitioners or their Attorney H.L. Robert the sum of four hundred & Ninety dollars & 38 cts.

Rowan County

Chapter Twenty-four

Rowan County

RUNAWAYS

State of North Carolina } To the Keeper of the Jail of
Rowan County } said County - I herewith send you the Body of a Runaway Negroe taken up by Michael Smith the said Negroe says his name is James Cleton and also says he belongs to a Certain Jesse Robinson living in Lincoln County N. Carolina the said Negroe appears to be fifty years of age and about 5 feet ten Inches high Grey head &C which said Negroe you will safely Keep untill duly Discharged According to Law.
Given under my hand and Seal this 25 July 1815
D. Woodson J.P. (Seal)

State of N. Carolina } This day Personally Came before
Rowan County } me David Woodson One of the Justices of the peace for said County Jesse Robinson of Lincoln County in the State above Mentioned and made Oath that a Certain Negroe Slave by the name of Jim Committed as a Runaway now in the Jail of Rowan County is the Property of the said Robinson.
Sworn to and Subscribed to this 2nd day of August 1815
D. Woodson J.P.   Jesse Robinson

****

Cartersville 20 July 1815

D. Sir

Your letters respecting a negroe confined in your Jail have been rec'd their is foure William Millers in this part of the Country neither of

Rowan County

which as far as I can learn have negroes out. The slaves and names mentioned all agree with the negroes Statement and from that Circumstance he is acquainted in this neighborhood - but he has not given you a correct Statement who is his real master - Your several Letters have been made as public as possible in the neighborhood - by getting him to give you a history where he was born & sold & the names of some other owners perhaps he can be traced to the wright owner.

      Yrs John G. Daniel
      Frm
      J.G. Daniel

Cartersville
20 July 1815
Mr. Roberts Nanny
Jailor Salisbury
North Carolina

****

State of North Carolina }
Rowan County   }

  To the Sheriff or Keeper of the Jail of the County aforesaid - I herewith Send you the body of a Negroe Jacob who was this day brought before me by Jacob Miller who Saith on Oath that he believes Said Negroe Jacob to be a Runaway and the property of John B. Moss of Randolph County state Aforesaid - These are therefore to command you to receive into your Custody the Said Negroe Jacob and him Safely Keep in the Common Jail until he shall be there discharged by due Course of Law given under my hand and Seal at Salisbury 7th day of February 1815
J. Murphy JP (Seal)

****

State of North Carolina } To the Sheriff or Jailor of
Rowan County   } said County

Rowan County

You are hereby commanded to receive a Black Boy by the name of Joe a Runaway which was taken up by William B Ward of said county and keep in your jail until he is released by his master or someone acting for him.
Given under my hand this 17th day of May 1818
N Grider J.P.
****

State of N. Carolina   }
Rowan County   } To the Jailer of said

County. I herewith send you the body of a Runaway Negroe who says her name is Sally and that she belongs to a certain Mr. Buddy Wheeler of Lincoln County in this State. You will therefore receive sd. Negroe Wench into your custody and her keep until duly proven according to Law.
Given Under my hand & seal this 16th day May 1816
N Grider (Seal)

State of North Carolina } This day personally appeared
Rowan County   }

W. Wheeler before me one of the justices for said county and made oath that the negroe Woman that is in the said jail by the name of Sally is his property.
Sworn to & subscribed the 18th of May 1816
N Grider J.P.   Buddy W. Wheeler

****

No. Carolina
Rowan County

    This day John P. Moore So. Carolina Lancaster district personally appeared before me one of the Justices of the peace in and for the County of Rowan and made oath that the negro fellow now confined in the Salisbury Jail by the name of Joe is the property of his Father John Moore Living in So. Carolina & Lancaster district - and the said John P. Moore is legally authorised to take him away.
Sworn to & subscribed before me this 31st May 1818

Rowan County

S L Ferrand JP   John P. Moore

Probate of John Moore's Negroe

****

State of N. Carolina   } To the Jailer of said
Rowan County   } County I herewith send
you the body of a Runaway Negroe Who says his Name is Peter and that he belongs to a Mr. Thomas McClain of Lincoln County the said Negroe appears to be between 25 & 30 yeares of age dark Complexion you will therefore Keep said fellow untill duly Proven according to Law.

Given Under my hand and Seal this 12th May 1816
A. Woodson J.P. (Seal)

State of North Carolina   } Richard D. Spaight McClain
Rowan County   } this day personally Appeared

before me Lewis Beard a Justice of the peace for said County and made Oath that the negro Peter as named & Described in the within now in the public Jail for Rowan County is the property of Thomas McClain of Lincoln County North Carolina.

Sworn & Subscribed to before me May 25th 1816
Richard D.S. MacLean
Ls. Beard J.P.

Peter Comt.
12th May 1816

Taking up $.75
12 Miles

****

To the jailer of Rowan County - you will take into your custody a Mulatto boy supposed to be a runaway taken up by Michael Smith and him safely Keep till the proper owner calls for him.

Rowan County

Salisbury 21st Septr. 1818   S L Ferrand JP

****

Rowan County this day personally appeared James Harrison and made oath in due form of law the Molatta fellow by the name of George now in Jail in Salisbury is the property of Doct. Thos. Brice and that he the said Harrison liveth in Fairfield district South Carolina.
Sworn & subscribed this 8th of Nov. 1818
James Harrison
N Grider J.P.

This is to Certify that I James Harrison of South Carolina, Fairfield District, have this day Received of Roberts Nanny Jailor of Rowan County a Mulatto boy by the name of George, the property of Doct. Thomas Briggs which said boy I am accountable for to his master or to the Jailor aforesaid, & the Award if any, all which I promise to cause to be paid unto the said Roberts Nanny Jailer as aforesaid when I can ascertain what the Amount of the Award may be.

Witness my hand this 8 day of November A. Dom. 1818

James Harrison

****

David Craige of the County of Rowan State of North Carolina has taken up A Negroe man by the name of Moses supposed to be A runaway. These are therefore to Command as Sheriff of the County aforesaid to take the body of the said negro and him safely keep Untill legally discharged.

Moses A. Locke JP

Wheeler
Near Charlston &C.

****

Rowan County

State of North Carolina } To the Sheriff or the
Rowan County } Keeper of the Jail for

the County of Rowan, you are hereby Commanded to receive the body of the negro boy Bill or Jack, taken up by Willa. H. Herak[**Horah?**] as a runaway and him Safely keep untill he is legally discharged.

Given under my hand this 10th day of July A.D. 1818
Moses A. Locke J.P.

****

To the Jailor of Rowan County
Greeting
You are hereby commanded to receive into your Custody the Negroe Girl Lydia as a Runaway & Keep here untill further order from me or some other Justice of the Peace this 1st Septr. 1818.
Moses A. Locke J.P.

****

Rowan County N. Carolina
To the Jailer of said County
    You are hereby commanded to take into your care the bodies of two negroes named Charles & Tom taken up by Dr. Scott as runaways & them safely keep untill released according to Law.
Novbr. 11th 1818   Moses A. Locke J.P.

Comt. & Releasing 2 Negroes	$1.20
Apprehending }	
Mileage }	2.10
15 day Subsistence	9.00
	$12.30

Rowan County This day James W. Speede came before me and made oath in due form of law that Tom belongs to Mr. Prescott[?] and Charles to the said Speed and they liveth both in South Carolina Mr. Prescott in Columbia & Speed in Abeville.
Sworn & subscribed this 25th of Nov. 1818

Rowan County

N Grider JP James W. Speed
Commitment of Charles & Tom
Nov. 11 1818
$25. each

****

North Carolina } To the keeper of the Goal of
Rowan County } Said County

    I herewith Sind you the body of a Negro fellow brought before me this day, who says he belongs to a Mr. William Miller of Cumberland County Va. that his name is Billy, after a strict examination he appeared confused and told many contradictory stories, -- you will therefore receive the Said Negro into your Goal and custody untill discharged by due court of Law Given under my hand and Seal the 14th day of August 1819
B [?]wood JP (S)

****

State of North Carolina } To the Sheriff or Jailor
Rowan County   } of Salisbury

    You are hereby commanded to receive in your Custody a negro boy by the name of Primus the property of Jonathan Hartsele the said negro was runaway and taken up by Eliza Morgan and Brian Fry. Given under my hand this 27th of November 1815.
N Grider JP (Seal)

Rowan County
    I do hereby Certify that the negro man by the name of Primus committed on the 27th of Nov. 1815 is Hartseles property and that he has sworn to the same.
    I do hereby command you that you deliver the same negro to Hartsele after paying charges &C.
Given under my hand & seal this 2d of December 1815.
Jonathan Hartsle

Rowan County

State of North Carolina } To Mr. Robt [Faded] Jailer
Rowan County   } of Rowan County at Salisbury

please to pay Over my fees for conveying a Certain Negro Man named Primus which negro was Deliver'd to your Jail in the first part of November Last pay same to Lewis Iyer and this my order shall be your Receipt for the same.
January 3rd 1816
Bryant Fry

****

State of North Carolina } The Jailor of the County of
Rowan County   } Rowan will receive into
his Custody the Body of a Negro or Molatta Girl named Ann a Runaway, and her Safely keep untill hir Owner may apply for hir & prove hir According to Law, she being brot before me as taken up by Mr. Daniel Bailey - Given under my hand this 4th day of April 1815.
D. [?] J.P.
Negro Anns
Committ

State of North Carolina}
Rowan County,

This day Peter Parker came before me Chas. Anderson One of the Justices of the peace for the County aforesaid And made Oath that a Certain Negro Woman; of the Name of Ann is confined in the Jail in the County aforesaid is the present property of him the said Peter Parker Sworn to & Subd. this 11th day of April 1815.

Test Cha. Anderson JP   Peter Parker

****

State of N. Carolina   }
Rowan County   }

Rowan County

This day Andrew Murray made oath before me that a Mulatto girl Priscilla now in jail the property of Mrs Barnwell of Beaufort S. Carolina.

Andrew Murray
HZ[?] Gatshele[?]
June 20th 1815
[Editor's Note: the name "Catharine" is written on back of document]

State of N. Carolina }
Rowan County } To the Jailor of said County

You are hereby requested to retaon priscilla a Molatto Girl the property of Mrs Ann Barnwell until call'd for June 21 1815
Andrew Murray

****

State of N. Carolina } To the public Jailor
Rowan County } of said County

You are hereby commanded to receive a Black boy by the name of Peter the property of Alex Lany who was a run away and taken up by Wm Kelly and then keep in close confinement until the property is proved as the law directs.
Given under my hand & seal
this 15th of Oct 1817
N Grider JP (Seal)

****

State of Nort Carolina } To the Keeper of the
Rowan County } common Jail of Said County

I herewith Send you the body of a Negro man who was this day brot before me by Henry Cline. Said Negro is of Dark Complexion and appears to be about twenty years of age. Says his name is Tom and that he is Runaway that he belongs to William Sanford of Putnam County, Georgia State. These are therefore to command you to Receive the said

Rowan County

negro Tom into your custody and him safely keep until he is discharged by [?] of Law given under my hand and Seal at Salisbury 18th day of September 1818.
J Murphey JP (Seal)
Taking up $.75 11-22 miles
Ferriage & 1 Guard

****

State of North Carolina } The Jailor In Salisbury
Rowan County   } for the County afsd

You are hereby Commanded to Receive In to your Custody The body of Harry a Negro Man As he confesses that he has Left his Master Livery In Georgia and says he was taken up And Put in Jaol at Concord And broke the Jaol Last Friday Night And him Safly keep In your Custody Untill he be taken aught of Jaol According to Law given under my hand And Seal this 10th of Febuary 1818
Willson JP
27 Miles, 1 guard, Ferriage
Reward $5   Harry or Henry
State of North Carolina
Rowan County

  Know all men by these presents that I George Kluttz & Rynhold Sooter of the County of Cabarrus & state aforesaid are held and firmly bound unto Roberts Nanny Jailor of the Town of Salisbury & State foresaid in the sum of Five hundred pounds for the delivery of a Negro Boy of the name of Harry now in Salisbury Jail which said negro broke Jail in Concord Cabarrus County which payment well and truly to be made unto the said Roberts Nanny we and each of us bind ourselves our heirs & executors and administrators faithfully in the performance of the above obligation

  The Condition of the above obligation is such that if the above bounded George Kluttz & Reynold Sooter doth keep the said Roberts Nanny undemnified for the delivery of Said Negro this obligation to remaine void otherwise to remain in full force & virtue. Witness whereof we have hereunto set our hands and affixed our Seals this 16th day of February 1818.

Rowan County

Witness	Geo. Kluttz	(Seal)
Michael Brown	Rinehold Suter	(Seal)

Committment of Harry	Taking Up	.75
Taken from Salisbury	Ferryage	.31 1/4
Jail by G. Kluttz	54 miles	5.40
Jailer at Concord	Guard	.40
	Reward	5.00
		11.86
		.60
		1.80
		$14.26

State of No. Carolina }
Rowan County } This day personally
appeared William Sandford and made oath in due form of law, that Henry
(a negroe) man 21 years old now in jail in Salisbury is the property of
Jesse and William Sandford and liveth in the State of Georgia
Sworn & Subscribed the 28th of October 1818
N. Grider J.P.　　　Wm. Sandford

****

State of North Carolina }
Rowan County } To the Jaler of Said
County at Salisbury　You are hereby Commanded to Receive in your
Custody and Safe Keep in your Jaol a Negro man by the Name of Francis
He Says he Belongs to James Hitchcock In South Carolina Pendleton
District the Said Negroe Is Charged With Stealing and Carrying away a
Looking Glass from Mr. Hayes, the Said Negro Man you are to Keep in
Jaol Untill He is taken aught of Your custody According to Law. Given
Under my hand And Seal this 26th of November 1818.
Willson　JP

State of North Carolina, Rowan Cty
　　　　This day personally appeared Joseph Dickey and made oath that
the Negro as committed per the within is his right and property. Sworn to
before me this 30th Nov. 1818 B. Howard & Joseph Dickey
Conv. of Francis

Rowan County

****

State of No Carolina }
Rowan County } This day personally

appeared before me Joseph Pruitt and made oath in due form of Law that a negro man by the name of John now lodged in Jail at Salisbury is the property of Robert W. Pruitt in Franklin County Georgia, and that I was authorised to recover Said Negroe
Sworn & Subscribed before me at Salisbury No. C.
N[?] Grider J.P.

****

This will Certify that Mrs. Mary Scruggs has Occasion to Travail to [Torn] North Carolina in Pursuit of some Negros taken from her first Husband Mr. Hillary Brett During the British Usurpation and Signifying her Business to us We hope that she may be favoured with every Encouragement Necessary for the Recovery of Said Negroes As we think her very Worthy and on no Bad Intention [Torn] Our hands This 21st day of February 1785
[?] Lunday J.P.
[Torn] Howell J.P.
[Torn] Howell [Torn]
[Torn] Hudson J.P.

****

State of No. Carolina } To the Sheriff or
Rowan County } Jailor of said County
You are hereby commanded to receive a Negro woman by the name of Fillis a run away which was taken up by Albert Peebles of said County
Given under my hand & seal this 12th of April 1818
N Grider (Seal)

****

Rowan County

Nanny
    The negro that I committed by Claybrooks you will not discharge until I see you.
    Her Master with several other negroes went round town or the Back street evidently to avoid the fare. Her Masters Companion, offered to Claybrook a $5 counterfeit Newark note as the reward for taking her up. For these reasond I committed her to jail in order if practicable to secure the case as he has 10 or 15 and see that he pays good money in the morning for fees &c.
              Yours &c
Moses A. Locke [?]
1st September 1818

****

State of North Carolina }
Rowan County }

    To the Jailor of Rowan County Greeting You are hereby Commanded to receive into your Custody the Negroe Man Jack a Runaway taken up by George Willis, and him Safely Keep until legally discharged.
    Given under my hand and sealthis 8th day September A. Dom. 1818
Taking up   .75   AM Srote JP (Seal)
Ferriage
9= 18 miles}
& 2 Guards }
State of North Carolina }
Rowan County   } Andrew Springs personally appeared before me and made Oath that the name of the negro mentioned on the Other Side [Editor's Note: Other side of document] of the paper is rightly Peter that he is Owner of the Said Slave Peter, that he is right and property   Sworn and subscribed at Salisbury 29th September 1818
Andrew Springs
J Murphey JP
Negro Jack

Rowan County

Committment by Geo. Willis

****

Commitment   }
    of   } Roberts Nanny Jailor
Letty a negroe   }
    girl   }
Letty   in Jail
Viney[?]
[Torn]
Molly
Betsey
Milly
Kitty
Nancy
Charity
Charles
Jerry
Gregory
Stephen   14
John   5
                           70
Reason Bealle was the   30 reward
principal person concerned $100

Mr. Nanny
      Mrs. Watson is paid & satisfied for her taking up of the negro girl Letty. You have therefore only to see as to the state fare (is such exists) your fees, and discharge her as the law directs.
Yours &c
Moses A. Locke

Chapter Twenty-five

Rowan County

TRANSPORTING SLAVES

State of North Carolina }
Rowan County }
    This day Nathaniel Erving, of Augusta Georgia personally appeared before me one of the Justices of the peace in and for the County of Rowan and made oath that the negroes he has in possession, he purchased for his own use. Sworn to & Subscribed before me the 2d Septe 1818 at Salisbury
Nathaniel Erving
FL Ferrand[?] JP

Index and Table of Cases

Table of Cases

CASES

Absalom Taylor Vs. John Hanglighter [1786]
Civil Action
Rowan County, NC ------131

Anne R. Robertson Vs. John Wright [1802]
Civil Action
Rowan County, NC ------160

Burton Craige Vs. R.H. & H.G. Burton [1834]
Civil Action
Rowan County, NC ------134

Elizabeth Helton Vs. Josephus Helton [1823]
Civil Action
Rowan County, NC ------139

Ezra Allemong Vs. Elizabeth Parker [1830]
Civil Action
Rowan County, NC ------141

Harris Vs. Nicholas Drury [1798]
Civil Action
Rowan County, NC ------121

Isaac (Free Man) Vs. Benjamin Abbit [1783]
Indebtedness
Rowan County, NC ------132

J.T. Avery Vs. J.B. Allison [1857]
Civil Action
Burke County, NC ------94

Index and Table of Cases

James Bowman Vs. Wade Hampton [1782]
 Indebtedness
 Rowan County, NC --133

James Cowan Vs. Alexander Silliman [1818]
 Civil Action
 Rowan County, NC --169

John Cook Vs. Solomon Hall [1810]
 Plea of Debt
 Rowan County, NC --157

M.F. Nesbitt Vs. Isaac A. Witherspoon [1860]
 Civil Action
 Rowan County, NC --177

Margaret West Vs. Joseph West [1844]
 Civil Action
 Rowan County, NC --146

Myer Myers Vs. M.L. Bost [1853]
 Civil Action
 Rowan County, NC --192

Patsey Williams Vs. Wm. & Nancy Presswood [1833]
 Civil Action
 Burke County, NC -- 87

R.J. West Vs. J.W. Hall [1870]
 Civil Action
 Rowan County, NC --159

Samuel Edwards Vs. Meshack Gentry [1818]
 Civil Action
 Rowan County, NC --162

Index and Table of Cases

State Vs. Bett (a Slave) [1818]
Attempted Poisoning
Rowan County, NC ---154

State Vs. Abel (a Slave) [1837]
Burning a Dwelling House
Lincoln County, NC --- 14

State Vs. Abner (A Slave) [1840]
Murdering his Master
Lincoln County, NC ---3

State Vs. Abraham (A Slave) [1837]
Crime Not Given
Lincoln County, NC --- 13

State Vs. Barbara Treffinger [1849]
Trading With a Slave
Rowan County, NC ---155

State Vs. Ben & Edmund [1835]
Felony (Stealing)
Lincoln County, NC ---8

State Vs. Bett (a Slave) [1818]
Felony, Stealing
Rowan County, NC ---152

State Vs. Bob (a Slave) [1827]
Burning a Barn
Lincoln County, NC --- 23

State Vs. Catherine Barringer [1815]
Murdering a Slave
Lincoln County, NC --- 21

Index and Table of Cases

State Vs. Charles (a Slave) [1831]
  Murder
  Rowan County, NC --125

State Vs. Daniel (a Slave) [1820]
  Horse Stealing, Felony
  Lincoln County, NC ---43

State Vs. David (a Slave) [1845]
  Assault & Battery
  Burke County, NC --105

State Vs. Dick (a Slave) [1839]
  Murder of Slave Named Adam
  Lincoln County, NC ---30

State Vs. Edward Mobley [1822]
  Liable Suit
  Lincoln County, NC ---32

State Vs. Isaac & Cyrus (Slaves) [1828]
  Murder of Joshua M. Irby
  Lincoln County, NC ---50

State Vs. Jacob (a Slave) [1812]
  Misdemeanor
  Rowan County, NC --130

State Vs. Jesse (a Slave) [1824]
  Attempted Rape & Murder
  Rowan County, NC --137

State Vs. Jesse Valintine [1842]
  Cohabiting With a Slave
  Rowan County, NC --144

Index and Table of Cases

State Vs. Joel Shaver [1832]
Trading With a Negroe
Rowan County, NC ---140

State Vs. John Collins [1817]
Stealing Corn
Lincoln County, NC ---25

State Vs. Joseph Wear [1825]
Accessory to Burglary
Lincoln County, NC ---34

State Vs. Mack Rankin (Free Negroe) [1858]
Misdemeanor, Carrying a Pistol
Rowan County, NC ---164

State Vs. Mary Myers [1850]
Trading With a Slave
Rowan County, NC ---156

State Vs. Morgan Jones [1826]
Stealing a Slave, Felony
Lincoln County, NC ---39

State Vs. Negro Man [1832]
Crime Not Given
Lincoln County, NC ---42

State Vs. Peter Best [1812]
Grand Larceny, Stealing Goods
Lincoln County, NC ---26

State Vs. Ramsour & 0thers [1827]
Assault & Battery on a Slave
Lincoln County, NC ---29

Index and Table of Cases

State Vs. Reuben Throgmorton [1851
Trading With Slaves
Burke County, NC --119

State Vs. Thomas Kelly (Freedman) [1866]
Possessing a Gun
Rowan County, NC ---148

State Vs. Tom Bailey (a Negroe) [1866]
Felony, Stealing
Rowan County, NC ---158

State Vs. Tony & Jacob (Slaves) [1812]
Conspiring an Insurrection
Rowan County, NC ---150

State Vs. William Hager & Others [1835]
Assault & Battery on a Slave
Lincoln County, NC -- 19

State Vs. William Shavers [1845]
Stabbing a Negroe Slave
Rowan County, NC ---146

State Vs. William Swink [1844]
Trading With a Negroe
Rowan County, NC ---141

State Vs. Wilson Sides [1844]
Cohabiting With a Slave
Rowan County, NC ---145

State Vs. Young Harris [1868]
Murder
Rowan County, NC ---166

Index and Table of Cases

Thomas Haggins Vs. John Brevard, Jr. [1787]
Civil Action
Rowan County, NC ---129

William B. Atrell Vs. David H. Patterson [1855]
Civil Action
Rowan County, NC ---142

William R. Darby & Others Vs. Joseph W. Hall [1859]
Civil Action
Rowan County, NC ---174

Wm. F. McKisson Vs. Wm. F. Gibbs [1869]
Civil Action
Burke County, NC ---101

Index and Table of Cases

Index

A

Abbets
  Benja., 132
Abbett
  Benja., 132
Abbit
  Benjamin, 132
Abbitt
  Benjamine, 133
Abbott
  Benjamine, 132
Abernathy
  David, 76
  Dr., 72
  E., 71
  Ezekiel, 71
  Franklin, 62
  Frederick, 12
  Green D, 69
  Green S., 71
  James, 45
  Jas., 45
  John, 61
  John B., 62
  John D, 62
  M N, 12
  M W, 63
  Miles W, 65
  Moses, 12
  Moses D, 11, 12
  Robt Senr, 10
  Turner, 10, 13
  William, 44, 45, 46, 47
  Wm, 47, 49
  Wm., 48
  Wm. N., 46
Abernathys
  Capt., 63
Abernaty
  Dr Jas, 71
Abett
  Benja., 132
Acott
  Wm A, 63
Adams
  James L., 52
  Mr. James L., 51
Adler
  Dr. E., 225, 227
  E., M.D., 224
  E., M.D., 225
  Emanuel, 223, 224, 226
  H., 224
AL County
  Choctaw, 213
  Green, 213
  Merengo, 213
  Sumter, 213
AL Towns
  Demopolis, 213
Alexander
  J.S., 31
  James T., 5
  John, 72
  John Y., 72
  N.W., 87
  Nat. W., 89
  Neman, 75
  R.W., 141
  William J., 21
  Wm J, 11
  Wm. J., 87, 89
  All[?]
  Ezra, 152
Allbrook
  William, 131
Allemong
  Ezra, 141, 142
Allen
  Burrell, 18
  Burwell, 18
Allison
  J B, 95, 97, 98, 99
  J.B., 94, 95
  John B, 100
Allon
  James, 67
Anderson
  Cha., 236
  Chas., 236
  Isaac, 65, 67
Andrews
  John, 137
Annett
  Saml., 161
  Samuel, 162
Armsworthy
  John, 152
Arney

Index and Table of Cases

Christian, 29, 30
Atrell
  William B., 142, 143
  Wm. B., 142
Attorneys
  Caldwell & Mitchell, 93
  Caldwell & Tate, 102
  Craige & Caldwell, 1
  G Folk, 101, 102, 105
  G.A. Folk, 105
  H.L. Roberts, 228
  Kerr & Fleming, 181
  Lomax & Prince, 213, 214
  Mitchell & Caldwell, 94
  Singleton & Clack, 224, 227
Austin
  E.A., 141, 146
Avery
  Clark M, 110
  j T, 98
  J T, 95, 96, 97, 98, 99, 100

B

Bagley
  W.H., 160
Bailey
  Mr. Daniel, 236
  Tom, 159
  Tom (a negro), 158

Baker
  Philip, 14
Baley
  John, 134
  Tom, 159
Ballew
  P., 90
Barber
  Mr., 126
  Thos., 148
  Will, 128
Barnhardt
  Jas. C., 165
Barnwell
  Mrs, 237
  Mrs Ann, 237
Barret
  Nathaniel, 58
Barringer
  Catherine, 21, 22, 23
  David, 157
Bealle
  Reason, 242
Beard
  Alexander, 121, 122
  Alexander, Esquire, 122, 123
  Alexr., 123, 125
  John, 130
  Lewis, 130, 152, 232
  Ls., 232
Bell
  James, 170, 171
  John, 52, 53
Bell[?]
  Moses, 201
Berdges
  Elisha, 75
Berry

B.A., 103, 105
Berryman
  G., 140
  Gilson, 140
  J., 139
Best
  Boston, 75
  Peter, 26, 27, 28, 29
Betz
  George, 152
Birch
  Richard, 76
Birchett
  T.F., 89
Bird
  Ann, 141
Bitz
  George, 130
Bivings
  Jas, 37
  Jas., 34
Bivins
  James, 23
Blackburn
  J.J., 69
  Joseph R, 70
  Maj Jo R, 69
  Robert Esqr, 70
  Wm., 69
Blair
  James, 83, 84
Boman
  James, 133, 134
Boon
  Jn., 91
  John, 90
Bost
  M.L., 192, 193
  Mr. M.L., 193
Boughrous
  Allen, 211
Bowman

Index and Table of Cases

Ann, 80, 81, 82
Anne, 81, 82
Elizabeth, 80, 81
Groves, 81, 82
James, 133
Sherwood, 80, 81, 82
Boyce
Isaac, 107, 113
Isaac (a free man of color), 111
Isaac (Free Negroe), 113
Isaac (free person of color), 107
John, 107, 113
John (free negro), 111
John (Free Negroe), 113
John (free person of color), 107
Boyd
Edward, 59, 60
Edwd., 59
Boyden
Nathaniel, 176
Bradshaw
D.R., 144
David R., 142
Brett
Mr. Hillary, 240
Brevard
Jno jr., 129
John jr., 129
John junior, 129
John junr., 129
Brice
Dr.Thos., 233
Bridges
Alfed, 67
Alpherd, 65
Elish, 67

Elisha, 65
James, 65, 67
Briggs
Doct. Thomas, 233
Brittain
H, 49
Brough
Doctor, 162
John, 160, 161, 162
Brown
G.W., 215
Geo., 215
Jeremiah, 130
John, 84
John Junr., 85
Michael, 141, 239
sarah, 215
Sarah, 215
W, 98
Walter, 96, 100
Brutons
Squire, 164
Bryant
James, 71
Buff
Henry, 72
Buford
William, 131
Burton
H W, 71
H.A., 134
H.G., 135, 136, 217, 218
H.G. & Robert H., 136
H.W., 71
Hutchins G., 134, 135
R H, 19
R.A., 135

R.H., 20, 30, 48, 75, 134, 135, 136, 218
R.M., 198
Robert H, 21, 31
Robert H., 21, 31, 135, 136
Robert M., 192, 193, 198
Robt H, 31
Robt. H., 58, 134
Butler
Hall, 119
Butts
Daniel, 72
Danl, 72
Bynum
J.S., 68

C

Caldwell
D.F., 207
Dav., 133, 134
F.H., 177, 180
Julias A., 199
Richard A., 199
Saml., 164
W.P., 186
Callaway
William, 203
Callicot
Pascall, 199
Campbell
Milos, 70
Campble
M., 69
Canseller
Mr, 37
Cansler
H, 53, 54
H., 24, 51, 52, 57

Index and Table of Cases

Henry, 37, 38
Philip, 52
Canup
  Martin, 15
  Mr, 15
Carlton
  C.A., 180, 221
  CA, 221
Carpenter
  David, 75
  Lawson, 76
  Nicholas, 65
  Sol., 69
  Solomon, 70
Carson
  Hugh, 211
Casper
  Henry B., 199
  John, 199
Chaffin
  Pleasant, 205
  Thomas, 199
Chambers
  Max, 125, 207
  Maxwell, 207
  W., 146
  William, 146
Chandler
  Henry, 160, 161
Christian
  Fady, 121, 122, 123, 125
Clark
  James (Capt.), 199
  James W., 223, 225
  Jas., 228
  Jas. W., 224, 227
  W.R., 6
Clarke
  James, 199
Claunch

Miss Polley, 150
Cline
  Henry, 17, 237
  James, 128
Cluts
  Peggy, 215
Clutz
  Martin, 215
Cobb
  Clizby, 52
Cody
  B., 199
Coffey
  Reuben, 117
Coffin
  John M., 199
  John M. (2nd Capt.), 199
Coleman
  Henry E., 160, 161, 162
Colleges
  Richmond Medical College, 194, 197
Collet
  Charles, 82
Collins
  Capt., 62
  John, 25, 26
Connor
  W.H. Alexr., 69
Conrad
  Danl, 55
Cook
  John, 157, 158
Corill
  Daniel Esqr, 152
Correll
  H.A., 199
  Jacob, 215
  John C., 199

Coulter
  J., 33
  Jno, 43
  John, 75
Cowan
  Abel, 128
  David, 169
  James, 76, 169, 170, 171, 172, 173, 174
  John, 169
  Thomas L., 130
Cox
  Green, 71
  Green W, 69
Craig
  Burton, 134
  David, 152
  Mr. B., 134
  Robert, 52, 53
  Thomas, 130
  Thos., 152
Craige
  B., 217
  Burton, 134, 135, 136, 199, 217, 218
  David, 233
  Robert N., 136
Cranford
  B, 207
  T., 178, 179
Crawford
  Thomas M., 199
Crawley
  Thomas, 113
  Tom, 105
Crawly
  Tom, 111
Creeks
  12 Mile Creek, 58
  Canoe Creek, 78

Index and Table of Cases

Liles Creek, 66
Lilses Creek, 67
Lockharts Creek, 70
Sugar Creek, 58
Cress
  Danl., 152
Crider
  Henry, 130
  Wm, 152
Crimes Against Slaves
  Assault & Battery, 19, 29
  Murder, 21, 30
  Stabbing, 146
Crudup
  J.D., 214
  John D., 214
Crump
  Mack, 130
Cry
  William, 81
Crye
  Wm, 81, 82
Cul[?]
  William A., 199

D

Daniel
  J.G., 230
  John G., 230
Darby
  W.R., 174, 176, 177
  William R., 174, 175, 176, 177
Davis
  Alex, 68
  Alex., 71
  Benjamin, 192, 193, 195, 196, 197, 198
  Henry, 192, 193, 194, 195, 196, 197, 198
  J W, 96, 100
  John, 68, 71
  John W, 100
  Mr., 196
  Mr. Benj., 195
  Mr. Benjamin, 196
  Mr. Henry, 195
  Solomon, 193, 197, 198
Day
  James, 83, 84
  John, 84
  Nicholas, 83, 84
  Nicholas Jr., 83
  Nicholas Junr., 83
Deal
  Mr, 114
  Mr., 111
  W R, 113
  William, 107
  Wm, 106
  Wm R, 113
Dellinger
  Fred, 75
  Lewis, 75
Derr
  Jonas W, 67
Dickey
  Joseph, 239
Dodge
  James R, 3, 7
  Jas R, 16, 18
Dole
  Jacob Senr., 85
Dolton
  William, 203
Dorchester
  James, 203, 204
Dorsey
  E.W., 104, 105
Dotson
  Thomas, 201
Douglas
  Isaac, 13
Douglass
  Isaac, 12
Downs
  Mary, 137, 138, 139
Drennan
  William A., 186, 192
Drury
  Mr., 122, 124, 125
  Nicholas, 121, 122, 123

E

Earnheart
  David, 1
  Isaac, 1
  Philip, 1
Edwards
  Nath, 13
  Samuel, 162
  W R, 72
  Wm R, 72
Eller
  Eve, 157
Emmons
  F.A., 221
  Fountain, 221
  James W., 221
  Jas. W., 221
  Hampton, 151
Ervin

Index and Table of Cases

John M, 169
Erving
  Nathaniel, 243
Erwin
  j., 115
  J., 77, 80, 81, 82, 83, 84, 117
  John, 173
  S.S., 90, 91, 92, 93, 94
  Sidney S., 90, 92
Estes
  Leu, 84, 85

F

Falls
  Andrew, 52, 53
  John, 75
Fauling
  Jno H, 153
  John H., 153
Felps
  Jane, 151
Ferguson
  Andrew, 52, 53
  Thomas, 52
Ferrand
  F L, 243
  S L, 233
  SL, 232
Ferree
  J D, 95, 96, 97, 98, 99, 100, 101
  Joseph D., 95, 96
Ferrer
  J.S., 119
Fike
  William, 61
Filhous
  Margaret, 147
  Michael, 146
Finger
  D., 69
  Daniel, 70
  Michael, 69
  S., 68
Fleming
  N.V. Esq., 213
Folk
  G, 101, 102, 105
  G., 103
  G.A., 105
Forsyth
  John A., 3, 4, 5, 6, 7
Forsythe
  John A., 3
Fraly
  Dr., 166
Free person of color
  Isaac, 132
  Isaack, 132
  Isack, 133
Freeland
  MF, 221
Freeman
  John, 71
  Samuel, 132
Frohock
  A., 154
Fry
  Brian, 235
  Bryant, 236
Fryday
  Ephraim, 75
Fulenwider
  H., 6, 30
  Henry, 5, 7, 31
  Hy., 31
Fulton
  John, 130

G

GA County
  Franklin, 240
  Putnam, 237
GA Towns
  Augusta, 243
  Cartersville, 229
Gabriel
  Abraham, 11, 12, 13
  Jacob, 9, 62
  Joseph, 63
  Wilson, 11, 62
Gaines
  James L., 209
Gaither
  B.S., 120
Gamble
  James C., 211
Gardem
  G.L., Jr., 224
Garden
  Gustave L., Junr., 224
Garner
  William, 61
Garrison
  Alfred, 68
Gast[?]
  Capt., 203
Gasten
  R, 62
  Robert, 63
  Robt., 63
Gatshele[?]
  HZ[?], 237
Gentry
  Allen, 163
  Allen D., 163
  Jordan, 164
  Meshac, 163

Index and Table of Cases

Meshack, 162
Ruben, 162, 163
Rubin, 164
Gibbs
  W.F., 104
  William F, 101
  Wm F, 102, 103, 104
  Wm F., 102
  Wm. F., 103, 104
Gibson
  John, 52, 53
  Saml., 58
Giles
  Hy, 137
  John, 131, 152
Gillespie
  Otho, 185
Goff
  John, 119
Gold[?]
  R.D., 228
Goodson
  Aaron, 67, 68
  Eph., 76
  Henry M, 68
  Jacob, 68
Grace
  I.W., 186
  James W., 191
Gracey
  James B., 5
  Jas. B., 6
Graham
  Alexr., 169
  John, 137
  William, 39, 40
Grant
  James Esqr, 117
Graves
  Thomas, 52, 53
Green
  Robert, 121, 125

W, 101
Wm, 97, 98
Greenlee
  E.M., 85
  Ephraim M., 85
  George, 105
Gregory
  John M., 193
Grice
  Nancy, 61, 62
Grider
  N, 235, 237, 240
  N., 231, 233, 235, 239
Guyol
  Theo, 224
  Theodore, 223, 224

H

Haffner
  Mo, 38
Hagar
  Henry, 71
  James, 71
  John, 71
  Michael, 70
Hager
  Henry, 69
  James, 69
  John H, 69
  Simon, 21
  William, 20
  William C, 19
  William C., 21
  William M, 20, 21
  Wm C, 19
  Wm H, 21
  Wm M., 20
Haggins

Thomas, 129
Hall
  Allmand, 220, 221
  J.W., 159, 176
  Joseph W., 174, 175, 176, 177
  Solomon, 128, 158
Halman
  Daniel, 69
Halton
  R.H., 157
Hamelton
  Reuben, 65
Hamilton
  Reuben, 67
Hampton
  Ephraim, 150, 151, 152
  Jas. W., 136
  Mr., 151
  Wade, 133
Hamton
  Waid, 133, 134
Hanes
  M., 139, 140
  Michael, 140
Hanglighter
  John, 131
Hanna
  Capt, 63
Hannah
  Capt, 62
Hannon alias Casper
  Polly, 215
Hansel
  Henry, 61
Harden
  John, 49
Harman
  Daniel, 15
Harmon

Index and Table of Cases

Daniel, 16
J.D., 14
Harris
  Joshua, 122, 123
  Maxamillian, 43, 45
  Mr., 121, 124
  R., 209, 210
  Richard, 155, 156
  Saml., 152
  Wm., 142
  Young, 166
Harrison
  James, 233
Harriss
  Jane, 167
  Samuel, 151
  William, 142
  Young, 166
Harshaw
  A, 106, 110, 114
  Abr, 107
  Abr., 110, 112, 113
  Abraham, 107
  Abram, 113
Hartsle
  Jonathan, 235
Hattern
  Wm, 98
Hause
  A.J., 72
Hauss
  And, 72
Havner
  Levy, 72
Hayes
  Mr., 239
Hayne, 171, 172
Haynes
  Robert G., 70
  Robt, 69
Hays

Robert, 163
Heatleman
  Wm., 155
Heffner
  Michael, 15
  Michel, 15
Hefner
  Michael, 17
  Michal, 14
Helderman
  J, 67
  Jacob, 67
  John F., 68
  Rufus M, 67
Helper
  H.H., 143
Helton
  Elizabeth, 139, 140
  Joseph, 139
Heltons
  Elizabeth, 140
Henderson
  C.C., 50
  John, 72
  L., 3, 5, 8, 9, 11
  Lawson, 11, 32, 44, 49
  Lwn, 25, 30, 32, 38, 39, 40, 42, 44, 45, 50, 55
  Lwn., 23, 29, 41, 49, 50
  Wallace A, 47
  Wallace A., 45, 46
  WL, 151
Henry
  John, 61
Herak[**Horah?**]
  Willa. H., 234
Herman
  J. Daniel, 17

J.D., 17
Heserman[?]
  Cornelius, 164
Hill
  James D., 52
  John, 52, 53
Hillard
  Catharine, 145
  Catherine, 145
  Thomas, 145
Hilton
  Elizabeth, 139, 140
  J., 139
  Josephus, 140
Hitchcock
  James, 239
Hobbs
  A L, 70
  A.L., 69
Hoffan
  David, 159
Hoffman
  Daniel, 148
  Danl., 148
  Margaret L., 148
Hoke
  A L, 72
  Col Daniel, 36
  Daniel, 37, 40, 46, 47
  Fr., 16
  Frederick, 15
  Jno, 31, 57
  Peter, 76
Holesclaw
  James, 75
Holland
  I., 5, 6
  Isaac, 3, 52
Holman
  Daniel, 70
Honeysicker

Index and Table of Cases

Joseph, 15
Hood
  J.P., 30
  Mr., 32
Hoover
  Absalom, 75
Horn
  Christian, 78, 79, 80
Hovis
  Andrew, 27, 28
  Andw, 29
Howard
  B., 239
  Benjamine, 132
  freeman, 63
  John, 133
Howley
  Govrnr, 131
Hoyle
  Peter, 33
Hudspeth
  George, 163, 164
  John, 163
Hughes
  James H., 228
  Jas. H., 227
Huie
  Robert, 136
Hull
  Major, 75
hunsicker
  Polly, 17
Hunsicker
  Joseph, 17
  Polly, 14
Huston
  O.P., 177, 178
Hyne
  Mary, 23
  Philip, 23

I

Irby
  Joseph, 51, 53
  Joshua M, 51, 53, 54
  Joshua M., 50, 51, 52
  M.H., 53
  Mary H, 53
  Will., 51
Irvin
  F.D., 103, 104, 105
Iyer
  Lewis, 236

J

Jackson
  William, 165
Jacobs
  J.M., 72
  John M., 72
James
  T.R., 103
  Thos. R., 103
Jemison
  Alexander, 138, 139
  James, 137, 138, 139
Jenkins
  Joel, 146
Jenning
  Mary, 125
Jennings
  Mary, 121, 123
  Thos., 125
Jianes[?]
  Beal, 158
Johnson

B S, 9, 10, 14, 18, 21, 31
B.J., 51
Carter P., 196, 198
Doctor, 194
Doctor Carter J., 193
Doctor Carter P., 194, 195
Doctr., 192
J.S., 146
John S., 146
Rob, 76
Johnston
  Dr T H, 71
  R.E., 72
  Robert, 68
  Robert Senr, 71
  William, 61
Jones
  C., 211
  Charity, 137, 138, 139
  Chs., 211
  E., 138, 139
  E.P., 147
  Ed, 155
  H.C., 145
  Johnston, 169
  Morgan, 39, 40, 41, 42
  Stephen, 160
  Wiley, 139
  Wilie, 139
Jones[?]
  Johnston, 160
Joy
  Abraham P., 21
Judges
  Judge Mitchell, 103

Index and Table of Cases

K

Keever
  L., 69
  Lawson, 70
Keistler
  Paul, 42
Kellar
  Jacob, 113, 114
  Mike[?], 111
  Mr, 114
Keller
  Jacob, 106, 107
Kelley
  Charles, 68
  Jackson, 68
Kelly
  Jackson, 71
  Thomas
    (Freedman),
    148, 149
  Tom, 148
  Tom (Freedman),
    149, 150
  Wm, 237
Kerns
  Peter, 157
Kerr
  J.E., 155
  James E., 156,
    165, 174, 175
  Joseph, 171
Kesiah
  Dunning, 42
  William, 41, 42
Killian
  John, 7
  Levi, 76
Kincade
  George, 20
  George W., 20
  Joseph, 130

Kincaid
  John, 113
King
  J.D., 71
Kiser
  Adam, 24
Kistler
  Paul, 3
Klutts
  Alfred, 149
  C., 155
  Caleb, 228
Kluttz
  Alfred, 148
  G., 239
  Geo., 239
  George, 238
Knight
  Thomas, 131
  Thos., 131
Knipe
  Martin, 14
Knup
  Martin, 17

L

LA Parishes
  Greenville, 225
LA Towns
  Jefferson, 225
  New Orleans,
    197, 223, 224,
    225, 226, 227
Labron
  Polly, 23
Landford
  Henry, 38
Langford
  Henry A., 35
Lany
  Alex, 237

Latham
  W.G., 224
  William G., 224
Laws
  John, 15
Leach
  R., 161
Ledbetter
  George, 103, 104
Lehmons
  F.L., 68
Lemly
  Saml., 152
  Samuel, 130
Leonard
  Carlos, 31
Lifford
  Soloman, 69
Linard
  Henry, 3
Linbarger
  Fred, 76
Linebarger
  John, 75
Lineberger
  Frederick, 63
Link
  Peter, 23
Little
  George, 76
  Sharad, 69
  Sherod, 19
  Sherod S, 19
Locke
  Dr. M.A., 178
  Fran., 211
  Moses A., 233,
    234, 241, 242
Loftin
  Langdon A, 68
  M.L., 68
Lomax
  John T., 213

Index and Table of Cases

Long
  Capt, 62
  R.N., 144, 145
  Thomas, 9
  William, 63
Lorance
  E., 43
  L., 43
Love
  Dillard, 95, 97, 99
  J R, 95, 97, 98, 99
  Robert E., 155, 156
  Robt. E., 165
Lowe
  Wash., 75
Lowrance
  J L, 65
  Lwn, 67
Lowrans
  Lawson, 65
Lyon
  John L., 184, 185
Lyttle
  Sherod Junr, 71

M

M Call, 172
Mackie
  Robert, 132, 133
MacLean
  Richard D.S., 232
March
  John, 130, 152
Martin
  James, 25
  Saml., 215
Mason

A Judson, 149, 150
A. Judson, 149, 150
Massey
  John, 52
Maury
  Noah, 72
Maxwell
  Benja, 153
  Benjamin, 153
  Thomas, 153, 228
  Thos., 153
Mays
  Tho L, 11
  Tho. L., 13
  Thomas L, 11, 12
  Thomas L., 13
Mcafee
  Abner, 26
Mcaffee
  Esqr., 26
MCall, 171
  Robert, 59
  Robt, 59
  Robt., 59
McCall
  Samuel, 172
McClain
  Mr. Thomas, 232
  Richard D.
    Spaight, 232
  Thomas, 232
McClurd
  Nathaniel, 24, 25
McClure
  James, 52, 53
McClurg
  Mr. Nathaniel, 24
  nathl, 24
McCombs
  James, 61
McConely

James, 62
McConneaughy
  Joseph, 173
McCorcle
  Alex., 76
McCorkle
  Nancy, 215
McCulloch
  Geo., 171
  James, 201
  Rachael, 51
  Robert, 51
  Will., 51
McCullock
  Geo, 43
  Wm., 50
McCulloh
  David, 52, 53
  John, 52, 53
  William, 55
McDowell
  J., 80, 115
  John, 80, 115
McElrath
  Robert, 115, 119
  Robt., 115
McEntire
  Wm., 85
McGee
  Blair, 46, 47
  D., 20
  Thomas, 28
  Thos, 29
McGeehee
  E.S., 188, 190
McGehee
  E.S., 186
McGinnis
  Edward, 69, 71
McKay
  James M., 181
McKee
  Js., 29

Index and Table of Cases

Mckenzie
  M., 155
  M.S., 156
McKenzie
  Kenneth, 80
McKisson
  W F, 101, 102
  W.F., 104
  William F, 101
  Wm F, 102, 103, 104
  Wm. F., 103
McLaughlin
  J.H., 221
McLemore
  John, 121, 123, 125
McNeely
  Elizabeth, 138
  Jesse, 182
  Jno., 137
  Margaret, 179, 182
  Margaret (wife of Jesse), 179
  Mr., 177
  Thomas, 178, 179, 180, 181, 182, 183, 184, 185, 186, 187, 192
Mcorkle
  Thomas, 63
McRee
  W L, 106
  W.L., 107
Mendenhall
  Robert, 71
Mendinghall
  Robert, 69
Michael
  Jhn, 64
  Jno, 64

John, 15
Michaels
  John, 63
Michal
  J.M., 68
  John, 7, 8, 14, 18, 19
Michel
  John, 29
Millar
  George, 141
Miller
  H.S., 146
  Henry S., 146
  Jacob, 230
  Mr. William, 235
  William, 229
Mobley
  Edward, 33
Mobly
  Edward, 32, 33, 34
Mock
  A.J., 177
  D., 41
  David, 41
Monday
  Wesly, 76
Money
  James, 88, 89
Mooney
  Abram, 25
Moony
  George, 75
Moore
  Alexander, 29, 44, 49, 72
  Alexr, 72
  J.W., 75
  John, 231, 232
  John P., 231, 232
  William, 52, 53
Morgan

Danl., 79
Eliza, 235
Moss
  John B., 230
Mot[?]
  Robt., 207
Motz
  John Jr., 76
MS County
  Carrollton, 191
  Holmes, 186, 188, 192
MS Towns
  Lexington, 186, 187
Mullen
  James, 68
Murdoch
  William, 174, 175, 176, 177
Murphey
  J, 241
  J., 238
Murphy
  J., 230
  James, 78, 79
  John, 130
Murray
  Andrew, 237
Myer
  Myer, 192
Myers
  Jacob, 157
  Jacob S., 157
  Mary, 156, 157
  Mr., 194, 195, 196, 197, 198
  Mr. Myer, 194, 195, 197
  Mr. Myers, 196
  Myer, 192, 193, 194, 195, 196, 197

Index and Table of Cases

Myers, 194

N

Nance
  William, 68
  William Senr., 71
Nanny
  Mr., 242
  Mr. Roberts, 230
  Roberts, 233,
    238, 242
Nc County
  Rowan, 233
NC County
  Buncomb, 43
  Buncombe, 44,
    45, 48, 67
  Burke, 48, 147
  Cabarrus, 238
  Davidson, 40
  Halifax, 217
  Hallifax, 135
  Haywood, 94, 95,
    96, 97, 98, 99,
    100, 101
  Iredell, 180, 181,
    183, 184, 185,
    221
  Jackson, 95, 96,
    99, 100, 101
  Lincoln, 135,
    229, 231, 232
  Mecklenburg, 58
  Montgomery,
    121, 122, 123,
    142
  Randolph, 230
  Roan, 161
  Rowan, 181
  Rowan, 1, 129,
    130, 132, 133,
    135, 136, 137,
    139, 141, 142,
    143, 144, 146,
    149, 150, 151,
    153, 154, 155,
    156, 157, 160,
    162, 164, 165,
    171, 174, 176,
    178, 179, 180,
    184, 193, 203,
    215, 217, 220,
    227, 229, 230,
    231, 232, 233,
    234, 235, 236,
    237, 238, 239,
    241, 243
  Rutherford, 89,
    217
  Stanley, 209
  Surry, 163
  Wilkes, 77, 80
NC Districts
  Salisbury, 125
NC Towns
  Charlotte, 58,
    169, 172, 173,
    174
  Concord, 238
  Lexington, 41
  Morganton, 90,
    91, 95, 96, 97,
    98, 103, 105,
    107, 108, 109,
    110
  Salesbury, 134
  Salisbery, 133,
    162
  Salisbiry, 171
  Salisbury, 58,
    130, 136, 142,
    145, 147, 149,
    150, 156, 165,
    175, 180, 181,
    182, 183, 193,
    196, 197, 200,
    207, 218, 223,
    225, 230, 231,
    233, 235, 238,
    239, 240, 241,
    243
  Statesville, 35,
    185
  Webster, 97, 98
Neely
  Alexander, 125,
    126, 128
  Margaret, 125,
    128
  Mrs. Margaret,
    128
  Richard, 128
  Washington, 128
Nesbit
  M.F., 181, 182,
    183, 184, 186,
    187
  Mr., 188
Nesbitt
  M.F., 177, 178,
    179, 180, 183,
    185
Nixon
  Isaac, 68, 71
Noland
  John, 52, 53
Norman
  John, 23
Norwood
  William, 135

O

Oliver
  Thomas, 57, 58
  William, 58

Index and Table of Cases

Wm., 58
O'Neill
  N.C., 102
Orvell
  Daniel, 205
Osborn
  Edwin Jay, 29
Osborne
  A., 129
Owen
  James, 215
Owens
  James, 143
  Mr, 144
  Mr., 143, 144
Owing
  Mr., 143
Owins
  Mr, 144
  Mrs, 143

P

Parker
  Elisabeth, 142
  Elizabeth, 141
  Jacob, 182
  John, 142
  Mr. Jacob, 181
  Mrs., 142
  Mrs. Elisabeth, 142
  Peter, 236
Parks
  Ambrose, 83
Patterson
  David H., 142, 143, 144
  J.T., 103
  John, 52, 53
  Rebecca, 142, 143, 144

Patton
  Thos., 77
Peale
  Allen, 156
Pearce
  Vire, 117
Pears
  Joseph, 199
Pearson
  Ch. J., 159
  Charity, 108, 112, 113, 114
  J H, 105, 106, 107, 108, 109, 110, 113, 114
  J.H., 119
  John H, 109
  Mary, 109
  Mrs, 112
  R, 113
  W.S., 106, 107, 108, 109, 110
Pearsons
  Charity, 105
  Isaac, 113
  Mrs, 111
Peasson
  J.A., 205
Peebles
  Albert, 240
Peeler
  G.H., 157
Pelly
  James, 152
Penny
  Jesse, 76
Perkins
  Eli, 43
Phelps
  Jane, 130
  Mrs., 150
Phifer
  M.C., 59

Martin C., 59
Philips
  Capt., 150
Phillips
  David, 49
Piercy
  Blake, 44, 45, 48, 49
  Ephraim, 46, 48
Pinkston
  Wm., 152
Pir[?]y
  D.S., 207
Places
  Beaties Ford, 134
  Fulenwider Forge, 58
  Gullic[?] pine, 217
  Kellars Gold Mine, 113
  Kellars Mine, 111
  McKissons Store, 111
  Michael Finger's Mill, 69, 70
  Moore's Ferry, 58
  Ramsours Store, 36
  Summys Store, 35
  Waxaw Settlement, 58
Pool[?]
  D., 150
Poteat
  J.H., 48
Poteet
  J.H., 44
  James H., 45
Powell
  J, 103
  R., 158

Index and Table of Cases

Prescott
  Mr., 234
Prescott[?]
  Mr., 234
Presswood
  Nancy, 87, 88, 89, 90, 91, 92
  William, 88, 89, 90, 91, 92
  Wm., 87, 90
  Wm. T., 92, 93
Prestwood
  Nancy, 92, 93
  Thomas, 92
  W.T., 94
  William T., 92, 93
  Wm. T., 93
Prince
  Oliver H., 213
Printers
  Nichols & Gorman, 103
Pruett
  Harrod B., 130
Pruitt
  H.B., 152
  Joseph, 240
  Robert W., 240
Purkins
  Elisha, 67

Q

Queen
  James, 7
Quin
  James, 52, 53, 62

R

Raeder
  W., 177
  William, 174, 177
Rafel
  Mrs. Hannah, 223
Raider
  W., 176
  William, 174, 175
Ramsaur
  D.A., 25
Ramsour
  David (Sen), 76
  Jacob, 29, 34, 38
  Jonas, 65, 67
  Mr., 32
RAMSOUR
  D A, 30
Ramsours
  Mr, 35
  Mr., 35
Randolph
  E.S., 227
  Edward S., 228
  Mr., 225
Ranken
  Wm, 67
Rankin
  Alexander Junior, 63
  John D., 76
  M. (a free negro), 165
  Mack, 165
  Mack (a free person of color), 165
  Mack (Free Negro), 164

  Wm, 65, 66
Ravenal
  Benjamin, 226, 227
Reade
  Edwin G., 169
Reavis
  J.P., 165
Reeder
  W., 176
  William, 174, 176
Reeves
  E.B., 147
  Saml., 142
  Samuel, 142
Reinhardt
  C.E., 34, 37
  D, 57
  D., 31
  David, 75
  F M, 67
  Franklin M, 67
  J.P., 59
  Jacob, 30, 59
  Jno, 21
Renshaw
  Milly, 154
Revis
  JP, 164
Reynolds
  Hugh, 183, 184, 185
  reuben, 183
  Reuben, 183
Rickman
  Robert, 161
  Robt., 161
Riggs
  J.S., 227
Riley
  Robert, 61
Rivers

Index and Table of Cases

Broad River, 217
Catawba River, 58, 67
Linville River, 101
Roane
  William, 85
Roberson
  A.P., 63
  John, 63
Roberts
  H.L., 228
  J.M., 62
Robertson
  A.R., 161, 162
  Anne R., 160, 161, 162
Robinson
  Isaac, 65, 67
  James A., 52, 53
  Jesse, 229
  John, 69
Robison
  John, 71
  John H., 63
Rodes
  Rudolph, 33
Rodgers
  Sarah, 209
Rogers
  Sarah, 209
Root
  C.B., 169
Rose
  William, 27
Ross
  Benjamin, 109
  Jas. L., 70
Row
  William, 27
Rowe
  Danl., 75
Rudesil

John, 75
Rush[?]
  Jacob, 30
Russ
  Jas. L., 68

S

Sadler
  Jn, 29
Sandford
  Jesse, 239
  William, 239
  Wm., 239
Sanford
  William, 237
Sanxay
  Richard D., 192, 193, 198
Saunders
  W.L., 176
SC County
  Winton, 131
SC Districts
  Darlington, 88, 92
  Fairfield, 233
  Lancaster, 231
  Pendleton, 239
  Sparklingburg, 163, 164
SC Towns
  Abeville, 234
  Beaufort, 237
  Columbia, 58, 234
  Winnsboro, 58, 226, 227
  Yorkville, 58
Schenck
  Michael, 27
Schenk

Michl, 29
Scott
  Cy, 112
  Dr., 234
  John, 220
  Judah, 113
  Judah (a free woman of color), 111
  Judah (Free Negroe), 113
  Judy (a free woman of color), 108
  Mr Abram, 62
Scruggs
  Mrs. Mary, 240
Settlemyer
  David, 75
Setzer
  Paul, 52, 53
Shank
  Henery, 30
Shannon
  William, 224, 226, 227
Sharpe
  Dr., 213
Shaver
  Fredk, 157
  Joel, 140, 141
  John I., 200
Shavers
  Enos, 159
  William, 146
Shaw
  William, 158
Shelton
  Spencer, 75
Shenck
  Michael, 28
Shenk
  Elizabeth, 23

Index and Table of Cases

Shenter
  William, 23
Shepherd
  Joseph, 46
Sherell
  Hoseah, 66
  Lewis L, 66
  Lewis S, 67
Sheril
  Hosah, 67
Sherill
  Austen, 66
  Austin, 66
  Enos, 65
  Hosah, 67
  Hoseah, 66
  Mason, 65
Sherrall
  Absalom, 75
Sherrell
  Enos, 66
  H W, 66
Sherrill
  Austin, 67
  David L., 67
  Eli, 9, 13, 65, 67
  Enos, 65
  Hosea W, 66
  Isaac, 63
  Logan, 62
  Mason, 67
  Michael, 9, 10
Sherwood
  B, 41
  Benjamen, 40, 41
Shinn
  John, 65, 67
Sho[?]
  Frederick, 115
Shrum
  Daniel, 69, 70
  Levi, 69, 70
Shuford

And. H., 75
B H, 11
B S, 8
Daniel, 30
Elk L., 66, 67
Elkanah, 65, 66
Elkanah L., 65
George, 29
Jno J, 13, 65
Martin, 46, 47
T R, 72
Thos R, 72
Shuman
  John Jr., 165
Sides
  Wilson, 146
  Wilson (Free person of color), 145
Sifford
  Solomon, 71
Sigman
  George, 14, 15, 16, 17
  Mr George, 18
  Mr., 16
  Squire, 15
Sillimam
  Saml., 147
Silliman
  A., 174
  Alexander, 169, 172
  Alexr., 170, 171, 172, 173, 174
  Dr., 172
  John, 170, 171
  Sam., 136
  Saml., 137
  Samuel, 136, 147
Simmons
  Jas, 135
Simpson

Doct. J.P., 31
Doctr. J.P., 31
Sipe
  George, 15
  Joseph, 16
Slater
  F., 136
Slave Crimes
  Assault & Battery, 105
  Attempted Rape & Murder, 137
  Burning a Barn, 24
  Burning a dwelling house, 14
  Conspiring an Insurrection, 150
  Felony, 39
  Felony & Burglary, 34
  Felony & Housebreaking, 32
  Felony (Stealing), 8
  Felony, Stealing, 153, 159
  Grand Larceny (Stealing Corn), 27
  Horse Stealing, Felony, 43
  Misdemeanor, 130
  Murder, 3, 50, 125, 166
  Poisoning, 154
Slaves
  Abel, 14, 15, 16, 17, 18

Index and Table of Cases

Able, 16
Abner, 3, 4, 5, 6, 7, 8
Abraham, 14
Abram, 12
Adaline, 181, 187
Adam, 30, 31, 32
Adeline, 187, 188, 189, 190, 191
Albert, 12
Aleck, 146
Alexander, 8
Alfd, 137
Alfred, 12, 110, 217, 219
Alidia, 163
Altimore, 39, 40
Andy, 174, 175, 176, 177
Angus, 215
Ann, 154, 236
Anthony, 58, 150, 151
Ben, 9, 10, 11, 12, 13, 115
Benj., 113
Bet, 153
Bets, 114
Betsey, 59, 60, 107, 111, 112, 113, 217, 220, 242
Bett, 152, 153, 154
Bill, 82, 207, 221, 234
Billy, 235
Biner, 88
bob, 151
Bob, 24, 25, 31, 32, 33, 34,
150, 152, 160, 161, 162
Byner, 94
Caesar, 217, 218
Campble, 27, 28
Captain, 154
Caroline, 217, 219
Catharine, 145
Charity, 242
Charles, 29, 78, 125, 126, 127, 128, 158, 234, 235, 242
Charles Webb, 128
Cimon, 220
Clarissa, 217, 218
Clarrisa, 217
Clary, 21, 22, 23
Clase, 80
Cloe, 83
Cyrus, 50, 51, 53, 54, 55
Dad Charles, 127
Daniel, 43, 44, 45, 46, 47, 48, 49
Dave, 4, 5, 6, 14, 15, 17, 110, 111, 112, 113, 114, 126, 127, 211
David, 5, 7, 12, 13, 105, 106, 107, 108, 109, 110
Deal, 112
Dennis, 151
Derry, 78
Diana, 217
Dice, 80

Dick, 25, 30, 31, 32
Dinah, 219, 220
diner, 84
Dorcas, 170, 171, 172, 174
Duncan, 125, 126, 127
Edmon, 9, 10, 11
Edmond, 8, 9, 10, 13, 66, 67
Edmund, 11, 12, 13, 217, 219
Elick, 217, 220
Eliza, 88, 91, 217, 218
Emberson, 10, 12
Emerson, 13
Emsey, 109
Essex, 218
Esther, 1
Feba, 220
Fed, 217, 220
Fil, 217, 219
Fillis, 5, 240
Flora, 217, 219
Francis, 45, 47, 49, 239
Frank, 48
Fred, 61
George, 112, 113, 195, 196, 198, 233
George Myers, 194
George Young, 194, 195, 196, 197
Gracy, 4, 5
Gregory, 242
Gustin, 217, 220
Hagar, 217, 219
Hanible, 110

270

Index and Table of Cases

Hannah, 145, 217, 218
Hannah alias Minder, 129
Harriet, 88, 91, 217, 220
Harry, 157, 217, 238, 239
Harry (Scrog), 218
Harry or Henry, 238
Harry Scroggins, 217
Henry, 239
Hiram, 119
Homer, 217, 219
Hope, 68, 155
Hopey, 217, 219
Howell, 217, 219
Ira, 88
Isaac, 50, 51, 52, 53, 54, 55, 108, 112, 113, 215
Isabella, 72
Jack, 217, 220, 234, 241
Jacob, 55, 130, 150, 151, 230
James, 14, 16
James Cleton, 229
Jane, 14, 105, 111, 112, 113, 147, 217, 219
Jani, 17
Jenny, 85
Jerry, 242
Jesse, 137, 138, 139

Jim, 10, 12, 25, 217, 220, 221, 229
Jinny, 217, 219
Joe, 12, 231
John, 88, 91, 217, 219, 223, 224, 225, 227, 228, 240, 242
John Thomas, 226
John Young, 193
Jude, 137
Julius, 125, 126
June, 34, 35, 36, 37, 38, 39
Kiss, 211
Kitty, 242
Lawrence, 137
Letty, 242
Levi, 155
Lidia, 164
Liran, 25
Lucinda, 217, 218, 219
Lucy, 78, 221
Lydia, 234
Madison, 110, 111, 112, 113
Malissa, 217, 219
Martha, 111, 217, 219
Martin, 26
Mary, 78, 217, 218, 219
Mat, 26
Matilda, 105
Matthew, 217, 219
Milly, 141, 242
Minty, 105, 113, 114
Mira, 91

Molly, 242
Moses, 12, 217, 233
Nancy, 143, 144, 215, 242
Nanny, 217, 220
Ned, 77
Old Charles, 127
Patience, 207
peggy, 217
Peggy, 219
Peter, 25, 57, 72, 232, 237, 241
Pheby, 217
philip, 12
Philip, 10, 16
Philis, 4, 7, 55
Phillis, 4, 162
Primus, 235, 236
Pris, 111, 112, 114
priscilla, 237
Priscilla, 237
Rachael, 209, 220
Rachel, 217
Richard, 125
Richy, 125
Ricky, 126, 127
Robin, 217, 219
Rye, 77
sally, 231
Sally, 154, 231
Sam, 58, 81, 82, 217, 218
Samp[?], 219
Sampson, 5, 7, 131
Samson, 4, 134
Sanco, 68
Sara, 84
Sauco, 67, 68
Silvey, 94
Silvia, 91

Index and Table of Cases

Simon, 217
Stephen, 4, 5, 242
Suckey, 146
Susan, 217, 219
Sylvia, 88
Tilly, 111, 112, 113
Tom, 12, 225, 226, 234, 235, 237, 238
Tom alias John, 227
Tom alias John Thomas, 227
Toney, 78, 152
Tony, 150, 151, 152
Tracy, 7
Vincent, 151, 152
Viney, 242
Violet, 124
Wiley, 217, 219
Will, 19, 20, 21, 134
Willis, 88, 91, 217, 220
York, 59
Zilpha, 10, 12
Sleighter
  Henry, 152
Smith
  B., 77
  Ben, 77
  David, 66, 67, 76
  E.B., 165
  EB, 164, 165
  John, 152, 172
  M.A., 148
  MA, 149, 150
  Michael, 229, 232
  Sarah, 205
  Sary, 205

William, 155, 156
Smyer
  John, 76
Sneed
  F.[?], 145
Snider
  John, 139, 140
  Lucy, 139, 140
Sooter
  Reynold, 238
  Rynhold, 238
Speed
  James W., 235
Speede
  James W., 234
Spraggins
  Tho., 129
  Thomas, 129
Springs
  Andrew, 241
Srote
  AM, 241
States
  Alabama, 213
  Georgia, 164, 197, 237, 238, 239, 240, 243
  Louisiana, 223, 224, 226
  Mississippi, 186, 188, 192
  S. Carolina, 58
  South Carolina, 88, 92, 163, 203, 225, 226, 231, 233, 234, 237, 239
  Tennessee, 163
  Virginia, 192, 198, 235
Steele
  John, 130, 151

Steward
  Leander, 69
Stewart
  J.M., 186
  John M., 188
Stokes
  H.M., 154
  Jno, 129
Stowe
  Larkin, 5, 6, 7
  Leroy, 5, 6
  Miss, 5
Stuard
  N.T., 72
  Thos, 72
Stuart
  John M., 186, 187
  Mr., 188, 191
  Mr. Stuart, 189
Stuarts
  Mr. John M., 188
Summerrow
  James, 70
Summey
  Mr., 35
  P, 51, 52
  P., 50
  Peter, 50, 51, 52
Sumrow
  James, 69
Suter
  Rinehold, 239
Swink
  william, 141
  William, 141

T

Tate
  Hugh, 79
Taylor

Index and Table of Cases

Absalom, 131
Franklin, 72
James, 72
Terral
  Timmothy, 203
  Timothy, 203
Thattearn
  Wm, 96, 100
Thomasons
  Wm., 215
Thompson
  Noah, 209
  Tabbitha, 209
  William, 160, 161, 162
Throgmorton
  Reuben, 119
TN County
  Green, 162
  Washington, 84
Todd
  J.E., 207
  Tho., 221
Torrants
  James, 173
Torrence
  Albert, 130
Townsen
  John, 84
Townsend
  John, 84
Tracey
  James, 7
Treffinger
  Barbara, 155, 156
Troy
  M., 207
  Matthew, 207
Turner
  Hezekiah, 145

U

Ursery
  Thomas, 121
  Thos., 122, 123
Urssary
  Thomas, 122
Ussery
  Thomas, 123
  Thos., 123, 125
Utzman
  John, 152

V

VA County
  Cumberland, 235
  Halifax, 160, 161
  Henrico, 192, 193, 198
VA Towns
  Petersburg, 197
  Richmond, 192, 193, 198
Valintine
  Jesse, 145
  Jesse (Free person of color), 144
Vanderpool
  E., 117
  Elyas, 117
Vanhorn
  John, 112
  Mrs., 110
Venable
  Saml, 71
  Saml W, 68
Vick
  Eliza, 154
Vogler
  George, 146

Volentine
  Elijah (free man of color), 215
  Jesse, 145
  Susan (free woman of color), 215

W

Wakefield
  Charles, 82, 83
  Charles Senior, 82
Walker
  A.M., 183
  William, 85
Wallis
  Betsy (free woman of colour), 215
Wallon
  Solomon, 132
Walton
  Tho, 113
  W.A., 148, 178, 179
  W.W., 176, 181
  WA, 149, 150
Ward
  Alexander, 12, 13
  Tho, 19, 20
  Thomas, 12, 13, 20
  William B., 231
Warlick
  Absalom, 23
  david, 23
Wasson
  W.F., 180, 182, 183
  WF, 183, 184

Index and Table of Cases

Watson
  Mrs., 242
Watt
  WT, 183, 184
Watts
  W., 183
  W.T., 180, 182
Weant
  William, 148, 149, 150
Wear
  Joseph, 34
Weather Spoon
  Thos., 179
Webb
  Charles, 126, 127, 128
Weir
  Joseph, 39
Welch
  R V, 95, 97, 98
Wells
  Henry, 132
West
  J.S., 147
  Joseph, 146, 147
  Joseph S., 147
  Margaret, 146, 147
  Margaret Alias Margaret Filhous, 147
  R.J., 159
Wheeler
  Buddy W., 231
  Jno, 45
  Mr. Buddy, 231
  W., 231
White, 172
  George H., 183
  James, 225, 226
  Jas., 227
  Mr., 225, 226

Whitesides
  John, 57
Wier
  Joseph, 34, 35, 38, 39
  Mr, 37
  Mr., 36
Wiers
  Mr., 36
Williams
  Patsey, 87, 90, 91, 92, 93
  Patsy, 89, 90, 91, 92
  Patty, 88
Williamson
  Robert, 77
Willis
  Geo., 242
  George, 241
  W.J., 165
  Wm J, 164, 165
Wilson
  a Medical student, 225
  J, 54
  J W, 33
  J., 22, 23, 40
  J.D., 226
  James D., 226
  Mr. Wm. J., 53
  N, 25
  N., 24
  Thos., 75
  W., 34
  W.J., 52
  William J., 52, 53
  Wm J, 54
  Wm. J., 54, 55
Wintz
  John, 40, 41
Wit
  P.S., 38

Witherspoon
  D., 80
  David, 80
  Dr. Thomas, 179
  I.A., 178, 179, 182, 183, 185, 186
  Isaac, 180, 181, 184, 186, 187
  Isaac A., 177, 179, 183, 185
  Mr., 191
Wood
  Dr. D.B., 178, 179
  Wm., 128
Woodford
  Lyman, 76
Woodson
  A., 232
  D., 229
  David, 229
  Obadiah, 193, 198
Worsham
  Afftin, 154
  Tabitha, 154, 155
Wright
  James Jr., 52, 53
  John, 160, 161

Y

Yarbrough
  Wilie, 152
Young
  Mrs., 48
  Neomy, 48
Yount
  John, 75

Index and Table of Cases

Z

Zimmerman
  J., 33
  John, 33, 34, 57
  Martin, 17, 29
  Nicolas, 67

ABOUT THE AUTHORS

WILLIAM L. BYRD, III has been involved in genealogical and historical research for more than thirty years. His primary areas of interest are Native Americans, African Americans, West Indians, East Indians and Moors in Virginia, North Carolina, and South Carolina.

He has been published by the *North Carolina Genealogical Society Journal*, the *Magazine of Virginia Genealogy*, *The Rowan County Register*, and *The South Carolina Magazine of Ancestral Research*. He has also co-authored articles with Sheila Stover in the *North Carolina Genealogical Society Journal*, *The Augustan Society Omnibus*, the *Pan-American Indian Association News*, and the *Eagle: New England's American Indian Journal*. He has received an "Award of Special Recognition" from The North Carolina Society of Historians in the category of "The History Article Award" for preserving North Carolina history.

He is a U.S. Army Veteran from the Vietnam era, and served with the U.S. Armed Forces overseas. He is currently retired, and resides with his family in Hickory, North Carolina.

ଔ ଓ

JOHN H. SMITH holds a BA in psychology from Lenoir Rhyne College, and did his graduate work at Winthrop University. His professional memberships include American Psychological Association, and Phi Alpha Theta (National Honor Society in History.) In addition to his full-time career, Mr. Smith is a part-time continuing education instructor of genealogy and family history, and a part-time research assistant to Catawba County Historical Association.

Mr. Smith was the editor of *The Burke Journal* (1992-1995), a quarterly publication of the Burke County Genealogical Society, (winner of the *Excellence in Periodical Publishing Award* from the North Carolina Genealogical Society, 1995.) He has presented numerous programs to genealogical groups in North Carolina in the past fifteen years, and has twice been a speaker at the South Carolina Genealogical Society's summer workshop. His articles have been published in *The Burke Journal*, *Catawba Cousins*, the *Rowan Register*, the *South Carolina Magazine of Ancestral Research* and several other local/county quarterlies.

Other Heritage Books by William L. Byrd, III:

Against the Peace and Dignity of the State: North Carolina Laws Regarding Slaves, Free Persons of Color, and Indians

Bladen County, North Carolina Tax Lists: 1768 through 1774, Volume I

Bladen County, North Carolina Tax Lists: 1775 through 1789, Volume II

For So Long as the Sun and Moon Endure: Indian Records from the North Carolina General Assembly Sessions, & Other Sources

In Full Force and Virtue: North Carolina Emancipation Records, 1713-1860

North Carolina General Assembly Sessions Records: Slaves and Free Persons of Color, 1709-1789

North Carolina Slaves and Free Persons of Color: Chowan County, Volume One

North Carolina Slaves and Free Persons of Color: Chowan County, Volume Two

North Carolina Slaves and Free Persons of Color: Pasquotank County

North Carolina Slaves and Free Persons of Color: Perquimans County

Villainy Often Goes Unpunished: Indian Records from the North Carolina General Assembly Sessions, 1675-1789

Other Heritage Books by William L. Byrd, III and John H. Smith:

North Carolina Slaves and Free Persons of Color: Burke, Lincoln, and Rowan Counties

North Carolina Slaves and Free Persons of Color: Hyde and Beaufort Counties

North Carolina Slaves and Free Persons of Color: Iredell County

North Carolina Slaves and Free Persons of Color: Mecklenburg, Gaston, and Union Counties

North Carolina Slaves and Free Persons of Color: McDowell County

North Carolina Slaves and Free Persons of Color: Stokes and Yadkin Counties

www.ingramcontent.com/pod-product-compliance
Lightning Source LLC
Chambersburg PA
CBHW062004220426
43662CB00010B/1226